Brands Plucked from the Burning

Essays on Methodist Memorialisation and Remembering

Frontispiece 1 Henry Perlee Parker, 'Is not this a brand plucked out of the fire?' Oil; 161 x 221 cms approx.; original version; in Methodist Church House, Marylebone Road, London. Image courtesy of the Oxford Centre for Methodism and Church History, Oxford Brookes University. The back cover detail is from Parker's half-size copy of this original painting (see Illustrations 2.5 and 2.9).

Brands Plucked from the Burning

Essays on Methodist Memorialisation and Remembering

Edited by

David J. Hart and David J. Jeremy

Published in UK
by
Wesley Historical Society

Website: www.wesleyhistoricalsociety.org.uk
22 Broadway Road, Evesham, WR11 1BG, England

First published by Wesley Historical Society, 2013

ISBN 978-0-9554527-9-6
Printed by and available from Lulu.com

Frontispiece 2   Escape of John Wesley from the Fire.   Hand-coloured lithograph, 1870; 40.6 x 53.3 cms.   Box WF16, Frank Baker Collection of Wesleyana and British Methodism, David M. Rubenstein Rare Book & Manuscript Library, Duke University.   Image courtesy of Duke University.   Detail on the front cover.

Acknowledgements

The editors are particularly grateful to Professor Geoffrey Tweedale for the very considerable help he has provided in processing the manuscript and helping to design the cover of this book for printing by Lulu.com.

For Frontispiece 1, we are indebted to Dr Peter Forsaith, Research Fellow, the Oxford Centre for Methodism and Church History, Oxford Brookes University, who has provided the image and arranged permission to use it.

For Frontispiece 2, we are equally indebted to Mr David Pavelich, Head of Research Services, the David M. Rubenstein Rare Book and Manuscript Library, Duke University, North Carolina, USA for supplying and arranging permission to use this image. Other picture credits are given in individual chapters.

Contents

List of Tables   xi

List of Illustrations   xii

1   Memorialising and Remembering: Life Stories in
    Methodism
    David J. Hart   1

2   'What Mean Ye by These Stones?' Aspects of
    Memorialising and Remembering in Wesleyan
    Methodism
    David J. Jeremy   11

3   The Transformation of the *Arminian Magazine* from
    John Wesley's Theological Instrument of Control to
    His Vehicle for Expressing and Preserving the
    Evocative Voices of Early Methodism
    Barbara Prosser   104

4   In the Shadow of the Founder: Methodist
    Memorialisation of John Wesley
    Gareth Lloyd   143

5   Men Who Left the Wesleyan Methodist Ministry,
    1791-1932: a Database in Progress
    John Lenton   168

6   Biographies in Church Monuments: William Smith
    and Jane Vazeille of Newcastle upon Tyne
    Terry Hurst   197

7   Memorials of Motherhood: the Travels and Travails
    of Preachers' Wives
    Janet Kelly   219

8   Methodist Prosopography: Sources and Exemplars
    of Collective Biography in British Methodism
    Clive D. Field   238

Note
Professor Jeremy's essay is contributed by invitation.

List of Tables

2.1 Remembering the Wesleys: the Wesleyan Centenary
and Thanksgiving Funds   69

2.2 Nineteenth century biographies listed in Vickers (2000)   70

2.3 Appendix: Memorial tablets inside City Road Chapel,
as existing in 1872   101

5.1 Numbers entering the Wesleyan ministry in 1831-73   175

6.1 Vazeille family tree   218

List of Illustrations

2.1 Exterior of City Road Chapel, 2013   45

2.2 Interior of City Road Chapel, 2013   47

2.3 Enoch Wood's bust of John Wesley   53

2.4 C. E. Wagstaff engraving, after C.A. Duval, Wesleyan
       Centenary Meeting   56

2.5 Henry Perlee Parker, Epworth fire   58

2.6 Centenary medal, 1839, obverse and reverse   62

2.7 The Edinburgh portrait of John Wesley   75

2.8 Detail from Wagstaff, after Duval,Wesleyan
       Centenary Meeting   85

2.9 Detail from Parker, Epworth fire   88

3.1 First Contents page of the *Arminian Magazine*,
       January 1778   106

3.2 Alexander Mather, preacher and close adviser of
       John Wesley   139

4.1 John Wesley's Preaching Plan,
       May-June 1790   153

4.2   John Wesley being attacked in Wednesbury, 1743   154

4.3   John Wesley being carried to heaven   156

4.4   John Wesley accusing his modern-day
      followers   161

4.5   Commemorative mug, showing the head
      of John Wesley   164

6.1   St Andrew's Parish Church, Newcastle upon Tyne   199

6.2   William Smith of Newcastle upon Tyne   203

Abbreviation

MARC Methodist Archive and Research Centre, John Rylands Library, Deansgate, Manchester.

Note

Dimensions of pictures are cited as height x width, in cms.

Contributors

Clive D. Field, OBE, DPhil, DLitt, Honorary Research Fellow in the School of History and Cultures, University of Birmingham and the Institute for Social Change, University of Manchester

David J. Hart, PhD, Associate Faculty Member, Trinity College, Bristol

Terry Hurst, BA, retired Methodist Minister

David J. Jeremy, PhD, Emeritus Professor of Business History, Manchester Metropolitan University

Janet Kelly, PhD, Associate of the Leeds Centre for Victorian Studies, Leeds Trinity University

John Lenton, PhD, Honorary Librarian, Wesley Historical Society Library, Oxford Brookes University

Gareth Lloyd, PhD, Methodist Archivist, The John Rylands Library, University of Manchester

Barbara Prosser, PhD, Head of the Faculty of Adult, Sixth Form and Language Studies, Cardiff and Vale College, Cardiff; and independent researcher into early Methodist education and literacy

1

Memorialising and Remembering: Life Stories in Methodism

David J. Hart

'Brands plucked from the burning',[1] the title of this book and a (pluralised) Old Testament metaphor for the experience of deliverance from sin shared by the ancient Israelites and Christians of all times and places, was particularly applicable to the early Methodists: John Wesley, rescued as a small boy from a fire at his father's rectory at Epworth in Lincolnshire, came to view his own life and calling in these terms.[2] Driven by this sense of divine mission, Wesley and the many fellow Methodists treated in these essays were all too human. Their frailties and fallibilities emerge as much as their devout religious faith, tireless energy, and sacrificial commitment to their cause.

The essays in this volume resulted from the residential conference of the Wesley Historical Society in 2011 when the theme was *Memorialising and Remembering: Life Stories in Methodism.* The aim was to explore three distinct but related areas of Methodist history. First, the conference sought to probe ways in which the telling of life stories has contributed to a wider process of establishing identity for the Methodist movement, especially in the nineteenth century. Secondly, it sought to examine how the remembering of lives influenced

---

[1] Zechariah 3: 2; the AV text reads, 'is not this a brand plucked out of the fire?'

[2] Henry D. Rack, *Reasonable Enthusiast: John Wesley and the Rise of Methodism* (3rd edn., Peterborough: Epworth Press, 2002), pp. 57, 533.

later generations of Methodists. Thirdly, the conference explored the tools at the disposal of the historian that may assist in the task of examining memorialising and remembering the past.

The first, it is argued, was a deliberate and co-ordinated programme of education that started with John Wesley, where the lives of previous generations were built into a hagiography and even, perhaps, a martyrology. Barabara Prosser's work on the *Arminian Magazine* examines this process in some detail. First published in 1777, the *Arminian Magazine* set-out to widen Wesley's reach by creating a reading congregation whose knowledge and experience could be extended by the material he chose to publish month by month. An important aspect of the publication came with the inclusion of the auto-biographical material provided by the travelling preachers (also known as itinerants: the ministers or professional clergy as they became), as they described their early lives, conversion narrative, and experience of God's influence in their ministry. This spiritual pedagogy was further broadened by the inclusion of accounts of the 'good deaths' of Methodist members, presented to inspire and encourage, which in Dr Prosser's words 'gave the movement its equivalent of a martyrology'.[3] Prosser's thesis is that what began as a 'theological retort', a tool for teaching the core theological values of Wesleyanism and thus its doctrinal cohesion, developed into the means of preserving the memory of the past and the space within which spiritual inspirations could be disseminated.

Gareth Lloyd explores the manner in which collective memory, purposefully shaped and controlled initially by Wesley, and later by those who vied for leadership, was an important influence in shaping the historiography of his move-

---

[3] Barbara Prosser, 'The Transformation of the *Arminian Magazine* from John Wesley's Theological Instrument of Control to His Vehicle for Expressing and Preserving the Evocative Voices of Early Methodism' (Below, Chapter 3).

ment. While accepting Wesley's 'claim to primacy within the Methodist tradition', Lloyd examines 'how Wesley consciously laid the foundation of this personal primacy'.[4] This pre-eminence, argues Lloyd, was based on Wesley's unshakeable conviction that he had received a calling that was individual and unique. Such certainty gave rise to a movement that was inevitably and inextricably linked with John Wesley. Indeed, for historians it has been difficult to separate Wesley from Wesleyanism and histories of his movement have all too often been histories of Wesley. In part, this is due to the dominating influence of what Wesley published. His Journal, written for publication and dissemination, whilst being set in the wider context of eighteenth-century diary-writing, nonetheless by virtue of his longevity and the extent of his travels, opened a window on the British Isles scarcely matched by any other. The sheer quantity of his publications and especially the *Christian Library,* provided accessible texts to meet the growing demands of his followers and especially his preachers. Lloyd cites Vicki Tolar Burton's assertion that at his death, Wesley's bookstore contained over a quarter of a million volumes awaiting distribution.[5] The Methodism that Wesley developed included lay, itinerant, and local preaching, the development of lay leadership in the local societies, and reliance on a network of circuits: features that endured beyond his death in 1791. Moreover, it is clear that Wesley installed specific legal and institutional structures, like the establishment of the Legal Hundred in 1784, designed to ensure that the essence of his influence would also survive his death. Consequently Wesley's memorial was the movement he founded, a

---

[4] Gareth Lloyd, 'In the Shadow of the Founder; Methodist Memorialisation of John Wesley' (Below, Chapter 4).

[5] Vicki Tolar Burton, '"Something for the People to Read"; John Wesley's Book Inventory (1791)', *Bulletin of the John Rylands University Library of Manchester*, Vol.85 (2003), p. 230.

movement which still in some ways struggles to understand its founding father.

This process of deliberately creating a legacy that would influence and shape the future was a well-known historic phenomenon not restricted to Methodism. As David Jeremy shows in his essay (included in these papers but not given at the Conference[6]) the aesthetic and social culture of England between the late eighteenth and the late nineteenth century is redolant with examples of memorialisation aimed at preserving status, significance, and identity through ritual, physical memorials, and written recollections. Professor Jeremy reminds us that this drive to memorialise percolated down from the elite into the middling and, eventually, the lower classes. Victorian Britain rediscovered the power of the memorialising image in a way not seen since before the English Reformation. Now, instead of seeking to perpetuate the political elite's memory by effigies in chantry chapels or monuments in cathedrals or churches, the example of heroes was refreshed by methods sometimes initiated by Britain's early industrial technology, like factory-produced ceramics and colour printing.

While the first area the 2011 Conference sought to explore was the intentional creation of memorials to perpetuate collective memory, the second area was less deliberate and linked more to the invocation of their predecessors by later generations. Sometimes this provided inspiration in times of trouble, division, or uncertainty and at other times a means of reinforcing the historic narrative of a local Methodist society or institution. The search for inspiration from the past is well illustrated in the observation of Thomas Jackson (1783–1873), Wesleyan historian and Conference President :

---

[6] David J. Jeremy, '"What Mean Ye by These Stones?" Aspects of Memorialising and Remembering in Wesleyan Methodism' (Below, Chapter 2).

> The truest respect that the present race of Methodist preachers can show for their venerable fathers who now sleep in Jesus, is to imitate them in the zeal for the honour of Christ, and the salvation of souls redeemed by His blood; in the inflexible adherence to the truth; their power in prayer; their irresistible appeals to the consciences of their hearers; their self-denial; their pastoral visitation from house to house; their sympathy with the poor and afflicted; their mighty faith in God; their affectionate concern for the young; their enterprise in carrying the gospel into neglected districts; their fidelity in maintaining every part of Methodist discipline; their undying attachments and fidelity to each other; their intense earnestness in their attempts to alarm the unconverted to bring penitent sinners into Christian liberty and to bring all believers to the possession of the perfect love which casteth out fear. [7]

Jackson went on to express his concern that it would be a poor day when a 'converting and effective ministry', with lively payer-meetings, class-meetings, love-feasts and sacrament services should be a thing of the past. There is something about the tone of his comment, and more profoundly the need for a series of biographies of the early preachers which suggests that that time had indeed come. Jackson evidently sought to re-discover the past, to return to former glories which, by the time he was writing in the mid-nineteenth century, had been lost. His six volumes of preachers' lives well merited Bruce Hindmarsh's verdict on the genre: 'If these autobiographies were thus destined for canonization in the nineteenth century, they had their genesis in the eighteenth century

---

[7] Thomas Jackson, *Lives of Early Methodist Preachers*, (6 vols., London, 1865), vol. 1, p. xxxiii.

in a preoccupation with recorded experience that was altogether typical of the Evangelical Revival.'[8]

If Jackson sought to recall the memories of the past as inspiration in the face of a present-day crisis, there were also numerous examples of the way remembering the past reinforced the historical narrative of the Methodist communities across the world. Some were formal memorials to those who had been instrumental in establishing the societies, staffing Sunday Schools, or providing the financial means to erect preaching houses, chapels, and churches. There are many examples of local Methodist dynasties that were remembered both in local Methodist buildings, whose construction they often supported financially and in the historic narrative of the communities that used them. Then there were the dynasties that could trace their lineage to Wesley himself: Terry Hurst's detailed examination of the family of William Smith of Newcastle upon Tyne, who married John Wesley's step daughter Jane Vazeille in either 1767 or 1769 (records vary), remind us of the familial links that perpetuated Wesley's importance to Methodism.[9] These local Methodist dynasties, which often exercised considerable influence over local societies for generations, may have asserted their influence precisely because they were able to invoke legitimating memories from the past.

A similar phenomenon was found among the travelling preachers of Wesleyanism, around whom a complete hagiography came to be constructed. This, in part and as John Lenton points out in his paper in this collection, was a result of family connections between the preachers which served to

---

[8] D. Bruce Hindmarsh, *The Evangelical Conversion Narrative: Spiritual Autobiography in Early Modern England,* (Oxford University Press, 2005), p. 239.
[9] Terry Hurst, 'Biographies in Church Monuments: William Smith and Jane Vazeille of Newcastle upon Tyne' (Below, Chapter 6).

strengthen their status within the movement.[10] This strength
was due in part because travelling preachers were often members of significant families of the kind examined by Terry
Hurst. A further dimension to the importance of the family as
a memorial mechanism is Janet Kelly's work on the families
of itinerant preachers.[11] Of particular poignancy are the experiences of preachers who, having been sent abroad often to
inhospitable places, took their wives and families with them.
The experiences of some of these, recorded in the *Wesleyan
Methodist Magazine* for example, provided yet another type
of memorial to those who too often died as a result of disease
and the harsh conditions they encountered. As Dr Kelly points
out, climate and conditions could be exacerbated by local hostility to the preachers and the movement for whom they laboured. A record of over seventy preachers' wives was found
in the fifty volumes of the *Arminian Magazine* and its successors, in the period between 1780 and 1880. The extent and
size of this catalogue demonstrates the significance of the
published life-story in Methodism: the fact that such material
went on being published for so long strengthens the argument
that these life-stories were significant influences in shaping
personal piety and spiritual determination among the readership. While there is a need to recognise the danger of visiting
contemporary psychological and sociological judgements on
the behaviour of past generations, the accounts of family separation, hunger, and misery were, and to some extent remain,
touching testimony to the willingness of women to sacrifice of
themselves to serve the calling of their husbands. Perhaps
from such collective memories were drawn the assumptions of
later generations of Methodists who made heavy demands

---

[10] John Lenton, 'Men Who Left the Wesleyan Methodist Ministry, 1791-
1932' (Below, Chapter 5).
[11] Janet Kelly, 'Memorials of Motherhood: the Travels and Travails of
Preachers' Wives' (Below, Chapter 7).

upon the clergy partners in the support of their ordained ministers. These life-stories were dominated by the dangers to women who were pregnant, an experience in the nineteenth century that was risky at the best of times and even more hazardous when associated with extensive travel, demanding physical conditions, and poor living conditions. As Janet Kelly points out, it was all the more remarkable that, despite the adversities of their lot, many still found the energy to exercise a ministry of their own and often in the context of chronic ill-health.

This memorialising of heroic individuals and dynasties provided Methodism with a set of commonly shared values which served to inspire later generations. This inspiration pointed towards a collective goal; the Methodist Junior Missionary Society, for example, encouraged generations of children to collect weekly contributions from members of their local congregation by providing stories of the work of missionaries in far-away and apparently exotic places, precursor of the more contemporary 'sponsor a child' type of appeal.

The third area which the conference touched was the relationship between specific, biographical evidence on individuals and the use of collective evidence on groups of biographies. Clive Field's paper on Methodist prosopography provides access to a tool of historical enquiry which has not been widely used in modern Methodist studies.[12] Collective biography is valuable in establishing group norms, enabling the historian to see how far his or her local subjects vary from the prevailing behavioural patterns of their group. One of the as-

---

[12] Clive D. Field, 'Methodist Prosopography: Sources and Exemplars of Collective Biography in British Methodism' (Below, Chapter 8). John Lenton's *John Wesley's Preachers: a Social and Statistical Analysis of the British and Irish Preachers Who Entered the Methodist Itinerancy before 1791* (Milton Keynes: Paternoster, 2009) is an outstanding example of the prosopographical technique applied to a Methodist social group.

pects of historical data relating to Methodist individuals, and especially those in the eighteenth century, is that for any individual, there is often a very incomplete biographical profile. A collective biography allows an incomplete individual biography to be given the context of the wider yet similar social group. Clive Field's paper includes case studies to illustrate how this works.

By their very nature, formalised, physical memorials like those of St Andrew's Parish Church in Newcastle upon Tyne are more easily identifiable and their message is clearer than the implied memorialisation of a life, a family, or the demands of itinerant ministry. Nonetheless, historians who give careful attention to this more nuanced evidence can learn more about the ways people lived their lives, formed their beliefs, and shaped their values. The industry that surrounded the near-canonisation of John Wesley, at least within his own movement in the nineteenth and early twentieth century, with its productions of mementoes, portraits, and souvenirs is not always easy to interpret. Sometimes it represented the enterprise of manufacturers spotting and seizing a particular market, such as the Wesleyans' Centenary. Sometimes the initiative came from the church side (as seen in David Jeremy's essay) As a result, the exploitation of the status of John Wesley, as Gareth Lloyd has arguably shown, became ever more deeply embedded in and seminal to the organisation he had founded. For this reason the way Wesley was remembered by successor generations of Methodists is not a reliable way of assessing the man in his lifetime.

The character of John Wesley left its mark on later generations of Methodists, both positively and negatively. For Wesleyan preachers at least until the middle of the nineteenth century, he provided the primary role model not least because the legacy he left his preachers was bound between the covers of the 'Large Minutes' with which each was presented. As the papers by John Lenton and Janet Kelly show, the growth in the number of preachers was only part of the story. What the preachers did and their willingness to accept privation was in no small measure due to a belief that the project in which they were engaged was of God, a conviction that Wesley had held from the earliest period of his movement. These privations became even more challenging as the Wesleyan movement began to send ever larger numbers of preachers overseas, often to the most challenging environments of the further reaches of the British Empire.

A Conference which explored how life stories have been memorialised in Methodism can, by virtue of the limits of time and place, only examine limited aspects of a very large theme. These contributions are therefore offered to encourage wider debate and enquiry about how, unwittingly or deliberatly, the religious phenomenon that is Methodism is currently perceived and will be remembered.

2

'What Mean Ye by These Stones?'[1] Aspects of Memorialising and Remembering in Wesleyan Methodism

David J. Jeremy

Memory of the past has never before intrigued so many different disciplines, professionals, and relationships as today. Among others, politicians, geneticists, anthropologists, sociologists, psychologists, family historians, legal and medical professionals, clergy, and grieving relatives, friends, and admirers of the deceased, all have a stake in knowledge about our individual and collective pasts.[2] The construction and meaning of memorialising go back to ancient times, as the question asked by the Israelites entering the Promised Land, cited in the title to this essay, testifies. What have historians learned about the process of memorialisation (part of their trade, after all)? How have Methodists recalled their past and what significance does that hold for present-day Methodist Christians? Answers to the first question, which has a bearing on the second of course, are clear in broad outline on the vast canvas of the past but debatable when examined in narrow circumstances of time and place. One thing is plain, memorialising is closely connected to the sustaining of group identity.

---

[1] Joshua 4: 6 (AV).

[2] At the time of writing, the most recent political example is a new government scheme under which it is proposed to send teachers and pupils from every school in England to visit sites and memorials on the Western Front, partly because the Great War was the most awful in modern times which society should remember and learn from, partly because the Centenary of that war is next year and there are no survivors left alive. See *Daily Telegraph* 10 June 2013.

11

Locating the topic, this essay offers a framework for analysing the phenomenon of memorialisation and an outline of the pre-dominant nineteenth century practices of memorialisation which surrounded Methodists. It uses elements of the framework to understand some aspects of Victorian Methodist memorialisation.

One caveat must be entered. This essay does not consider the sacred rituals of Sunday worship, the celebration of Holy Communion (the Eucharist), or rites of passage (except some aspects of funerals), all of which Methodists largely derived from their roots in the Church of England. Nor is the Methodist Love Feast mentioned here.[3]

1   A FRAMEWORK

Remembering and memorialising have been important for every society and social group in defining and demarcating its identity, its perceived 'sameness over time and space'. If memories feed and support identity, 'what is remembered is defined by the assumed identity'.[4] So remembering and memorialising is not simply an antiquarian indulgence; above all it is crucial in sustaining and evaluating our social identity, a concern of enduring importance in the twenty-first century.

While the phenomenon of memorialising has been complex, varying between civilisations and periods of time, between public and private memorialisations, between memorialising of the famous and of the obscure, between remembering the young and the old in age, a number of features recur. First, the phenomenon has taken various forms. Primarily, these have been ritual, image (ranging from symbols to pic-

---

[3] For which see Frank Baker, *Methodism and the Love-Feast* (London: Epworth Press, 1957).

[4] John R. Gillis, 'Memory and Identity: the History of a Relationship' in John R. Gillis (ed.), *Commemorations: the Politics of National Identity* (Princeton NJ: Princeton University Press, 1994), p. 3.

tures and monuments), inscription (memories recorded in written language), and myth (stories, written down or transmitted orally). Second, specific social settings have modified the nature and extent of those forms. Third, collective memories have been deliberately shaped, usually by dominant elites, in order to establish or support particular identity goals. Last, dominant memories have been contested, by rivals, subordinates, or successors. This four-dimension anatomy of memorialisation, derived (and simplified) from John R. Gillis's essay on the subject,[5] is helpful for contextualising and understanding the meaning of memorialising and remembering among Methodists.

2   THE NINETEENTH CENTURY CONTEXT OF MEMORIALISATION IN BRITAIN

Memorialisation in Methodism has frequently revolved round the life and legacy of John Wesley. He was regarded as the founder. His theology and organisation shaped the movement. The branch which stayed closest to his perceived legacy, the Wesleyans, was the largest of the successor Methodist bodies and they ensured that the legacy of John Wesley, with its sacerdotal bias, was preserved. If not as hero, but certainly as a focus for denominational identification, the elevation of John Wesley had begun soon after his death in 1791. It is of some consequence therefore to understand the contemporary secular context, particularly society's treatment of great figures and of memorialisation in its various forms in the nineteenth century.

Traditionally Westminster Abbey was 'the sole church building in the country that could be classed as a national ter-

---

[5] Ibid., pp. 3-24.

ritory'.[6] It was the resting place of mediaeval kings and queens and the focus of divine right claims, particularly from aristocratic Jacobite sympathisers in the late seventeenth and eighteenth centuries. As a Royal Peculiar outside the jurisdiction of the diocesan system, its dean and chapter enjoyed administrative autonomy. Their patronage controlled the distribution of monuments, for the viewing of which they charged entrance and viewing fees. In the first half of the eighteenth century they acceded to a drift away from monuments commemorating court loyalties and towards the use of Abbey space to honour the competitive claims of elite families to recognition in the public domain. The accession of George III in 1760 and the growth of empire accelerated the trend.

Between the American Revolution and the First World War national commemoration moved towards outstanding public servants, particularly senior military figures, rather than mere aristocratic inheritors. Identifying with the state rather than the court served the new realities of monarchy, parliament, and empire. Through forms of memorialisation, particularly funerals, monuments, and myth, the public learned to lionise those individuals whose behaviour projected the ruling elite's image of Britishness.

This adulation of heroes came in two surges, the first during the American, French Revolutionary, and Napoleonic Wars and their aftermath, the second from the death of Wellington in 1852 until the disillusionment of the First World War. In the first surge, Britain's ruling elite exploited memorialisation of military heroes and commanders to excite widespread patriotism and to legitimate their own position in the nation.

---

[6] Matthew Craske, 'Westminster Abbey, 1720-1770: a Public Pantheon Built upon Private Interest' in Richard Wrigley and Matthew Craske (eds.), *Pantheons: Transformations of a Monumental Idea* (Aldershot: Ashgate, 2004), p. 58. The rest of this paragraph comes from this source.

St Paul's Cathedral, a public space subject to diocesan and parliamentary authority, had long been one of the sights for London tourists. It took on a new character in the late eighteenth century, eclipsing Westminster Abbey as the site of a national pantheon of military heroes. Monuments to thirty-two senior commanders were erected in St Paul's Cathedral at the behest of Parliament between 1794 and 1823, with John Flaxman's monument to Nelson occupying a prime space. In death blue-blooded military heroes were associated with red-blooded ones like Nelson, a Norfolk parson's son and the most glory-laden hero of the time. Thereby the status of the ruling aristocracy was cemented into the country's wartime solidarity.[7]

In effect St Paul's Cathedral became a Christianised military pantheon. The compromising of sacred space, however, was contested both within and outside the Established Church. 'Influential counter-traditions to "the heroic" in eighteenth-century philosophy, historiography and fiction drew on general pacifist impulses fed by Roman stoicism, traditional Christian beliefs, and humanism. 'More specifically, there was strong, especially evangelical and Methodist, resistance to the celebration of earthly heroism in monuments sited in churches, because of its inferiority to Christ's sacrifice.'[8] Wil-

---

[7] Linda Colley, *Britons: Forging the Nation, 1707-1837* (London: Pimlico, 2003), pp. 177-87; Holger Hoock, 'The British Military Pantheon in St Paul's Cathedral: The State, Cultural Patriotism, and the Politics of National Monuments, ca. 1790-1820' in Wrigley and Craske (eds.), *Pantheons*, pp. 81-105. Not every single one of the thirty-two commanders was a hero in the Nelson tradition. Major-General Thomas Dundas, whose brigade of light infantry captured the islands of Martinique, St Lucia, and Guadeloupe, in 1794, died on the latter of yellow fever. The French shortly after recaptured Guadeloupe, disinterred his body, and fed it to the birds. Parliament voted a monument to Dundas in retaliation for this desecration. Ibid., p. 91.

[8] Ibid., p. 90, quoting Emma Vincent Macleod, *A War of Ideas. British Attitudes to the Wars against Revolutionary France, 1792-1802* (Aldershot: Ashgate, 1998).

liam Wilberforce deplored the lack of acknowledgement of divine providence in the official announcement of Nelson's victory at Trafalgar. Later, in the 1830s, the cathedral authorities expressed unease about the conflicting functions of worship space, meeting place, and sculpture gallery.[9]

In the nineteenth century Britain's rising industrial middle classes, whose economic interests were bound up in free trade and imperial expansion and whose radical tendencies were sometimes worrisome to the old landed order, were assimilated into the country's political structures and dominant sense of shared values. Assimilation of the new working classes took longer. Three constituents of memorialisation developed to advance a modified national identity. One was a new theory justifying recognition of individual greatness. A second was the manifestation of that theory in public funeral rites and monuments. The third was the production of popular heroic biographies inviting emulation.

Thomas Carlyle expounded the new theory in his essays *On Heroes, Hero-Worship, and the Heroic in History* (1841). The book was particularly important because it widened the definition of national greatness from the military hero to the concept of the great man. In these essays Carlyle proposed a typology of heroes, of great men: the hero as divinity (Scandinavian mythology), as prophet (Mahomet), as poet (Dante, Shakespeare), as priest (Luther, Knox), as man of letters (Johnson, Rousseau, Burns), as king (Cromwell, Napoleon). It rested upon his premise that,

> as I take it, Universal History, the history of what man has accomplished in this world, is at bottom the History of the Great Men who have worked here. They were the leaders of men, these great ones; the modellers, patterns, and in a wide sense creators of whatsoever the general mass of men contrived to do or to attain; all things that we see standing accom-

---

[9] Hoock, 'The British Military Pantheon in St Paul's Cathedral', pp. 95, 99.

> plished in the world are properly the outer material
> result, the practical realisation and embodiment, of
> Thoughts that dwelt in the Great Men sent into the
> world: the soul of the whole world's history, it may
> justly be considered, were the history of these.[10]

Carlyle's heroes had messianic character, perceiving the will of God they changed the course of nations by their pre-eminent capacities and their force of personality. One view is that they were such rare individuals that they defied emulation. Emulation related to a different type of hero: 'where the individual life had a didactic purpose with no necessary relationship to historical narrative.'[11] The problem with this distinction lay in its blurring of who might or might not be the model for a potentially great person. The assumption in Victorian hero worship was that the career of all those commonly regarded as heroes was worth study and could lead to realistic and achievable imitation.

The notion that social change depended upon a few remarkable individuals ran counter to the ideas of Auguste Comte, Herbert Spencer, and the early pioneers of sociology who emphasised group behaviour as the key to understanding how social change could be understood. Nevertheless until the end of the nineteenth century the great man theory held sway. It fitted the class structure of English society, the observed nature of economic and technological change, and the

---

[10] Thomas Carlyle, *On Heroes, Hero-Worship, and the Heroic in History* (1841; Oxford University Press, 1904), pp. 1-2.

[11] Christine MacLeod, *Heroes of Invention: Technology, Liberalism and British Identity, 1750-1914* (Cambridge University Press, 2007), pp. 21-22 , quoting Walter E. Hamilton, *The Victorian Frame of Mind, 1830-1870* (New Haven, Yale University Press, 1957), pp. 305-40 and Geoffrey Cubitt, 'Introduction: Heroic Reputations and Exemplary Lives' in Geoffrey Cubitt and Allen Warren (eds.), *Heroic Reputations and Exemplary Lives* (Manchester University Press, 2000), pp. 1-27.

opportunities and burdens of empire.[12] The memorialisation of heroes was never more vividly evident than in the funerals of those deemed to be the social giants of the Victorian age.

The funeral in 1852 of the Duke of Wellington, a front rank hero, the general perceived to have delivered Europe from tyranny, was a turning point in national memorialisation ritual: it shifted forwards the public sense of British identity, from the aristocratic towards the democratic.[13] Nothing like it had been seen in living memory apart from the funeral of Nelson. Funerals for royalty were private affairs: the first three monarchs of the nineteenth century died, lay in state, and were buried at Windsor Castle. Wholly exceptionally, in 1821 the cortege of Queen Caroline, the estranged and humiliated but widely popular wife of George IV, sparked riots on its way from Hammersmith to Brunswick. Conversely, Nelson's funeral in 1806 accorded with the idolised Olympian, triumphant in the battles of the Nile, Copenhagen, and Trafalgar. His body lay in state in Greenwich, was conveyed by barge to Whitehall, and thence to St Paul's on a funeral car resembling a ship, besieged by huge crowds. Obsequies concluded with Evensong and burial in the crypt under the dome of St Paul's.[14]

Wellington's state funeral was the grandest public funeral of the century. At least one million in a population of 18 million (England and Wales) turned out on 18 November to see the funeral cortege, which took two hours to pass - the six wheeled, purpose-built funeral car costing £11,000 painfully

---

[12] A view which derives from an impression of the celebration of centenaries, the installation of civic statues to local heroes, and the publication of biographies and collective biographies of philanthropists, politicians, entrepreneurs, engineers, and inventors.

[13] Information on funerals of royalty and the eminent Victorians mentioned here comes almost entirely from John Wolffe, *Great Deaths: Grieving, Religion, and Nationhood in Victorian and Edwardian Britain* (Oxford University Press for the British Academy, 2000): on Wellington, pp. 28-55.

[14] Ibid., pp. 15-23.

lumbering along.[15]   Ten thousand mourners headed by the Queen and Prince Albert packed into St Paul's where a choir of 200 led the obsequies. All of which suggested a huge national interest and participation in the Duke's extravagant state funeral.

If Wellington's funeral marked a new departure in memorialisation, it was followed by other memorable funerals, not least and widely popular those of two men perceived as Christian hero-martyrs, dying in the service of the Christian gospel and the British Empire: David Livingston in 1874 and General Gordon in 1885. Despite initial doubts about the identity of the bones that were carried across Africa by Livingston's faithful followers, and in the absence of Gordon's body, both men were memorialised in Westminster Abbey. The former's remains were interred in the Abbey. For Gordon, memorial services there and in many other cathedrals reflected a wide consensus edged with political implications. Soon after, Khartoum fell, Gladstone's Liberal government, tardy in sending a relief column and therefore held responsible for Gordon's death, also fell.[16]

The funerals of Disraeli (1881) and Gladstone (1898) reasserted a private, less grand tone to the funerals of great men. Disraeli's executors, obeying his will's instructions, ensured that he was buried at Hughenden, his beloved Buckinghamshire estate. Gladstone, unashamed Anglican and champion of Nonconformist causes, died at his home, Hawarden Castle in North Wales. Simple family observances at Hawarden were shared by local people before his body was taken by train for a three-day lying-in-state in Westminster Hall, followed by interment in Westminster Abbey.[17] All these four men (Livingston, Gordon, Disraeli, and Gladstone) originated below

---

[15] The cost is given in Pat Jalland, *Death in the Victorian Family* (Oxford University Press, 1996), p. 196.

[16] Wolffe, *Great Deaths*, pp. 136-53.

[17] Ibid., pp. 154-91.

England's aristocratic classes. Together they represented the newly-emerged worlds of empire and 'improving' industrial society.

Queen Victoria's state funeral in 1901 and Edward VII's in 1910 were the last great funerals in the high Victorian tradition. Queen Victoria, was buried as Empress of India (a title taken at the instigation of Disraeli in 1876) and ruler of nearly 25 per cent of the world's land mass and 25 per cent of the world's population.[18] The great funeral that terminated her life marked the closing of an age and simultaneously successfully projected the British identity as imperial, aristocratic, and democratic.[19] Edward VII's funeral, more open to the public because of the lying in state in Westminster Hall, as Wolffe observes, gave ritual expression 'to the mediating role of constitutional monarchy, in bridging the divide between the aristocratic and the democratic, and the sacred and secular'.[20]

Four years later the appalling slaughter of the First World War utterly democratised memorialisation. In its aftermath the names of vast numbers of soldiers, sailors, and airmen, mostly infantrymen of low rank, could be found across the country, on monuments in local parish church and chapel or on the village green. At Port Sunlight, for example, a memorial listed almost 500 names. In Whitehall the Cenotaph commemorated the dead of the British Empire.[21]

For Victorian royalty and national heroes, funerals were usually very expensive, large-scale, very public, metropolitan rather than provincial, and culminated in ceremonials, and sometimes burial, in one of the two London pantheons,

---

[18] Lance E. Davis and Robert A. Huttenback, *Mammon and the Pursuit of Empire: the Political Economy of British Imperialism, 1860-1912* (Cambridge University Press, 1986), pp. 27-29.
[19] Wolffe, *Great Deaths,* pp. 221-42.
[20] Ibid., pp. 243-58, quote from p. 252.
[21] William J. Reader, *'At Duty's Call': a Study in Obsolete Patriotism* (Manchester University Press, 1988), pp. 1-6, 110.

Westminster Abbey or St Paul's Cathedral. Rather different were middle-class funerals. Knowledge of feudal baronial conventions for conducting great public funerals, preserved for royalty and aristocracy by the College of Heralds, percolated downwards to the landed gentry. By the late eighteenth century these conventions were imitated by the prospering middle classes of industrialising England. Great public funerals and the handbooks of London undertakers also suggested middle-class norms. An aristocratic funeral could be as much as £1,500 in the early nineteenth century, an upper gentry one £100 to £400, and an upper middle-class one as little as £130.[22] The cost structure of the £130 funeral is revealing. Nearly a third (£47 3s 6d) went on hats and dress accessories. A sixth (£23 18s 6d) went on two coffins (£7 7s for an outer lead one, £5 15s 6d for an inner elm one), the hearse, four horses, and one mourning coach-and-four. The rest (about £60) was expended on paying and dressing appropriately nine gentleman-mourners, the clergymen, six servant-mourners, two mutes, six hearse-pages, four coach-and-feather pages, and two coachmen. The roles of ushers, pages and mutes, symbolising castle retainers of various ranks, and emblems like the plume of black ostrich feathers carried on a cushion (tokening shield and helmet), harked back to baronial times. Patricia Jalland argues that these funeral conventions faded among the middle classes after 1850.[23] Mourning rituals did not.

Deficiencies in public health, medical knowledge, diet, and housing conspired to make disease and death ever present realities in nineteenth century Britain. In the face of the transience of life the urban middle classes imitated the aristocracy

---

[22] These prices may be compared to the annual earnings of a farm labourer (about £25 in the late 1830s) or a skilled cotton mule spinner (about £100 in the 1840s). See John Burnett, *A History of the Cost of Living* (Harmondsworth: Penguin Books, 1969), pp. 250, 252.

[23] Jalland, *Death in the Victorian Family*, pp. 194-203.

in practising ancient lugubrious customs. Black silk dominated. Between the 1840s and the 1890s and beyond, widows (men wore sombre suits everyday), influenced by the Court and journals of fashion, wore black for a year and a day. The fashionable did not escape mourning garments entirely for another year. In supplying demand for crape (hard silk with a crimped or curled effect), the family of Samuel Courtauld (1793-1881), Unitarians, became the largest silk manufacturers in the country. As their sales reflected, habits of conspicuous grief only faded after the death of Queen Victoria.[24] Victorian middle-class funerals, especially of civic dignitaries, also mirrored albeit faintly, the funerals of national heroes, in their attention to the impressiveness of the cortege. For example, of 18 Rochdale mayors dying between 1873 and 1914, only two were mourned with less than 10 funeral carriages, ten had 30 or more.[25] Such practices played the commonality of private grief into a civic identity often managed by middle-class elites.

The middle class funeral (which widows did not usually attend because they were assumed to be unable to control their feelings) was followed by a period of mourning. Besides the wearing of black, sending out black-edged memorial cards, and receiving condolence letters, widows visited the grave, possibly weekly for a year, certainly at the anniversary of their husband's death. They were expected to find this thera-

---

[24] Donald C. Coleman, *Courtaulds: an Economic and Social History*, vol. 1 *The Nineteenth Century, Silk and Crape* (Oxford: Clarendon Press, 1969), pp. 24-32, 82, 128-33, 158, 160, 192. Courtauld's sales of crapes (overwhelmingly mourning crape) rose from 3,542 packets in 1832-34 to 15,316 in 1842-44 and 24,504 packets in 1852-56, most evidently going into domestic outlets. Their sales doubled to 49,000 packets in 1883-5 and doubled again to 93,019 packets in 1901-3; by 1896 Courtaulds reckoned to sell more crapes abroad than at home - still about 40,000 packets distributed to the domestic market.

[25] Jalland, *Death in the Victorian Family*, pp. 210-24, 284-317; author's data on late nineteenth-century Rochdale mayors' funerals.

peutic. A widower grave-visiting for as much as three weeks was regarded as self-indulgent: he was expected to return to work. The deaths of children, ravaged by epidemic diseases like scarlet fever, were particularly devastating: Darwin avoided the funeral of his daughter Annie and never visited her grave. Queen Victoria's prolonged mourning, lasting twenty rather than the usual two or three years, was, according to Jalland, a highly exceptional and abnormal practice that did not reach down to the upper and middle classes.[26]

Least influenced by the mourning habit of middle-class Victorians were the Society of Friends (Quakers) and the very poor. In keeping with their belief in living a plain lifestyle, the Quakers eschewed mourning dress, carried the simple coffin without a pall to a cemetery where graves were in rows in order of date of death, performed the ceremony in silence, and refused the 'use of sepulchres, underground vaults, tombstones, monuments, or epitaphs'.[27]

The growth of public cemeteries facilitated mourning practices. Population growth, urbanisation, and overcrowding in churchyards demanded alternatives for the disposal of the dead. Despite a few precedents in the eighteenth century and the Arcadian model of Père Lachaise Cemetery in Paris (1804), the movement for the establishment of cemeteries outside the consecrated ground of the parish churchyard tarried until after the defeat of Napoleon. One of the first was The Rosary in Norwich (1819) promoted by a Nonconformist minister Rev Thomas Drummond, not least to overcome the disabilities practised against Dissenters by the Anglican clergy and, sometimes, civic authorities. Other Nonconformist cemeteries followed in the 1820s: in Manchester, Chorlton Row (1821), Every Street in Ancoats (1824); in Liverpool, Low

---

[26] Jalland, *Death in the Victorian Family*, pp. 221-22, 258-59, 291, 348.

[27] Ibid., p. 220. There were exceptions: Professor Edward Royle tells me that one was at Farfield Meeting House, Addingham, Ilkley where the Quakers had table tombs.

Hill (1825); and in Newcastle on Tyne, Westgate Hill (1825).[28]

Rising mortality rates and then the cholera epidemic of 1831 led to a cluster of city cemeteries: in Birmingham (Key Hill, 1836), Sheffield (General, 1836), Manchester (General, 1837), York (Public, 1837), Nottingham (General, 1837), and Bristol (Arnos Vale, 1840). Seven commercial cemeteries ringed London: Kensal Green (1833), South Metropolitan, West Norwood (1836), Highgate (1839), Nunhead (1840), Abney Park, Stoke Newington (1814), Brompton (1840), and Tower Hamlets (1841). The 1850s saw 100 of the 160 open architectural competitions held between 1843 and 1900, spurred by the Burial Acts of 1850-57 which enabled local authorities to manage public cemeteries. The largest cemetery of all was Brookwood near Woking, Surrey (1854). At over 2,200 acres and served by a railway with two stations on different sides of the cemetery, it was the largest in Europe. Differing charges for positions and plots in the cemetery landscape, as well as the possibilities of monumental sculpture (increasingly neo-Gothic after the 1840s) preserved in death the social divisions of life.

Images, the second form of memorialisation in this analysis, had a much more enduring role in remembering than death rituals. Furthermore, images such as monuments, paintings, pottery busts and the like, memorialising great figures, imbued a sense of national identity in the minds of viewers. The development of Westminster Abbey and St Paul's Cathedral as pantheons has already been noted. They memorialised royalty, military heroes, and political colossuses. It was a struggle to get any representation for inventors, engineers, or entrepreneurs into those pantheons. James Watt, inventor of

---

[28] This and the next paragraph are drawn from Chris Brooks, *Mortal Remains: the History and Present State of the Victorian and Edwardian Cemetery* (London: Wheaton, 1989) and Sarah Rutherford, *The Victorian Cemetery* (Botley, Oxford: Shire Publications, 2008).

the steam engine who died in 1819, after ten years of lobbying became the first engineer to be so monumentalised - in St Paul's with a marble statue by Sir Francis Chantrey, in 1834. Other first generation industrialists and engineers, like Smeaton, Boulton, Brindley, Arkwright, or Wedgwood, were slow to be recognized.[29] Watt was honoured with statues (both by Chantrey) in Glasgow (1832), scene of his early career, and in Greenock, his birthplace.[30] As Christine Mac-Leod observes, 'Until the 1850s, it was as though James Watt had obtained a patent on glory'.[31]

Thereafter, and chiefly in civic halls and squares, numbers of other engineers were honoured with statues. For example, George Stephenson, the railway engineer, who died in 1848 was commemorated with a marble statue in St George's Hall, Liverpool in 1851 and another one three years later in the grand hall of Euston Station, London.[32] Isambard Kingdom Brunel, engineer and inventor, who died in 1859, was recalled by a subordinate portrait in the stained glass window honouring George Stephenson in Westminster Abbey; Brunel's statue, denied a place in Trafalgar Square or Parliament Square, finally stood on a site on the Victoria Embankment in 1877.[33] Partly because monuments were contingent upon circumstances, William Fairbairn's proposal of 1836 for a monument to Sir Richard Arkwright never materialised, though there was a good life painting and a variety of engravings.[34]

---

[29] For Arkwright's contested reputation see David J. Jeremy, 'British and American Entrepreneurial Values in the Early Nineteenth Century: A Parting of the Ways?' in Robert A Burchell (ed.), *The End of Anglo-America: Historical Essays in the Study of Cultural Divergence* (Manchester University Press, 1991), pp. 24-59.

[30] MacLeod, *Heroes of Invention*, pp. 91-124.

[31] Ibid., p. 181.

[32] Ibid., pp. 204-5.

[33] Ibid., pp. 233, 319.

[34] Ibid., p. 117; Judy Egerton, *Wright of Derby* (London: Tate Gallery, 1990), p. 256; David J. Jeremy and Polly Darnell, *Visual Mechanic*

Portraits of course were much easier to accommodate and many more could be accumulated in a limited space than statues. The nation's pantheon of portraits, the National Portrait Gallery was founded in 1856 and opened to the public in 1859. Its political promoters, inspired by a gallery honouring the most illustrious men of France in the Palace at Versailles, believed that it would promote the moral good of the nation. Crowds thronged to it and its first director George Scharf, who saw it as an educational tool, noted with approval the receptiveness of the young and the orderliness of adults.[35]

Inscriptions, a third form of memorialisation, most widely appeared as biographies and collective biographies. Epitaphs of course were confined to the tombstone or monument, unless they were published in print form (and are not considered in this chapter). Decades before Carlyle's *Heroes*, a sprinkling of inventors, engineers, and business leaders, pioneers of Britain's industrial expansion, were accorded modest recognition in print. John Aikin, a dissenting physician, and William Enfield, a Unitarian minister, published their *General Biography; Lives, Critical and Historical, of the Most Eminent Persons of All Ages, Countries, Conditions, and Professions* (1799-1815). It included entries for Arkwright, Brindley, Smeaton, Harrison, and Wedgwood but, surprisingly, not for Watt, Boulton or Edward Jenner, pioneer of inoculation against smallpox. Another work, *British Public Characters* by Richard Phillips, was projected in several volumes, of which the first appeared in 1798. Its author also had radical connections, testified by the inclusion of Joseph Priestley and Erasmus Darwin. One subject, Edmund Cartwright, a Church of England clergyman and inventor of an early power loom,

---

Knowledge: The Workshop Drawings of Isaac Ebenezer Markham (1795-1825), New England Textile Mechanic (Philadelphia: American Philosophical Society, 2010), pp. 49-56.
[35] Gertrude Prescott Nuding, 'Britishness and Portraiture' in Wrigley and Craske (eds.), *Pantheons*, pp. 256-58.

was also brother of Major John Cartwright, political reformer and agitator.[36]

If Carlyle was the British originator of the great man myth, Samuel Smiles was its secular, and Edwin Hodder its Christian, exponent. Smiles's *Self-Help with Illustrations of Conduct and Perseverance* (1859) exalted leaders of industry, industrialists, scientists, artists, businessmen, financiers, social reformers, poets and politicians, men of energy, courage, industriousness, frugality, and honour,   inspiring emulation. Smiles was far more popular than Hodder.   *Self-Help* sold 20,000 copies in its first year, 55,000 by 1863, and 258,000 by 1905, the year of the author's death. 'The book later came to stand for the coarsest strain of Victorian materialism, but in fact it reflected an association of the moral aspects of the Calvinism Smiles had been taught as a child with the educational values of the Unitarians and the radicalism of the Anti-Corn Law League.'[37]

Edwin Hodder (1837-1904) was a brother of Matthew Henry Hodder, a founding partner in the publishing firm of Hodder & Stoughton. Edwin went into the Civil Service and by the mid-1870s was an FRGS and part-time editor for Messrs Thomas Cook & Son, the travel agents and fellow Nonconformists. He edited the eighth number (1875) of their travel magazine *All the World Over.*[38] Hodder's *Heroes of Britain in Peace and War* (2 vols., London: Cassell & Co, 1878-80) was about 'the progress of Christian civilisation, especially in connection with missionary enterprise', during the previous hundred years.[39] He took a narrative approach,

---

[36] MacLeod,, *Heroes of Invention*, pp. 71-73; Rory T. Cornish, 'John Cartwright', *ODNB*.

[37] H. Colin G. Matthews, 'Samuel Smiles', *ODNB*.

[38] Clyde Binfield, *George Williams and the YMCA: a Study in Victorian Social Attitudes* (London: Heinemann, 1973), pp. 77, 228-29, 338-40; *Bristol Mercury*, 9 October 1875.

[39] *Bristol Mercury*, 9 April 1888.

in Volume 1 relating the fight against the slave trade, mentioning Sharp, Clarkson, Wilberforce, Buxton, and 'Livingstone's heroic labours as explorer and missionary'; struggles of 'everyday heroes' as well as Humphry Davy who brought safety lights to coal mines; others who pioneered lifeboats. There were heroes of Afghan wars; Victoria Cross heroes; prison heroes and heroines; Arctic explorer-heroes; and Indian Mutiny heroes. In Volume 2 Hodder told the story of 'more heroes of the coast' like Grace Darling; and of the Indian mutiny like the Baptist Sir Henry Havelock. He also included chapters on great engineers like blind John Metcalfe, the road engineer, and Brunel; on Florence Nightingale; missionaries to China and Japan; more on David Livingstone; explorer heroes of Australia; inventors like Wedgwood, Watt, Boulton, Stephenson; heroic men of science; missionary martyrs in Africa and the Pacific; and great philanthropists like Raikes the Sunday School pioneer, and Jonas Hanway champion of chimney sweeps and poor children. Here and there obscure women, such as Miss Johanna Chandler and Miss Adeline Cooper (in public health), appear. Hodder's approach was not entirely satisfactory. His selection avowedly favoured Christian heroes though in some cases faith was retrospectively imputed by the author. Over the two volumes there was also some duplication of cases. It is significant that Hodder switched to writing single subject biographies of men of indubitably Christian persuasion such as Lord Shaftesbury (1886) and Samuel Morley (1887).

The Victorian interest in great lives reached its zenith with the most ambitious biographical dictionary of all, *The Dictionary of National Biography*. This privately funded enterprise sponsored by George Smith of the publishing firm Smith & Elder appeared between 1885 and 1900 edited by Leslie

Stephen and Sidney Lee.[40] It ran to 63 volumes, contained 29,104 entries of which 27,195 were full substantive articles and the rest briefer subsidiary pieces, and was written by 653 contributors. Looking back, the editors pronounced a modestly nationalistic verdict on the huge project:

> Such a work of reference may be justly held to serve the national and the beneficial purpose of helping the present and future generations to realise more thoroughly than were otherwise possible the character of their ancestors' collective achievement, of which they now enjoy the fruits.[41]

Carlyle's hero theory of history soon percolated into the consciousness of middle-class Victorian youth. John George Edgar (1827/28-64), a Border-born author inflamed by the novels of Sir Walter Scott, preceded his fellow Scot, Samuel Smiles, when he published *The Boyhood of Great Men* (1853), *The Heroes of England* (1858), and *The Footprints of Famous Men* (4th edn, 1858). The latter was clearly a morally instructive work with emulation in mind: its subtitle was *Designed as Incitements to Intellectual Industry*.[42]

Victorians understood that if history hinged upon the lives of great individuals, then greater resources should be invested in the production and motivation of those individuals: hence the significance of public schools and memorialisation. In

---

[40] Bill Bell, 'George Murray Smith', *ODNB*; Alan Bell, 'Sir Leslie Stephen', *ODNB*.

[41] '*The Dictionary of National Biography*: A Statistical Account' in the last volume of the *DNB*.

[42] *Footprints*, arranged in four parts (men of action; men of letters; artists; men of science) included a number of Scots such as Lord Erskine, David Hume, Dr William Hunter, James Watt, and Adam Smith. There is a copy in the John Rylands Library but it is not in the British Library Catalogue. Nor is it mentioned in Guy Arnold, 'John George Edgar', *ODNB*.

public school chapels or assembly halls, honour boards fed the memorialisation phenomenon.[43]

Yet another Scot who exploited the hero myth was Alexander Hay Japp (1836-1905).[44] A prolific author (writing under seven known pseudonyms) and publisher, friend and biographer of Robert Louis Stevenson, and flagrant redactor of the works and papers of Thomas de Quincey, Japp offered an early business pantheon. After *Leaders of Men. A Book of Biographies Specially Written for Youth* (1880) and *Good Men and True: Biographies of Workers in the Fields of Beneficence and Benevolence* (1890), he published (with the assistance of F. M. Holmes) *Successful Business-Men: Short Accounts of the Rise of Famous Firms with Sketches of the Founders* (1892). Japp's Preface explained that he had contacted the principals of most of the firms, that his selection carefully avoided firms that were competitors, and that his information would not 'publish any secrets either as to machinery or to methods'. Fourteen firms and their founders were included: ranging across the industrial spectrum from a brewer (Allsopp) to a gunmaker (Armstrong) and a travel agent (Thomas Cook). The longest and most informative entries were those on Cook, Price's Patent Candle Co, Salt & Sons, and Sir Josiah Mason, Birmingham steel pen manufacturer. Inevitably a number figured Nonconformists, like Wilberforce Bryant (Quaker and match manufacturer), Cook (Baptist), Jeremiah Chubb (Wesleyan-raised lock maker), Charles E. Mudie (Congregationalist and circulating library pioneer), and Titus Salt (Congregationalist and worsted manufacturer). This gallery was unusual for its time. Late Victorian heroes were military men, explorers, missionaries, engineers, inventors, not

---

[43] Pertinent to this might be a study that I have not seen: N. G. Hamilton, *A History of the Architecture and Ethos of the School Chapel* (University of Bristol PhD; published Ann Arbor MI, 1985).

[44] G. Le Norgate and Laura E. Roman, 'Alexander Hay Japp', *ODNB*.

men in trade or business. In an aristocratic, landed society, trade was deemed inferior to professional or political callings.

The *fin de siècle* presented the opportunity for enterprising publishers to take collective biography into the world of county, middle-class society, and in so doing to dilute the elitist hero myth. Of several publications the most ambitious was the series edited by William Thomas Pike of Brighton. Between 1888 and 1912 his firm produced 33 volumes each of which combined a topographical section on the cities and counties they covered with an illustrated biographical dictionary of distinguished citizens.[45] As the element common to all titles, 'Contemporary Biographies', indicated, the appeal of the series (and no doubt the way in which it was financed) was that it gave county and city leaders a chance to exhibit, and memorialise, their achievements. Each volume had distinct sections in its biographical part: descending from the Lord Lieutenant, Bishops, High Sheriff, and MPs to the nobility, gentry, and magistrates, clergy, volunteers, and last the professional and commercial classes. Nearly all entries were accompanied by photographs, 'mug shots'. No editorial (in the reprinted version at least) explained the criteria for inclusion. It must be assumed that local status and the willingness to subscribe to a volume were prerequisites. Pike's volumes neatly harmonised class snobbery with memorialisation. Britain was still an essentially male-dominated hierarchical society. Although trade union and working class leaders seem to have been excluded from Pike, the presence of the professional and commercial classes represented a shift in memorialisation towards the democratic end of the spectrum and the perception of a British identity which included entrepreneurialism and professionalism.

---

[45] The British Library Catalogue seems not to have a convenient list of the Pike titles. However, in the 1980s the biographical sections of all 33 volumes were reprinted by Peter Bell, an Edinburgh bookseller, and this information comes from his advertisement at that time.

Bombarded by such a throng of heroes, witnessed in funeral rites, monuments, paintings, and literature, and searching for enduring meaning and larger identity for precarious lives stalked by death, it would be surprising if Victorian Methodists were unaffected.

3   ASPECTS OF METHODIST MEMORIALISATION IN THE NINETEENTH CENTURY

Focusing on Wesleyan leaders, this section examines Wesleyan expressions of memorialisation (ritual, image, inscription). The elements come together in the following section which explores the dimensions of control and challenge, mostly before the 1860s.

As a general preface, it should be noted that Methodists, like other Nonconformists, were discriminated against throughout much of the nineteenth century by laws governing burial. 'Until 1880 burials in consecrated ground had to be in accordance with the rites of the Church England. Only a clergyman could read the service; he was forbidden to use it in unconsecrated ground'.[46] Final irritations were swept away in 1900.[47] These seem to have affected ritual rather than monuments. Nevertheless there were cases of clergymen interfering with proposed inscriptions on Nonconformist tombstones.[48]

---

[46] Edmund C. Rawlings, *The Free Churchman's Legal Handbook* (London: National Council of the Evangelical Free Churches, 1902), p. 46.

[47] The fullest account of the struggle to remove Nonconformists' burial disabilities is found in Bernard Lord Manning, *The Protestant Dissenting Deputies* (Cambridge University Press, 1952), pp. 286-332.

[48] Ibid., p. 315; Clive Field, 'Demography and the Decline of British Methodism, III Mortality' *Wesley Historical Society Proceedings,* vol. 58 (2012), 251-53.

In this context some Wesleyans chose to be buried in the parish churchyards of the Church of England,[49] others could access the relatively few Dissenters' burial grounds, and yet others like Thomas Farmer (see below) preferred the new corporate cemeteries springing up in major cities (see above).[50]

(A) WESLEYAN FUNERAL RITES

Memorialisation began with funeral obsequies. Comparisons between the funerals of John Wesley, his brother Charles, or other early Wesleyan leaders and those of the military heroes lodged in the national pantheons during the wars against France and afterwards demonstrate the middle-class, sometimes relatively restrained, character of some Methodists' rituals.

John Wesley died at the age of eighty-seven on Wednesday 2 March 1791, after a short illness, at his house in City Road, London; he was interred in a special vault in the adjacent burying ground on 9 March. During the intervening week he was laid out in his coffin clothed in his clerical habit, cassock, and bands and, for a day, viewed by crowds in the entrance hall to the City Road Chapel (the New Chapel, as it was known) which stood on an adjacent side of the burying ground. So great was the throng that his close attendants decided to hold the funeral at 5 a.m. on 9 March. Even so many managed to be there at that hour. Buried in two coffins, an inner one of lead and an outer one of oak, the identification plate on the lead coffin had the Latin inscription 'Johannes Wesley, A.M., Olim. Soc. Coll. Lin. Oxon., Ob. 2do die. Martii, 1791, An. Aet. 88' (John Wesley, Master of Arts, formerly Fellow of

---

[49] For an example of this see Terry Hurst, 'Biographies in Church Monuments: William Smith and Jane Vazeille of Newcastle upon Tyne' (Below, Chapter 6).

[50] The South Metropolitan Cemetery Company, West Norwood, for example, advertised its mixed facilities for both Anglicans and Dissenters in *The Watchman*, 29 April 1840

Lincoln College, Oxford, died on the second day of March 1791, in the eighty-eighth year of his age.) Wesley left his robes to the Chapel for use by visiting preachers and was buried in woollen, as he wished, conforming to the law. In accordance with the last (1789) of several earlier versions of his will, six poor men were paid £6 to carry him from the Chapel to the vault. Perhaps with some pride, he noted in his *Journal* two years before his death, 'I left no money to any one in my will, because I had none.' About 40 of his preachers and his executors followed the coffin. Huge crowds missed the interment but when Wesley's physician, Dr John Whitehead, preached the funeral sermon later at 10 a.m. they surged in 'great peace and quietness', restrained by 'a vast number of constables' who made way for the mourners coming into the Chapel.[51]

Wesley's rejection of the use of a hearse and insistence on being buried in woollen symbolised the economic self-denial he advocated. It also contrasted sharply with the practices of the wealthy of his time. Burial in woollen, for example, enacted as a protectionist measure for the woollen industry in 1666, and repealed in 1814, was regarded as 'odious' and invariably ignored by the upper classes who could afford to use silk and pay the £5 fine.[52] However, a double coffin, including one of lead, was not within the ambit of the poor, for as seen above it could be as much as £7.

---

[51] The information in this paragraph comes from Richard P. Heitzenrater, *'Faithful unto Death': Last Years and Legacy of John Wesley: Catalogue of an Exhibition in the Elizabeth Perkins Prothro Galleries Commemorating the Bicentenary of John Wesley's Death* (Dallas, TX: Bridwell Library, 1991), pp. 1-25. The quotes are from Elizabeth Ritchie's well-known eyewitness account published later that year.

[52] D. G. C. Allan, 'Burials in Woollen, 1667-1814' in *Centuries of Achievement in Wool* (London: International Wool Secretariat, 1959), pp. 39-42. Allan quotes Alexander Pope's satire on the funeral of the actress and beauty Anne Oldfield (1683-1730): 'Odious! In woollen! T'would a saint provoke Were the last words that poor *Narcissa* spoke'.

Charles Wesley, who predeceased John by three years, died in circumstances different from those of his brother John in at least one important respect. Charles was survived by his wife and his daughter Sarah, intimate relatives. Their mourning was unmatched by any for John recorded in the contemporary accounts. John Wesley, driven by his sense of God's calling and the peripatetic life that constantly took him up and down the land, had separated from his wife. He had no children, though as an essay in this volume shows, his stepchildren were very fond of him.[53] Nevertheless the judgement of recent historians is that he was insensitive to grief. His eyes were so fixed on the glory hereafter that he minimised the pains of sorrow here and now.[54]

When in 1749 Charles married Sally Gwynne the paths of the two brothers began to diverge. Within a few years domestic responsibilities drew Charles away from the life of the itinerant preacher and his priorities changed 'from those of the single-minded and footloose evangelist to a devoted husband and loving father'.[55] The Gwynne family had two estates in the Welsh borders, her father had served as High Sheriff of Radnorshire, Sally and her eight siblings were brought up in comfort, and in the faith of the Church of England, though her churchmanship was not very distant from that of Charles. For his part, he settled into a loving family relationship which produced eight children, though no fewer than five died before the age of two. At their London house they mixed with more aristocratic members of society: a class with whom John Wesley had little sympathy. In old age Charles was closely

---

[53] Terry Hurst, 'Biographies in Church Monuments: William Smith and Jane Vazeille of Newcastle upon Tyne' (Below, Chapter 6).

[54] Henry D. Rack, *Reasonable Enthusiast: John Wesley and the Rise of Methodism* (3rd edn., London: Epworth Press, 2002), pp. 542-43

[55] Gareth Lloyd, '"My Dearest Sally": the Marriage of Charles Wesley and Sally Gwynne', *Wesley Historical Society Proceedings,* vol. 56 (2007), 114. Information in this paragraph comes from this source.

supported by his wife and daughter Sarah and at his death they keenly felt the bitterness of parting. To his grief stricken sister-in-law John could only dispassionately quote Job: 'The Lord gave, and the Lord has taken away: blessed be the name of the Lord!'[56]

Charles Wesley, 'the sweet singer of Israel' died on 29 March 1788. 'His remains, by his own desire, were interred in the churchyard of St Mary-le-bone, near his own residence in Chesterfield-street. The pall was supported by eight Clergyman of the Church of England'.[57] Given that Charles Wesley was a prolific and popular hymn writer (with about 8,000 hymns to his name), the lyrical quality of many matching those of Isaac Watts, the father of the Nonconformist hymn, and given his Anglican predilections, it was not surprising that he received a more fashionable funeral than that of his brother John. In Methodist chapels the passing of Charles Wesley was widely mourned, with pulpits and desks hung in black.[58]

Little has been written about the funerals of the post-Wesley generation of preachers. John Lenton's collective biography of Wesley's preachers comments on deathbeds, burials, funeral sermons, and obituaries but does not probe funeral ceremonies. This is not surprising because few sources are available. However, Dr Adam Clarke, one giant among the 883 Wesleyan clergy alive when he died in 1832, was given considerable detail by his biographers. [59] It cannot be taken as

---

[56] Thomas Jackson, *Memoirs of the Reverend Charles Wesley* (2 vols., London: John Mason, 1848), vol. 2, p. 456, quoting Job 1: 21.

[57] Ibid., vol. 2, p. 459.

[58] Ibid., vol. 2, p. 461.

[59] John Lenton, *John Wesley's Preachers: a Social and Statistical Analysis of the British and Irish Preachers Who Entered the Methodist Itinerancy before 1791* (Milton Keynes: Paternoster, 2009), pp. 397-401; Robert Currie, Alan Gilbert and Lee Horsley, *Churches and Church-Goers: Patterns of Church Growth in the British Isles since 1700* (Oxford: Clarendon Press, 1977), p. 203.

typical of the Wesleyan ministry except, perhaps, for the wealthier Wesleyan clerics.

Adam Clarke, born in County Londonderry in 1762, the son of a schoolmaster, became the most erudite linguist among John Wesley's preachers. An autodidact, he gained a command of Latin, Greek, Hebrew, Syriac, and Chaldean as well as several oriental languages.[60] He used these skills in the service of the Bible Society, the Wesleyan Methodist Missionary Society, and in the compilation of his eight-volume commentary on the Bible (1810-26), now unfairly remembered for its identification of the serpent in Genesis as an ape. He received an honorary LLD from the University of Aberdeen (1808) and was elected to various learned societies which brought him in contact with members of the Establishment including His Royal Highness the Duke of Sussex. In his fifty-year-long and active preaching ministry he served on the periphery of the British Isles, in the Channel Islands, Cornwall, Ireland, rural Lancashire, and the Shetlands. In the upper echelons of the Wesleyan denomination he was a moderating influence, if at times theologically unconventional. He was President of Conference in 1806, 1814, and 1822. By his later years he had a library of 10,000 volumes at his home Haydon Hall near Pinner, luxuries enabled through his mar-

---

[60] Outlines of Adam Clarke's life are George John Stevenson, *Methodist Worthies: Characteristic Sketches of Methodist Preachers* (6 vols., London: Thomas C. Jack, 1884-86), II, pp. 222-37 and Ian Sellers, 'Adam Clarke (1762-1832)' *ODNB*. Fullest available biographies are William Jones, *Memoirs of the Life, Ministry, and Writings of the Rev. Adam Clarke, LLD, FSA* (London: J. M'Gowan, 1834) and the tendentious James Everett, *Adam Clarke Portrayed* (2 vols., London: W. Reed, 1866). John Wesley Etheridge, *The Life of the Rev. Adam Clarke, LLD* (London: John Mason, 1859) is derivative. Samuel Dunn, *The Life of Adam Clarke, LLD* (London: William Tegg, 1863) is a much more popular treatment. Both Everett and Dunn had defied Jabez Bunting and the authority of Conference, seeing Clarke as their champion in efforts to bring greater democracy to Wesleyan governance.

riage in 1788 with Mary Cooke, heiress of a wealthy Trowbridge clothier (her sister married Joseph Butterworth, London law publisher and pillar of Wesleyan Methodism). Adam Clarke died of cholera at the age of seventy in the epidemic of 1832, at the home of his friend George Hobbs in Bayswater, survived by his wife, three sons, and three daughters.

The funeral of Adam Clarke took place in the City Road Chapel on Wednesday 29 August 1832, three days after he died. The hearse left Hobbs' house in Bayswater at about noon accompanied by three mourning coaches and reached the Chapel at one o'clock. Despite the exceedingly wet weather and arrangements to make the funeral strictly private, 'a great number of friends were assembled'. They included the preachers able to attend, such as the Revds. Henry Moore and Joseph Beaumont MD. Rev. Joseph Entwisle, a former President of Conference, 'read the solemn service, and delivered a short address, which was concluded with prayer'. Clarke's remains were taken into the burial ground adjoining City Road Chapel. 'Closely soldered in a coffin of lead' they were buried in a newly-dug vault, 20 feet deep, 'resting on a foundation of brick and cement ... the sides and ends secured with masonry'. Presumably it was dug so deep to accommodate future occupants, and incidentally deterred grave-robbers. Clarke's vault was next to that of John Wesley.[61]

For his eldest son, John Wesley Clarke, the loss of his father was almost too much. Before the day of the funeral he went to his mother, his brothers, and his sisters separately, and unbeknown to the others, took from each of them a lock of hair. These he pressed into a small piece of paper then folded tightly. When the customary earth was given him at the graveside, unseen by spectators he squeezed the wet earth around the paper and dropped it onto the coffin. Everett

---

[61] These details come from Everett, *Clarke,* vol. 2, p. 286, except the names of the preachers, given in Jones, *Clarke,* p. 655.

comments: 'an interesting instance of filial affection! depositing a portion of himself and of the family, while yet living, in the tomb of a parent.'[62]

Funeral sermons eulogising Adam Clarke were preached at several chapels by half a dozen ministers including Revs. Heny Moore and Joseph Beaumont MD.[63] The former was one of John Wesley's literary executors and twice President of the Conference, the latter a staunch opponent of Jabez Bunting's hegemony of Conference. Clearly Clarke was given a restrained middle-class funeral. Mourning coaches, the lead coffin, and the 20 foot vault bore the marks of a prospering member of the middle classes and could never have been afforded by an ordinary Wesleyan minister. On the other hand, there were no reports of any of the flummery of baronial symbolism, detailed above.

Hints of those cryptic funeral symbols appeared in the funeral of the nigh-eighty-year old Rev Dr Jabez Bunting at City Road Chapel on 22 June 1858.[64] Three or four features singled out Bunting's funeral as a distinctively upper middle-class one. From Bunting's residence at 30, Myddelton Square to the City Road Chapel, mostly along City Road, the cortege was headed by the undertaker followed by mutes; then two mourning coaches containing the officiating ministers and Bunting's medical man; then the hearse; followed by two mourning coaches containing the family; then 12 mourning coaches containing various Wesleyan clergy and laymen; and last, six private carriages. Since a modest upper middle-class funeral in 1843 comprised one mourning coach, plus sundry undertaker's minions, and cost £130 17s, 16 mourning coaches (all of which had to be hired from the undertaker) sounds lavish. The second feature which echoed earlier baronial custom was the presence of mutes, men usually holding staves

---

[62] Everett, *Clarke*, vol. 2, pp. 286-87.
[63] Ibid., p. 287.
[64] *The Watchman*, 23 June 1858.

and standing at doorways: vestiges of the roles of castle por-ters.[65] Third, three coffins (a shell of elm enclosed in a lead coffin which in turn was placed in a black oak coffin) again suggested a wealthy funeral.

After fifteen minutes the cortege was met by 'a large num-ber of ministers and friends' 152 in number walking in pairs and headed by the Committee members of the Wesleyan Methodist Missionary Society and the Theological Institution, who wore hatbands, having left the Chapel at 1.0 pm. They led the cortege back to the Chapel. The public were freely admitted to the balcony and the side aisles. The service, dur-ing which Rev John Bowers offered a 45- minute long extem-pore prayer and the Rev John Scott, former President of Con-ference, gave the eulogy, lasted four hours. Afterwards the coffin was removed from the Chapel to a grave in the grave-yard behind the Chapel. Over two weeks later the funeral sermon was preached in City Road Chapel, on Friday morn-ing 9 July 1858, by the Rev Thomas Jackson, Wesleyan histo-rian and former President of Conference. The sermon, and the memoir of Bunting which was read on that occasion, required two hours to deliver.[66]

These ministerial obsequies may be compared to those for one of the leading Wesleyan laymen in the middle decades of the nineteenth century. Thomas Farmer (1790-1861), retired sulphuric acid manufacturer and merchant, was a munificent donor to the British and Foreign Bible Society and the Wes-leyan Methodist Missionary Society of which he was for many years Treasurer.[67] A wealthy industrialist, he left a very

---

[65] Jalland, *Death in the Victorian Family*, p. 196.

[66] *The Watchman*, 23 June, 1858; George J. Stevenson, *City Road Chapel, London and Its Associations* (London: George J. Stevenson, 1872). pp. 225-26. According to W. R. Ward, 'Jabez Bunting', *ODNB*, the burial in this location needed the special permission of the Home Secretary.

[67] Stevenson. *Methodist Worthies*, vol. 4, pp. 569-71; England, Census, 1851. He held patents for processing sulphuric acid and japanned goods. GB Patents 8398 (1840) and 10,224 (1844).

considerable estate of £120,000 (which may be compared to Rev Dr Jabez Bunting's estate of £1,500, still a comfortable one).[68] On 16 May 1861 Farmer was buried in a catacomb (underground burial chamber, usually owned by a family) in the presumably unconsecrated part of the relatively new Highgate Cemetery.

During the morning, the cortege made its ponderous way from Farmer's home, Gunnersbury House, Acton to Highgate led by the hearse, six mourning coaches containing relatives and friends and another containing his servants, followed by many private carriages. On approaching the chapel in Highgate Cemetery the hearse was met by 60 or 80 ministers and lay gentlemen, walking in pairs. On reaching the cemetery gates the pairs parted to form parallel lines between which the cavalcade passed. At the chapel the President of Conference, Rev William Wood Stamp[69], read the service, after which the coffin was carried to the tomb, situated on 'the upper side of a curved, and therefore secluded, cutting near the brow of the hill', a location chosen by Farmer weeks before he died. A short ceremony, led by the President of Conference, was held beside the tomb, in which 'the assembly sang with cheerful solemnity one of Mr Wesley's hymns commencing –

> Hark! A Voice divides the sky, --
> Happy are the faithful dead!
> In the Lord they sweetly die,
> They from all their toils are freed!'

The chief mourners then withdrew and the tomb was visited by those who had stood back a little distance. Nearly three

---

[68] England and Wales, National Probate Calendar, 1858, 1861. See note 22.

[69] See Terry Hurst, 'Biographies in Church Monuments: William Smith and Jane Vazeille of Newcastle upon Tyne' (Below, Chapter 6).

weeks later the funeral sermon was preached, on the evening of 6 June 1861 in the City Road Chapel by the Rev Dr John Hannah who had twice been President of Conference. A long memoir of Farmer was read on that occasion.[70]

Whereas Jabez Bunting was buried with elements of baronial flummery and 16 mourning coaches, and Adam Clarke only three mourning coaches, Farmer's funeral was simpler but nevertheless expensive, with its seven mourning coaches and interment in a catacomb on one of the new sites in Highgate Cemetery. Early eminent Wesleyan ministers in comparison to eminent Wesleyan laymen were privileged in death to be buried in the graveyard adjacent to City Road Chapel, the Wesleyan equivalent of Westminster Abbey or St Paul's Cathedral. Both leading ministers and laymen were accorded long funeral sermons, usually some days or weeks after the actual funeral. In all cases, the distinguished successors of John Wesley were given the kind of funerals of which he might well have disapproved. Their defence would be that they were conforming to the prevailing Victorian customs of the prospering urban middle classes: following conventions that their memberships may well have expected of them - signalling, as they did, the superior social status that the Wesleyan community had achieved by 1840. Their mid-Victorian funeral rituals clearly established the Wesleyan identity as associated with wealth and power. These conclusions, however, are based on a handful of examples which need testing by means of a much wider survey. This evidence and a survey of pre-1914 Rochdale mayors, many of whom were Nonconformists, confirm Jacqueline Williams's finding on the death rituals of Methodist families, that until 1914 (and perhaps later) they could be expensive middle class occasions.[71]

---

[70] *The Watchman*, 22 May, 7 June 1861.
[71] Jacqueline D. S. Williams, 'Methodist Families ca 1850-1932' (University of Wolverhampton, PhD thesis, 2003), p. 299. Author's survey of Rochdale mayors.

(B) WESLEYAN MONUMENTS AND OBJETS D'ART

For nineteenth century Wesleyans the foremost national memorial was John Wesley's City Road Chapel. With its adjacent burial ground (which apparently was not consecrated[72]) it became the Wesleyan pantheon. Nearby was Bunhill Fields, the *Campo Santo* of Dissenting England, the last resting place of Bunyan and Defoe, of Isaac Watts, and William Blake. That was finally secured from the clutches of the Ecclesiastical Commissioners (who proposed selling it for building development) after the City of London authorities stepped in and took the Fields over in 1867.[73] Wesley's City Road premises were different because they not only had a burial ground but also a busy premises with Chapel and Book Room (printers and publishers), which was built under John Wesley's direction.[74]

The Foundery, formerly a royal arsenal, was the multi - purpose premises which accommodated the first Methodist Society in London, from 1739-40 until 1778. It included a 1,500-seat preaching house. This was replaced by a purpose-built Chapel, the 'New Chapel', a short distance away on City Road. To pay for the Chapel, John Wesley raised £6,000 from the Methodist societies in the United Kingdom. It opened in 1778. In the mid-nineteenth century the Chapel had 500 free seats, 936 other (appropriated) seats, and standing room for 500 – accommodation for 2,000 people.[75] After

---

[72] Lenton, *John Wesley's Preachers*, p. 399.

[73] Manning, *Protestant Dissenting Deputies*, pp. 311-15.

[74] The Book Room was moved in 1808, the first of several moves over the next the century. Frank Cumbers, *The Book Room: the Story of the Epworth Press and Methodist Publishing House* (London: Epworth Press, 1956), p.18.

[75] The National Archives, HO 129/16/4/1/2, Ecclesiastical Returns for the Religious Census of 1851, Middlesex, St Barnabas District, St Luke's parish.   For digitised access see http://discovery.nationalarchives.gov.uk/ Search UI/hbrowse?uri=C8993, accessed 22 August 2013. My thanks to Dr Clive Field for this reference.

Wesley's death in 1791 the trustees decided to memorialise the founder and other major figures in the early Methodist movement.[76] See Appendix for a list.

Several points emerge from the list of monuments inside the City Road Chapel before 1872. None was installed until well after the death of John Wesley. Thereafter these tablets recorded the lives of three groups of people: associates of John Wesley; London laity of wealth and influence exerted in the interests of Wesleyan Methodism and the Wesleyan Methodist Missionary Society; and the giants of the denomination in the decades after Wesley, men who held the denomination together in the face of threats of schism and whose talents allowed them to contribute complementary roles to the denomination's development. Also noticeable is the absence of any of the opponents in Conference of the disciplinarian of the denomination, Jabez Bunting, apart from Joseph Fowler. Two others who might have been included were Rev Joseph Beaumont MD and Rev James Dixon DD though he died in 1871, a bit late to be included in the City Road pantheon before Stevenson's record of it. At any rate Beaumont defied Bunting in the Fly Sheets controversy of 1844-49, which led to the expulsion of three ministers over the issue of the concentration of power in Conference, the exclusively clerical body that determined and governed Wesleyan Methodism.

---

[76] 'Wesley's Chapel, City Road, London', online *Dictionary of Methodism* ed. John A. Vickers; http://wesleyhistoricalsociety.org.uk/dmbi/ (accessed June 2013); Stevenson, *City Road Chapel*. For Wesley's Chapel and other Methodist sites, see *Methodist Heritage Handbook: Information for Visitors to Historic Methodist Places in Britain* (2nd edn., London: Methodist Church House, 2012).

PREVIOUS PAGE

Illustration 2.1
Exterior of City Road Chapel, 2013. Reproduced with the permission of The Trustees of Wesley's Chapel, City Road, London. Photographer: Graham Portlock.

NEXT PAGE

Illustration 2.2
Interior of City Road Chapel, 2013. Reproduced with the permission of the Trustees of Wesley's Chapel, City Road, London.

Adjuncts to the City Road Chapel were public monuments and statues. John Wesley's remains were exhumed (the burial of others in the vault having allowed inspection of Wesley's coffin) and in 1828, under the direction of Lancelot Haslope the Chapel treasurer, 'were deposited in a plain and neat sarcophagus' of Portland stone. That in turn was modified and enlarged in 1839 during the Centenary of Methodism. The tomb was entirely renovated in 1870 and in Stevenson's volume has the shape of a Gothic Revival shrine-tomb.[77]

Efforts to secure a public statue of John Wesley took over twenty years to come to fruition, as Donald Ryan has shown.[78] They began in 1820 when John Manning, a linen draper in Bloomsbury, a godson of John Wesley, and a long-time Methodist, first suggested the project. His motive in part was to promote the careers of one of his sons, all three of whom were sculptors. John Manning found a sponsor in Joseph Butterworth, MP and legal book publisher (see above), and his middle son, Samuel Manning the elder, was commissioned to carve the statue for one thousand guineas. Delay was occasioned by the death of Butterworth in 1826. Having earlier obtained the marble, Samuel Manning the elder, drew up a proposal to complete the statue of John Wesley so that it could stand in the Committee Room of the Wesleyan Mission House in Hatton Garden, London. There was some difficulty about the facial features and Rev Dr Adam Clarke advised Manning to use as his model the life bust of John Wesley made in 1781 by Enoch Wood. Then for over ten years noth-

---

[77] Stevenson, *City Road Chapel,* frontispiece, pp. 368-70; for the typology of tombstones see Frederick Burgess, *English Churchyard Memorials* (1963; repr. Cambridge: Lutterworth Press, 2004), pp 64-65.
[78] Donald H. Ryan, 'Wesley Statues and Sculptures: Part I, The Manning Marble Statue of John Wesley', *Wesley Historical Society Proceedings,* vol. 56 (2008), 306-19; idem, 'Wesley, John: Statues and Sculpture' online *Dictionary of Methodism* ed. John A. Vickers; online version at http:// wesleyhistoricalsociety.org.uk/dmbi/ (accessed June 2013).

ing is heard of the project. Samuel Manning the elder died in 1842 and Samuel Manning the younger, his son, took it over. A new backer, Thomas Farmer (see above) was found. Farmer required that it be placed within 10 miles of London and in 1849 the first full length statue of John Wesley was publicly unveiled at the Wesleyan Theological Institution in Richmond. At the inaugural service Rev Thomas Jackson, the Institution's theological tutor, President Designate, and biographer of Wesleyan leaders, declared, 'he should delight, in future, to gaze on that statue, while he remained in that place; and he believed the sight of it would not fail to awaken remembrances of Mr Wesley which would be of benefit to him and would stir him up to increase diligence and zeal in the discharge of his duties.'[79]

Whether the Manning statue immediately inspired other projects is unknown. However, in 1856 a medical doctor and Anglican from Doncaster, Dr George Dunn, was reported in *The Times* as launching a project to erect a statue of John Wesley at his birthplace, Epworth in Lincolnshire. Henry Tilbury, a well-known water-colourist of Doncaster, took his drawing of the proposed statue to a meeting at Epworth and it was later published in the *Illustrated London News*. In the event, the scheme never got off the ground but it did inspire an unidentified Staffordshire potter around 1860 to make 'large numbers of commemorative Staffordshire flat back ornaments in two sizes, based on the drawing of the proposed Epworth statue'. Surviving copies show John Wesley standing preaching with the Bible in his left hand.[80]

The pace of installation of Wesleyan statuary increased in the last quarter of the nineteenth century. As Donald Ryan

---

[79] Ryan, 'Wesley Statues and Sculptures: Part I', quoting *The Watchman,* 20 June 1849.
[80] Donald H. Ryan, 'The John Wesley Millennium Statue', *Wesley Historical Society Proceedings,* vol. 54 (2003), 115-19.

has detailed,[81] a bas-relief profile of John and Charles was unveiled in Westminster Abbey in 1876; a full-length bronze statue of John Wesley was erected in the forecourt of City Road Chapel in 1891 (see Illustration 2.1); and a stone statue of him was placed in the reading room of the John Rylands Library after it opened in 1899. The City Road Chapel statue marked the centenary of Wesley's death and Methodist Union in 1932 was celebrated by an equestrian statue of John Wesley placed in the forecourt of the New Room, Bristol. In 1988, on the 250th anniversary of John Wesley's conversion, a bronze copy of the Manning statue was placed in the churchyard of St Paul's Cathedral. The tercentenary of John Wesley's birth was celebrated with a bronze statue at Epworth. If memorialisation shaped identity, Methodism had become part of the English identity after 1876.

A variety of objets d'art commemorating John Wesley and the Methodist leaders were manufactured and sold in substantial numbers during the nineteenth century. Peter Forsaith suggests three reasons for this 'Wesleyana' phenomenon. Commemorative pottery, such as busts and tableware, could be produced for chapels where a strong social life was developing, very often expressed in shared meals. Secondly, the country's major centre of pottery manufacture was North Staffordshire which was also a stronghold of Methodism. Thirdly, commemorative ware was highly collectible. Forsaith rightly observes that in this phenomenon Methodism was wholly different from other Christian traditions owing much to one man. 'Neither Lutherans, Calvinists, Jesuits nor Franciscans make such play of the image of their founding fa-

---

[81] Idem, 'Wesley, John: Statues and Sculpture', *Dictionary of Methodism* ed. John A. Vickers; online version at http://wesleyhistoricalsociety.org.uk/ dmbi (accessed June 2013).

ther'.[82] The Methodist 'Wesleyana' phenomenon can only be understood when the three factors cited by Forsaith are overlaid by two more: the powerful impression of himself that Wesley projected into succeeding generations by his writings and organisation and the first generation of his preachers; above all, the conducive receptor culture of Victorian memorialisation centring on hero worship.

The first and most authentic three-dimensional portrayal of John Wesley was the bust made and retailed by Enoch Wood (1759-1840) of Burslem in 1781. Wood had some training under Josiah Wedgwood and was apprenticed to Humphrey Palmer of Hanley Green. He emerged a skilful modeller and became known to John Wesley when the latter met his wife on visits to the Potteries. Five sittings were required to get a lifelike bust and, once made in unglazed terracotta, Enoch Wood took samples of it to the Methodist Conference which was meeting in Leeds that year. It was greatly admired and when John Fletcher, the Vicar of Madeley and staunch follower of John Wesley, met the young Wood he congratulated him, placed his hands on the young man's shoulders, and for twenty minutes preached the Gospel to him.[83] Wood remained a loyal Anglican but, not without significance, his daughter Sarah married into the Budgett family, pillars of Wesleyan Methodism in Bristol.[84]

---

[82] Peter Forsaith, 'Material and Cultural Aspects of Methodism: Architecture, Artefacts and Art' in William Gibson, Peter Forsaith, and Martin Wellings (eds.), *The Ashgate Research Companion to World Methodism* (Farnham, Surrey: Ashgate, 2013), p. 400. See also idem, 'Methodism and Its Images' in Charles Yrigoyen Jr. (ed.), *T&T Clark Companion to Methodism* (London: T&T Clark International, 2010).

[83] Arthur D. Cummings, *A Portrait in Pottery* (London: Epworth Press, 1962); Frank Falkner, *The Wood Family of Burslem* (London: Chapman & Hall, 1912), with the report of the Fletcher meeting on p. 56; *'A Brand Plucked from the Burning': John Wesley, a Potteries Portrait* (Stoke-on-Trent: The Potteries Museum & Art Gallery, 1988).

[84] *Bristol Mercury*, 23 May 1840.

Wood's busts of Wesley continued to be made but after 1784 they were produced as coloured hollow backs, which would have been more expensive than the terracotta version, and in black basalt, until shortly after the death of Wesley.[85] The French and Napoleonic wars created a time of rising prices which probably subdued demand for ornamental ceramics. The next fillip for the market in Wesleyan memorabilia came with the celebration of the Methodist Centenary in 1839. It It would be surprising if Enoch Wood did not contribute some of his busts to the celebration: he then employed over 1,000 people. Regrettably his business papers have been lost. This author could find no trace of an advert for his productions in the 1839 summer issues of *The Watchman*.

If Wood's ceramic busts of John Wesley were on sale at Liverpool, the site of the Wesleyan Conference in summer 1839, the question arises as to who might be able to afford to buy them. Two sources for the 1780s and from then until 1815 show that the wholesale price of a pair of white earthenware figures (like a shepherd and a shepherdess) fetched anywhere between 1s 6d and 3s while coloured and gilded ware cost around 5s since they required a double firing.[86] This would make these ceramics well above the ability of a farm labourer on 10 shillings a week to purchase, and not easy for a skilled worker on £2 a week to afford.

---

[85] Cummings, *Portrait in Pottery*, p. 36.

[86] I am grateful to Miranda Goodby, ceramics specialist at the Potteries Museum & Art Gallery in Stoke-on-Trent, for a telephone conversation on 11 June 2013 when I enquired about the prices of ceramic busts in the 1830s. She kindly checked the ledger book of John Wood for wholesale prices in the 1780s and, for the period up to 1815, Ann Eatwell and Alex Werner, 'A London-Staffordshire Warehouse, 1794-1825', *Northern Ceramic Journal* vol. 8 (1991) for this information. Pat Halfpenny, *English Earthenware Figures, 1740-1840* (London: Antique Collectors Club, 1991), p. 314 indicates that John Wood bought wholesale from his brother Enoch Wood.

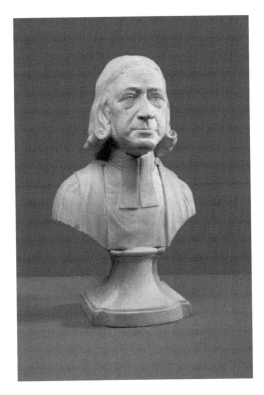

Illustration 2.3
Enoch Wood's bust of John Wesley; biscuit (unglazed pottery); 29.5 cms high; in collection at Wesley's Chapel, London. Reproduced with the permission of the Trustees of Wesley's Chapel, City Road, London. Photographer: Graham Portlock.

Other manufacturers and artisans were busy. For example, 'Robinson & Leadbeater made an attractive copy of Wood's later bust in white Parian'. Staffordshire potters turned out tea services and mugs 'bearing the face of Wesley and a picture of the Centenary Hall and Mission House'. [87]   Maling of

---

[87] Cummings, *Portrait in Pottery*, p. 41.

Newcastle upon Tyne is believed to have made a plaque based on a portrait of Wesley by an unknown artist. [88] John Wesley's head was transmuted into pepper pots, dresser rests, and sash window stops.[89] During the nineteenth century it is estimated that as many as 50 or more different Staffordshire potters created Wesley busts.[90] The best were based on the Wood portrayal.

Of the several denomination-wide events celebrated by Wesleyans in the nineteenth century, the most significant was the Centenary of 1839.[91] It was an unprecedented occasion for celebrating memories. Reminders of mustard seed beginnings; of growth under John Wesley's leadership; of survival in the face of schism; of the apostolic Christian faith they preached: all were underlined in their celebrations. And all, like the ancient Israelites' stones in the Jordan, demanded indelible markers of some sort. Consequently, celebratory sermons and services were accompanied by a huge fundraising effort in support of home and foreign missions, like a new London headquarters for the denomination; properly-established theological training facilities in the south of England (at Richmond) and the North of England (at Didsbury); Centenary chapels; and a missionary ship for the Pacific: all summarised in the *Report* of the Centenary Fund. Accessory, but serving as future reminders of the meanings of the celebrations (as well as being a modest source of income), were

---

[88] *'A Brand Plucked from the Burning'*, Introduction.

[89] Cummings, *Portrait in Pottery*, p. 41; Donald H. Ryan, 'John Wesley Head Window Stop', *Wesley Historical Society Proceedings,* vol. 58 (2012), 275.

[90] Roger Lee, *Wesleyana and Methodist Pottery: a Short Guide* (London: R. Lee, 1988), p. 11.

[91] For these funds see John Lenton, 'Sources for the History of British and Irish Methodism and Genealogy: Some Printed Donation Lists', *Wesley Historical Society Proceedings*, vol. 55 (2005), 43-52 and idem, 'More Information on Methodist Donation Lists', *Wesley Historical Society Proceedings*, vol. 55 (2005), 121-22.

the tangible memorabilia of pottery, paintings, engravings, and medals.

For artists and manufacturers of objets d'art, the Wesleyan Centenary presented a heaven-sent opportunity. Some quickly seized it. Thomas Agnew (1794-1871), Manchester art dealer, promoted a painting by Charles Allen Duval (1808-72), portrait and subject painter in Manchester, recording one hundred portraits of Wesleyan ministers and gentlemen.[92] They had been present at the Wesleyan Centenary Meeting 'held in Manchester' (the preparatory meetings held in the Oldham Street Chapel, Manchester on 7-9 November 1838, when 250 gathered including the President and seven Ex-Presidents).[93] Despite Agnew's frequent advertisements in mid-1839, the Duval painting was not completed until March 1840.[94] The promised engravings, of a large size (see Illustration 2.4), did not appear until early in 1843, made by C. E. Wagstaff and marketed by Agnew.[95]

NEXT PAGE

Illustration 2.4

'The Wesleyan Centenary Meeting' (7-9 November 1838; held in Oldham Street Chapel, Manchester); First Class Proof, C. E. Wagstaff engraving of Charles Allen Duval's painting (first exhibited by Thomas Agnew in Manchester, March, 1840); engraving published by Thomas Agnew, Manchester and Messrs Ackerman & Co., London, 1 February 1843; 76.7 x 93.7 cms; Oversize Map Folder 3, Frank Baker Collection of Wesleyana and British Methodism, David M. Rubenstein Rare Book & Manuscript Library, Duke University. Reproduced by courtesy of Duke University Library. The published key to the individual portraits has yet to be traced.

---

[92] Denis Farr, 'Agnew family', *ODNB*; Albert Nicholson and Patricia Morales, 'Charles Allen Duval', *ODNB*.

[93] *The Watchman*, 3, 10, 24 July 1839; Thomas Jackson, *Recollections of My Own Life and Times* (London: Wesleyan Conference Office, 1873), p. 293.

[94] *Manchester Times and Gazette*, 28 March 1840.

[95] This publication date is based on the entry in the Duke University Library catalogue. See caption to Illustration 2.4.

Particularly enterprising was Henry Perlee Parker (1795 - 1873), another fashionable portrait painter, based in Newcastle upon Tyne. Apparently on his own initiative he executed a large painting (measuring 7 ¼ feet by 5 ¼ feet) showing 'the rescue of the Founder of Methodism from the fire at the Rectory House at Epworth' in 1709.[96] See Illustration 2.5. This became a major piece of Methodist iconography. It captured, in Peter Forsaith's words, 'the denominational creation myth of providential causality that Wesley himself had arguably originated as he described himself as "a brand plucked from the burning"'.[97] The original painting still occupies an inspirational position at the administrative centre of Methodism: it hangs in the Committee Room of Methodist Church House in Marylebone Road, London.

NEXT PAGE
Illustration 2.5
Henry Perlee Parker, 'Is not this a brand plucked out of the fire?' Oil; 91.5 x 122 cms approx.; artist's half-size copy of original; in Brunswick Methodist Church, Newcastle upon Tyne. Courtesy of the Minister (Rev Eden Fletcher) and Trustees of Brunswick Methodist Church. Photographer: David J. Jeremy.

The black-and-white engraving of the original painting (see Frontispiece 1) measuring 70.5 x 93.7 cms made by Samuel William Reynolds (see below) was evidently published several times: one was published in 1863 by A. J. Isaacs; a copy of this is in the Frank Baker Collection of Wesleyana and British Methodism in the David M. Rubenstein Rare Book & Manuscript Library at Duke University, NC, USA. They also have a smaller hand-coloured lithograph of the picture (shown as Frontispiece 2 and on the front cover).

---

[96] *The Watchman*, 26 June 1839. The original, owned by Oxford Brookes University, is leased to Methodist Church House; a half size copy, also by Parker and in better condition, is in the possession of the Brunswick Methodist Church, Newcastle upon Tyne.

[97] Forsaith, 'Material and Cultural Aspects of Methodism', p. 400.

Parker's picture was exhibited during the Centenary Conference meetings at the 2,000-seat Brunswick Chapel in Liverpool in August 1839, 'inspected by crowds of visitors, many of whom, we were happy to observe, gave substantial evidence of their approbation, by attaching their names to the Subscription List' [for copies of the engraving].[98] *The Watchman* profiled Parker's picture in November 1839, giving it a lengthy and glowing write-up, and naming the main characters in the scene. Parker shrewdly let it be reported that he intended 'to present the original as his centenary contribution, to the new Centenary Hall', eliciting *The Watchman* reporter's comment, 'an act of liberality which will not be without its influence upon our Wesleyan friends'.[99]   Parker presumably expected handsome returns because he had it engraved by S. W. Reynolds - Samuel William Reynolds, the younger (1794-1872) a well-known and skilled mezzotint maker and engraver whose father had engraved some of Constable's work.[100]   The engravings were advertised at three guineas for proofs and £1 10s 6d for prints which were expected to be available at Conference meetings in Newcastle upon Tyne the following year.[101]   Agnew increased the print price to £1 11s 6d when he exhibited the picture in Manchester in August 1839 and warned that all prices would be advanced 'as soon as subscribers are supplied'.[102]

Whether Enoch Wood was retailing his Wesley busts at Centenary meetings or not, his imprimatur was used to sell an

---

[98] *The Watchman*, 14, 28 August 1839.

[99] Ibid., 13 November 1839.

[100] Ibid.   Felicity Owen, 'Samuel William Reynolds', father and son, *ODNB*.

[101] *The Watchman*, 26 June, 10 July, 13 November 1839; Marshall Hall, 'Henry Perlee Parker', *ODNB*.

[102] *Manchester Times*, 17 August 1839.

engraved portrait of John Wesley, 'copied from the celebrated Bust executed from the life by Enoch Wood Esq and pronounced by the late Dr Adam Clarke to be the only correct likeness of Mr Wesley ever given to the world'. The publishers of the engraving, Simpkin Marshall & Co of Fleet Street and W. Dean of Stoke upon Trent, cited the testimonial given them by Wood who, it was claimed, superintended the execution of the portrait. Proofs sold at 6s, prints at 3s each.[103]

The Wesleyan Methodist constituency, to say nothing of other branches of Methodism, represented a very sizeable market. In 1839 there were (in round figures) 287,000 Wesleyans and a total of 455,000 Methodists of all kinds in the British Isles.[104] All of them traced their spiritual origins back to John Wesley, his conversion experience in 1738, and the foundation of the first Methodist societies in 1739. The Centenary would bring many of them to Liverpool and to centres such as Bristol, Manchester, Leeds, Sheffield, and London where District committees were organising their celebrations. What proportion of Wesleyan members were prosperous enough to afford three guineas or even 30s for a Parker engraving? An analysis of those who contributed to the nationwide Wesleyan Centenary Fund has shown that 591 Wesleyans donated £50 and upwards (to £1,500):[105] an almost guaranteed market for some of the dearer mementoes that were produced for the Centenary.

One class of these, about which little seems to have been written, were medallions. In their *Report* on the Centenary Fund the Central Committee mentioned that one item in the balance sheet which had raised substantial proceeds and had been organised by the Treasurer (James Wood, company director of Manchester) and Secretaries were 'Medals suitable to be presented to the children of our people, and those in our

---

[103] *Liverpool Mercury*, 16 August 1839.
[104] Currie et al (eds.), *Churches and Churchgoers*, p. 141.
[105] Author's data.

Sunday Schools, who wish to preserve a Memorial of so glad and important an occasion; and some, fitted by their being executed in bronze and silver, to be laid up in the cabinet, and preserved as works of art'. The *Report* added that five medals had been struck.[106]

Although various manufacturers produced Wesleyan Centenary medals, only this series of five medals was made under the direction of the Conference's Centenary Committee. The manufacturers were James Heeley & Sons of Birmingham,[107] appointed by the Centenary Medal Committee (formed at the preparatory meetings in Manchester in November 1838). The five medals were described as follows:

> No 1, 1½ inches in diameter; on the obverse, the head of John Wesley, his life dates, and his motto, THE WORLD IS MY PARISH; on the reverse, a three-quarter length likeness of Charles Wesley, his life dates and the inscription 'Centenary of Wesleyan Methodism, 1839'. This medal was the official Sunday School Medal.
>
> No 2, nearly 2 inches in diameter; on the obverse, John Wesley in high relief and his life dates; on the reverse, an elevation of Centenary Hall and Mission House in London 'from the designs of Mr Pocock'; in the exergue [small space below main feature], John Wesley's motto THE WORLD IS MY PARISH.
>
> No 3, nearly 2 inches in diameter; on the obverse, a three-quarter face and bust of Charles Wesley; on the reverse, a stanza from one of his hymns 'embod-

---

[106] *General Report of the Wesleyan Centenary Fund* (Leeds: Anthony Pickard, 1844), pp. xxxiv-xxxv.
[107] Several Heeley family members manufactured steel or silver 'toys' (small clothing accessories, cutlery, and household items); three (presumably brothers or cousins), Francis, Clement, and Edmund, were Wesleyans. Clement took out two patents for clothing strap fastenings. Francis White & Co, *A New Commercial Directory of Birmingham, 1855* (Sheffield, 1855), p.166; *General Report of the Wesleyan Centenary Fund*, Birmingham and Shrewsbury District, second page. GB Patents 7802 (1838), 8938 (1841).

ying that point of theology which has ever distinguished the Wesleyan Ministry, -- *universal redemption.*

O for a trumpet voice,
On all the world to call!
To bid their hearts rejoice
In Him who died for all!
For all my Lord was crucified!
For all, for all, my Saviour died!'

In the margin was the inscription 'Centenary of Wesleyan Methodism, 1839' and one of Charles Wesley's favourite sayings, 'God buries His workmen, but carries on His work'.
Nos 4 and 5 were duplicates of 2 and 3 'in every respect' except that they were larger, more than 2½ inches in diameter.[108]

---

[108]*The Watchman*, 16 October 1839.

Illustration 2.6
Official Centenary medal, 1839, by James Heeley & Sons of Birmingham;
1½ inches (38mm) size; obverse (upper photo) showing the head of John
Wesley, reverse (lower photo) showing the head of Charles Wesley. It is of
the same size and design as No. 1 in the description of the Sunday School
medal in *The Watchman*, 16 October 1839. That medal was struck in white
metal; this is an example struck in silver, which was not at first available.
Photographed by Mr Martin L. Bower, the owner, and used by his kind
permission.

The price of none of these official Centenary medals was
initially widely advertised. However, James Wood, treasurer
of the Centenary Fund, and a member of its Medal Committee, circulated Wesleyan ministers with a price list in September 1839. The medals were struck in two metals at first, white
metal (a form of pewter) and silver. The white metal versions
ranged between 4d and 2s each, the silver between 7s 6d and
£1.00 each.[109] Evidently they sold so well that the maker,

---

[109] *The Watchman*, 16 October 1839 gives a full textual description. Circu-
lar letter from James Wood addressed to Rev John Stevens, Wesleyan minister, Manningtree, Essex, September 1839, MARC, MAW Pa 1839.60

James Heeley & Sons, by the end of 1839 advertised 'a few choice impressions in Bronze': the small size (No 1) 3s 6d; the middle size (Nos 2 and 3) 11s the pair; the large size (Nos. 4 and 5) 20s the pair; case included in each instance. The whole set in a handsome case was priced at 36s. In the same advertisement the firm announced that they had made new dies in order to execute silver medals, in bright or dead silver on the shortest notice.[110] For their part, the Medal Committee in the autumn 1839 announced they had agents in every circuit in the country ready to handle orders from Sunday Schools 'and the Wesleyan friends generally'.[111] Sales of this commemorative proved very profitable for the Medal Committee: they raised £900 from medal sales for the Centenary Fund.[112] If the Sunday School medal made by James Heeley & Sons, the small one at 4d each raised as much as £400 of the £900, then 24,000 of the cheapest official medals would have been distributed.[113]

This close inspection of a few images of John Wesley by no means exhausts this form of memorialisation. The National Portrait Gallery has records of 30 images of him, just three of his brother. For Adam Clarke it has six images. Their relative visual presence reflects the importance of the John Wes-

---

EMA1511. My thanks to Martin Bower for bringing this item to my attention.

[110] *The Watchman*, 11 December 1839.

[111] Ibid., 2 October 1839. Some agents thought it profitable to advertise the medals. See the *Newcastle Courant*, 13 September 1839 and the *Liverpool Mercury*, 25 October 1839.

[112] *General Report of the Wesleyan Centenary Fund*, pp. xxxiv-xxxv. For references to other medals see Joseph G. Wright, 'Two Scarce Wesley Medals' *Wesley Historical Society Proceedings*, vol. 6 (1907), 85-86; Graham Kirby, 'Wesley Medallions' Ibid., vol. 47 (1989), 59.

[113] The question then arises, what happened to these ca. 24,000 medals? A lot may have disappeared in the scrap metal drives of the Second World War. Pewter would survive neglect. At any rate the apparent loss of the medals since 1839 seems to reflect both the erosion of John Wesley's heroic image and the collapse in churchgoing in the twentieth-century.

ley image, cultivated by himself in his lifetime and thereafter by his followers. He was seen as the founder of the denomination. The occasion of the Centenary was particularly suited to celebrate the founder and the movement. It also presented ample opportunity for political and commercial interests to come into play (see below).

If neither John Wesley, nor his brother Charles, nor Adam Clarke, could be commemorated with a plaque or monument in one of the Establishment's national pantheons, then small-scale mementoes like pottery busts, mezzotints, and medals, all produced in quantity by means of emergent factory organization and technologies developed in the previous sixty or so years, would be distributed to the Wesleyan faithful – retailed by a much finer grained and larger organisational network across the country than other church denominations could mobilise.

(C) WESLEYAN TEXTUAL MEMORIALISATIONS

In the Reformation tradition, and like other Nonconformists, Methodists highly prized the communicative power of the word. Literacy, hymns and religious poetry,[114] libraries,[115] authorship, and above all the Bible were highly respected among nineteenth-century Wesleyans. John Wesley epitomised these characteristics, with his emphasis on literacy for his preachers, his composition of hymns, his printing press,

---

[114] For Wesleyan hymns see J. Richard Watson, *The English Hymn: a Critical and Historical Study* (Oxford: Clarendon Press, 1997), pp.205-64.

[115] Clive Field, 'The Allen Library: A Victorian Methodist Odyssey', *Bulletin of the John Rylands University Library of Manchester,* vol. 89 (2012-13), 69-106 details Wesleyan efforts to form a denominational library rivalling the Church of England's Sion College Library and Old Dissent's Dr Williams's Library. Through the dismal failure of successive trustees and Conference the enterprise failed, in contrast to the great John Rylands Library formed from the collections of the most wealthy nineteenth-century cotton manufacturer and Congregationalist, John Rylands (1801-88). I am grateful to Dr Field for bringing his article to my notice.

and his voluminous writings including published versions of sermons he preached.

In the essays which follow in this volume, those by Barbara Prosser[116] and Janet Kelly[117] demonstrate these characteristics of the founder of Methodism. Not only was he a remarkable organiser but, in the genre of the Puritan cleric, he used his writings both to communicate the Gospel and to control the theology and values of his itinerant preachers. His Journal, a huge work over the years, he may have seen as influencing posterity, thinking that his executors were unlikely to destroy it, though in his will he had given them permission to do so. Certainly he expected his sermons to keep future congregations of Christian believers in the path of orthodox evangelical Arminian theology.[118] All this has been much studied..

Within the topic of this essay only one question is of concern: how in the hundred years or so after his death was John Wesley regarded in their writings or other inscriptions either by his preachers, his professional clergy that is, or by Wesleyan Methodist laity? Was he singled out as a hero? A complete answer here is impossible but there are pointers.

Due reverence to the memory of John Wesley was paid at the meetings by the Committee appointed by Conference (then meeting at Bristol) in July 1838 to make arrangements for the Wesleyan Centenary in 1839. Leading laymen were

---

[116] Barbara Prosser, 'The Transformation of the *Arminian Magazine* from John Wesley's Theological Instrument of Control to His Vehicle for Expressing and Preserving the Evocative Voices of Early Methodism' (Below, Chapter 3).

[117] Janet Kelly, 'Memorials of Motherhood: the Travels and Travails of Preachers' Wives' (Below, Chapter 7).

[118] A collection of 44 of them became the standard statement of belief for Methodists until the late twentieth century: John Wesley, *Sermons on Several Occasions* (London: Methodist Conference Office n.d. but issued when Edgar C. Barton was Book Steward, 1932-48). My copy belonged to my father, a Methodist local preacher on the Wantage and Wallingford Circuit Plan, 1942-1980s.

admitted to these preparatory meetings in St Philip's Chapel, Bristol. One of them, Thomas Farmer (see above), advancing the case for a theological seminary where both the UK ministry and missionaries for foreign service could be trained, as well as the need for a secondary school for children of Wesleyan parents, prefixed his remarks with an expression of indebtedness to John Wesley:

> He then alluded to the national advantages, in a religious point of view, which had resulted from the instrumentality which God had raised up in the person and followers of Mr Wesley. That eminent man, he believed, had been divinely directed to the adoption of those means which had been in progressive use amongst the Wesleyans to the present day, and, by God's blessing on which it was owing that, at the expiration of a hundred years, the little one had become a thousand.[119]

James Wood, a wealthy Manchester businessman and important Wesleyan layman, said 'it would be a disgrace to them if they did not now take care to erect some monument which might hand down to posterity the opinion they entertained of their great founder, and their veneration for his memory'.[120] He favoured a Theological Institution (seminary). Dr Jabez Bunting not only linked gratitude to God, and veneration for Mr Wesley, to a monument of some kind but emphasised, farsightedly, 'It was to be not only a memorial to themselves, their children, and the Methodist Connexion, but a testimonial to the world. These were the general principles on which they all seemed to be agreed.' Bunting eventually steered the meeting (of which the chairman was Rev Thomas Jackson, the President that year) towards raising funds for two buildings (for the Theological Institution): 'that would be two monu-

---

[119] *The Watchman*, 8 August, 1838.
[120] Ibid.

ments, and of course a greater number of persons would be impressed by them'.[121]

The Centenary preparation meetings were continued in Manchester in Oldham Street Chapel over three days in November 1838. A series of resolutions, emerging from the Bristol meetings, were then unanimously adopted and published in *The Watchman*. The first two clearly demonstrated how the leading ministers and laymen regarded the first hundred years of Methodism and John Wesley's role in it:

> I That this Meeting cordially approves of the proposed Celebration (in 1839) of the formation of the Wesleyan Methodist Society in the year 1739, under the providential instrumentality of the ever-to-be-revered and venerated JOHN WESLEY; and deeply feels that the PRIMARY object of such Celebration should be the *religious* and *devotional* improvement of the Centenary by solemn PUBLIC SERVICES in all our Chapels, both at Home, and in the various Stations occupied by our Foreign Missions.
>
> II That this Meeting most cordially concurs in the opinion that, in connection with this primary object [there shall be a national fund] being intended as a practical THANK-OFFERING TO ALMIGHTY GOD for the personal, domestic, and public benefits derived, by his blessing, from the labours of MR WESLEY, and of his Co-adjutors and Successors, during the last Hundred Years, and from the direct and indirect influences of the various ministrations and agencies of Wesleyan Methodism, not merely on our own religious community, but also on the Christian Church at large, and on the spiritual interests of the World.[122]

The design and inscriptions on the official Centenary medals suggest that John Wesley shared official recognition with his brother Charles Wesley. His portrait and text were on two

---

[121] Ibid.

[122] Ibid., 14, 21 November 1838.

of the medals while John was on three (see above). Far more text was on the Charles Wesley medals where the opportunity was taken to quote his magnificent stanza expressing the theology of universal redemption.

Another pointer comes from the inscriptions accompanying donor dedications in the the Centenary Fund, launched in 1839 and kept open until 1844, and the Thanksgiving Fund of 1878-83, two of the three large, nationwide Wesleyan funds of the nineteenth century (the third was the Twentieth Century Fund of 1898). Two variables were counted, the mention of John Wesley or another Wesley in the dedications, with the John Wesley category being confined to those dedications that remembered him for himself, not for example, because grandfather knew him. The other variable was the presence of the Wesley name among the Christian names of the donors. The problems with the latter are that very often initials only were given and that J. W. could mean anything. The results of this exercise are in Table 2.1.

Table 2.1
Remembering the Wesleys: the Wesleyan Centenary and Thanksgiving Funds

Funds	*Mentions of a Wesley in dedications*	*In memory of John Wesley*	*In memory of Dr Adam Clarke*	*Donors' names incorporating Susannah, John or Charles Wesley or Wesley*
Centenary Fund, 1839-44	42	9	14	30
Thanksgiving Fund, 1878-83	1	10		13

Source
Reports of the two Funds; author's analysis.

The Centenary Fund *Report* contained approximately 31,800 donors' names and the Thanksgiving Fund *Report* 47,500 donors' names. In each case the numbers of dedications were in the hundreds rather than the thousands. If it has any validity, Table 2.1 demonstrates a waning at the articulate grass roots level of the adulation of John Wesley between the 1830s and the 1880s.

The multiplication of biographies of Wesleyan and other Methodist figures of distinction might be expected to diminish John Wesley's stature as Methodist hero. To ascertain this, the number, length, and sales of John Wesley biographies should be compared to those of other Methodist figures. Presently no convenient listing of all the nineteenth century biographies of ministers and lay people, Wesleyan or Methodists, exists, let alone an analysis of their lengths or book sales.[123] One crude interim estimate has been derived from the *Dictionary of Methodism in Britain and Ireland*. Because it reflects the limited preferences of late twentieth century historians, it may be quite misleading. See Table 2.2.

Table 2.2
Nineteenth century Methodist biographies listed in Vickers (2000)

Period	Number of titles	Years	Per annum rate	Increase over preceding period
1790-1825	20	35	0.57	
1826-1844	25	18	1.39	243%
1845-1899	91	54	1.69	121%

Source
John A. Vickers (ed.), *A Dictionary of Methodism in Britain and Ireland* (Peterborough: Epworth Press, 2000), pp. 412-38.

---

[123] Dr Clive Field suggests that the Methodist Book Room archive (in the John Rylands Library) or COPAC, the UK universities' search engine, could be used to construct a definitive listing.

While this cannot be regarded as definitive, it might be used as an interim measure. Evidently the rate of production of Methodist biographies after 1845, at 1.69 biographies a year, was much greater than in earlier periods, which neatly coincided with the ascendancy of Carlyle's heroic theory of history. One finding not evident in the table is that after John Wesley (5 biographies), the next most popular subject was Adam Clarke (3).

Several Methodist pantheons in literary form were compiled in the nineteenth century. [124] Thomas Jackson's *The Lives of Early Methodist Preachers* (1837-38 and later editions) dealt only with full-time professional ministers, 41 preachers' biographies in all, most reprinted from Wesley's *Arminian Magazine.* [125] The first collection of biographies spanning both eminent ministers and laymen (no women) in all branches of Methodism was George J. Stevenson's *Methodist Worthies* (6 vols., 1884-86). In Volume I, where more than half the volume treated the respective histories of the Wesleyans, Primitive Methodists, Methodist New Connexion, Bible Christians, and the United Methodist Free Churches, John Wesley's biography received only 20 pages. While he had the longest biography, Charles Wesley was given 17 pages, and John Fletcher and Thomas Coke 14 pages each.

By and large, laymen and women in the nineteenth century received much less attention in the Wesleyans' written sources than their ministers. Few had obituary notices in the *Wesleyan* (formerly *Arminian*) *Magazine*, though the position improved somewhat after *The Watchman,* at 4 ½d a weekly issue, first appeared in 1835. Single volume studies of a few prominent Wesleyan laymen did appear, particularly in the aftermath of Carlyle's *Heroes.* Best known is *The Successful*

---

[124] For biographies of groups of Methodist ministers and lay people see Clive D. Field, 'Methodist Prosopography: Sources and Exemplars of Collective Biography in British Methodism' (Below, Chapter 8).

[125] Lenton, *John Wesley's Preachers*, pp. 13-14.

Merchant: Sketches of the Life of Mr Samuel Budgett Late of Kingswood Hill by Rev William Arthur, a leading Wesleyan preacher. It was published in 1854 and four years later reached its 20th edition by which time 50,000 copies had been printed. Multiplying Methodist biographies appear not to have detracted in the slightest from the heroic view of John Wesley, the venerable founder of Methodism, as Dr Gareth Lloyd's essay on this volume demonstrates.

Biographical studies of John Wesley were massively assisted after 1982 by the appearance of the first volumes of *The Works of John Wesley*,[126] a large editorial project similar in scope and ambition to the numerous and magisterial editions of United States presidential papers that have graced a number of major American universities since the 1940s.[127] Well before the John Wesley project was complete, the verdict of Henry Rack, author of the most recent and rounded biography of the founder of Methodism, was decidedly unflattering. Wesley's lack of human sympathy and empathy towards the bereaved; his self-admission that the assurance of salvation which he preached was hardly ever his own experience; and the failure of his organisational structure to revive the church or to prevent internal schisms: all heavily dented Wesley's nineteenth century reputation as unblemished hero.[128]

Not all memories and stories about John Wesley or eighteenth and nineteenth century Methodists were captured in written records, not even in Sunday School materials (a vehicle of memorialisation not considered here).[129] Oral history

---

[126] Albert Cook Outler, Frank Baker, and Richard P. Heitzenrater (eds.), *The Works of John Wesley* (1982-).

[127] Beginning with Julian P. Boyd et al (eds.), *The Papers of Thomas Jefferson* (Princeton NJ: Princeton University Press, 1950--).

[128] Henry D. Rack, *Reasonable Enthusiast: John Wesley and the Rise of Methodism* (3rd edn., London: Epworth Press, 2002), pp. 535-54.

[129] One study, which I have not seen, might be relevant to this topic: Dorothy M. Entwistle, *Children's Reward Books in Nonconformist Sunday*

was another means by which memories were transmitted across the generations, while not always preserving accuracy. Little has been written about this, though Clive Field in an unpublished paper demonstrated that the early Methodists were well aware of the value of collecting oral history.[130]

In contrast to the short spiritual biographies and autobiographies treated in the present book's chapters by Barbara Prosser[131] and Janet Kelly,[132] the large-scale, volume-length biographies of Wesleyan heroes, primarily John Wesley, and secondarily Charles Wesley, Adam Clarke, and a number of other eminent Wesleyans, provided much more detail and insight into the humanity of these figureheads. In this they were facilitated by advances in papermaking, printing and book distribution, which lowered costs, and, after the 1830s, were not untouched by the rise of the popular Victorian novel. William Arthur's hagiographic portrayal of Samuel Budgett fell between the two genres, the earlier spiritual biography and the lengthy, detailed, honest profiles of a distinguished individual like Adam Clarke.

Schools, 1870-1914: Occurrence, Nature, and Purpose (University of Lancaster PhD; and Ann Arbor, MI: thesis, 1990).

[130] Clive D. Field, 'Communication: Methodism and the Origins of Oral History, 1817-1827' (typescript, ca. 1973). I am grateful to Dr Field for the sight of this.

[131] Barbara Prosser, 'The Transformation of the *Arminian Magazine* from John Wesley's Theological Instrument of Control to His Vehicle for Expressing and Preserving the Evocative Voices of Early Methodism' (Below, Chapter 3).

[132] Janet Kelly, 'Memorials of Motherhood: the Travels and Travails of Preachers' Wives' (Below, Chapter 7).

4 MEMORIALISATION AS A WINDOW ON CONTESTED CONTROL AMONG WESLEYAN METHODISTS

Outside Methodism, biographical portrayals of John Wesley were first contested by the poet laureate Robert Southey in a two volume biography published in 1820. Reactions to its appearance have recently been re-evaluated by Peter Nockles. Southey's main criticism of Wesley was that he was driven by power-seeking and the compulsion to control, and also by religious enthusiasm and self-delusion. Unsurprisingly this caused negative reactions with many inside Methodism. Henry Moore, one of Wesley's preachers, came to the defence with a two volume biography (1824-25) of Wesley, and Richard Watson, another leading Wesleyan preacher, wrote a critical review of Southey. Other clerics from the Church of England participated in this episode of contested memorialisation. Nockles concludes that Southey was much less critical of Wesley than Methodist defenders imagined.[133] While the scope of Edwin Hodder's *Heroes of Britain in Peace and War* (1878-80), (above) did not include John Wesley, neither did it include George Whitefield.

Again outside Methodism, John Wesley remained an iconic figure, visually sustained by one of the last portraits of him, sketched in 1790 by John Kay (1742-1826), Edinburgh portraitist and miniaturist. Kay made portraits of hundreds of inhabitants and visitors to Edinburgh, many of them reproduced as engravings or etchings. The best known of the two Wesley sketches showed the eighty-six-year-old John Wesley walking between fifty-year-old James Hamilton MD, a Wesleyan local preacher, and thirty-nine-year-old Joseph Cole, a Wesleyan itinerant preacher.

---

[133] Peter Nockles, 'Reactions to Robert Southey's "Life of Wesley (1820)" Reconsidered', *Journal of Ecclesiastical History,* 63 (2012), pp. 61-80.

Illustration 2.7
The Edinburgh portrait of John Wesley, by John Kay.   Probably H.
Longmaid's engraving; sold by George Ellison, 1853-81; 21 x 15cms. Au-
thor's copy, scanned.

The engraving appeared in a two volume collection of 360
of Kay's Edinburgh portraits, published 1838-39 (vol. 2, Plate
XXX), as a 'Triumvirate of Methodist Clergyman'.   Notes to
the portrait informed that Wesley was returning from preaching a sermon.   Later nineteenth century printers made variant
copies which circulated in Britain until the 1920s.   Two points
can be added to Donald Ryan's thorough account of the Wesley Edinburgh portraits.[134]   First, after appearing in monthly

---

[134] Donald H. Ryan, 'The Edinburgh Wesley Portraits', *Wesley Historical
Society Proceedings*, vol. 55 (2005), 1-13.

parts the book form arrived, fortuitously, precisely when the Wesleyans were celebrating their Centenary, which may well have added interest in the print, as well as sales for the printer. Second, the portrait showed Wesley, not as a thunderous preacher addressing the crowds but as a small figure in old age needing the support of younger followers: a venerable model nevertheless of longevity and persistence in Gospel proclamation. While this was not a subversive portrait, it did suggest a more vulnerable character than later heroic portraits allowed.

Before the waning of Methodist expansion in the late nineteenth century, the clerically dominated pyramidal structure of Wesleyan Methodism afforded two arenas with scope for effective control of (or resistance towards) memorialisation. One was the annual Conference, the clerical ruling body of the Wesleyans. The other was a fund-raising occasion when the support of the laity had to be widely mobilised, at national or regional (District) levels; of these there were not many before 1914, the first being the Centenary Fund of 1839-44.

Glimpses of the struggle for control of memorialisation at Conference level come from the 1820s and early 1830s. As is well known, Rev Jabez Bunting, pilot of Wesleyan Methodism between the 1820s and the 1840s, in preventing or minimising the dangers of schism, became hypersensitive towards any of the Wesleyan itinerant preachers who gave the slightest hint of stepping out of line. When the venerable Rev Dr Adam Clarke let his friends know that he wished to postpone retirement, the Bunting faction in Conference blocked any move. Bunting was behind the unpleasant treatment of Clarke, as is clear from Bunting's letter to Edmund Grindrod of 2 March 1831.[135] James Everett, the last biographer of Clarke, gave the story extra spin, suggesting that envy moti-

---

[135] W. R. Ward (ed.), *Early Victorian Methodism: the Correspondence of Jabez Bunting, 1830-1858* (London: Oxford University Press, 1976), pp. 8-12.

vated Bunting: by forcing Clarke's retirement, he prevented the most honoured minister in the Wesleyan Conference from becoming eligible for yet another honour of election as Wesleyan President for an unprecedented fourth time.[136]

This was the background to the situation shortly after Adam Clarke's death in 1832 when some of Clarke's friends mobilised allies such as the Duke of Sussex in an effort to erect a public monument to his memory, even in St Paul's Cathedral. Meetings were held and the support of the Wesleyan Conference was sought. At this juncture Rev Richard Watson, Bunting's protégé, made a countermove. He proposed that Adam Clarke and Rev Joseph Benson should be honoured with tablets to their memory in the City Road Chapel. This was agreed and once more the Bunting party checked steps to honour and memorialise a potential rival in death, if not to John Wesley, then to Jabez Bunting. Ironically, before the end of the year 1833 Watson himself was dead and another monument would be added to the interior of Methodism's cathedral. In this instance memorialisation became an instrument of control in the hands of Jabez Bunting. In writing biographies of Adam Clarke, Dunn and Everett challenged clerical autocracy in Conference, exposed Bunting's plotting, as they saw it, and exacted some justice.

Memorialisation was not only a political implement but a vehicle of inspiration. When reduced to stone and metal it diminished the personality and achievements of a great person whose reputation rested on his scholarship and learning. It was this tendency which worried Adam Clarke's first biographer, William Jones (1762-1846), Scotch Baptist minister who was 'deeply opposed to religious establishments'.[137] His last word on the Clarke Monument Committee was to quote Sir William Jones that 'the best monument which can be

---

[136] Everett, *Clarke*, vol. 2, pp. 264-69.
[137] Derek B. Murray, 'William Jones (1762-1846)' *ODNB*.

erected to the memory of an author is a good edition of his works', adding

> Sincerely respecting the memory of Dr Clarke as an
> amiable, laborious, and learned man, one could ar-
> dently wish that his friends would content them-
> selves with the testimony to his worth now referred
> to, leaving it to the Nelsons, the Wellingtons, the
> Chathams, and the Foxes, to have recourse to bronze
> and marble for perpetuating their illustrious
> deeds.[138]

A later example of Wesleyan contempt for statues of John Wesley was reported in the Wesleyans' national weekly, *The Watchman*. As seen above, support for a John Wesley statue was hesitant between the 1820s and 1840s, partly because of the accidents of life. When in October 1860 the members of City Road Chapel met to discuss raising an extra £9,000 to secure the freehold of the City Road Chapel estate and the minister the Rev Thomas Jackson moved a resolution express-ing thankfulness that the trustees had made the appropriate legal arrangements, Edward Corderoy, a merchant[139], second-ed the resolution with an eloquent speech. It included the fol-lowing powerful declamation:

> Something has been said about erecting a monument
> to Wesley. No! Very respectfully, no! Purchase
> this place, if you please, as a memorial of our vener-
> ation and affection for Wesley. Purchase it as an in-
> heritance for our children and our children's chil-
> dren, that they may worship here. Purchase it as a
> place of pilgrimage for Methodists from every part
> of the world, but John Wesley needs no monument.
> You may raise your columns and carve names on

---

[138] Jones, *Clarke*, p. 658.

[139] He died at sea on 10 May 1865, leaving an estate of (under) £8,000. National Probate Calendar, England & Wales, 1865. *The Watchman,* 17 May 1865.

them to men whose names are in danger of dying out and being forgotten; you may chisel the features of your warriors on marble, lest you should forget how heroes have looked; but Wesley needs no monument. He impressed the mind and heart of his time more than any other man of that age; and he is impressing the character of our age more than any Protestant divine ever impressed any age or any country. Wesley needs no monument. He is reproduced in every Methodist pulpit of our land by local as well as itinerant preachers, and wherever a holy man goes distributing your tracts, or visiting the sick or dying, or leading your classes, or the village prayer-meetings - John Wesley is reproduced in the Methodist Societies of every city, town, and village throughout this land, and reproduced in the countless congregations in the United States of America. John Wesley needs no monument! He is everywhere working on mankind by his sermons, his letters, his journal, his works, his Society, his system; and John Wesley never can die. His name will never be blotted out, and you need no monument to perpetuate it! Let each of us strive to be so like Wesley that we shall be living monuments unto his memory. The sun gleams on scarcely any portion of the earth where the name of Jesus has been preached where there are those who will acknowledge, mediately or otherwise, John Wesley as their spiritual father.[140]

Ironically, in denying the need for a statue of John Wesley, Corderoy let his rhetoric flights shape Wesley into an extraordinary prophet hero, not dissimilar to Carlyle's prototype Mohammed. He realised the hazard, continued, but then went further portraying Wesley with the perfection usually ascribed to Jesus Christ. The grace of God was almost an appendage to Corderoy's image of Wesley:

---

[140] *The Watchman*, 24 October 1860; also quoted in Stevenson, *City Road Chapel*, pp. 230-31.

> Other denominations may accuse us of honouring a
> man unwisely but let it be said once for all that no
> Society on earth can boast such a founder, so pure in
> his character, so simple in his motives, so truthful in
> his utterances, so superior to money and every petty
> and ordinary thing - a man who went about doing
> good the whole of his life, yet we will not glory
> even in Wesley apart from the grace of God, which
> made him what he was, and enabled him to achieve
> what he did.[141]

The stage for these two challenges to the memorialisation
projected by the dominant Wesleyan elite was relatively limited, one the Conference, the other London. By far the broad-
est stage was presented by a nationwide fund-raising event,
like the Centenary celebrations, developed in 1838 and nationally shared in 1839. Undercurrents to the Centenary help
to answer the question, 'who controlled Wesleyan memorialisation in the nineteenth century?'

On the one hand, the Conference and its Centenary Committee, in authorising the celebratory medals, three depicting
John Wesley, two Charles Wesley, exerted a forceful and
wide influence. The images were official, they were exclusively of the Wesley brothers and John more than Charles,
they were affordable by Sunday School children, and, sharply
executed, they encapsulated in metal (and before the age of
cheap steel) the Methodists' overriding Arminian theology:
the Gospel for the whole world. As seen, the medals were
very widely distributed across the denomination. Those in
charge of deciding medal images might have chosen a selection of early Wesleyan Presidents, including Adam Clarke
whose likeness was sold as a commemorative ceramic in

---

[141] Ibid., pp. 231.

about 1840.[142] Instead they ensured John Wesley topped the podium with brother Charles as runner-up.

On the other hand, men with an independent commercial interest played a part in the image making that was in the background of the Centenary celebrations. Several medals were produced, with designs figuring John Wesley.[143] Warnings against spurious Centenary medals were advertised by the Conference Medal Committee.[144]

While the medals gave prominence to John Wesley, the paintings occasioned by the Wesleyan Centenary presented

---

[142] One mug and four different plaques ca. 1840 depicting Clarke are listed in *'A Brand Plucked from the Burning'*, catalogue Section D.

[143] Several other manufacturers produced unofficial commemorative medals for the Centenary. The London medal, struck in several different metals, depicted John Wesley. It was based on a design by Philip Champ, with dies executed by W. J. Taylor of London. The gold version retailed at 8 guineas, the silver at 15 shillings, the bronze at 6 s 6d, and the Queen's or pure white metal, 1s. 'Through the liberality of some Friends to Methodism, who deprecate the idea of an inferior Medal to celebrate so important an event, the White Medals are to be furnished to Sunday Schools at £3 12s per gross, the orders for such to be accompanied with a Certificate from the Superintendents or Secretaries stating that they are for such Schools.' Chapel-keepers and pew-openers who might be appointed as agents for the sale of the medals were promised an inspection medal. Supplies were available from Messrs Clarke & Lewis of Crown Court, Threadneedle Street, London or Mr Champ of 5 Stepney Green Terrace, London. At 6d a medal, these were certainly affordable by the majority of Sunday School children, but dearer than the official 4d Centenary medal (above). *The Watchman*, 23 October 1839.

Edmund Heeley & Co (presumably not unconnected with James Heeley & Sons who won the official medal contract) advertised 'Centenary medals commemorating the annual Wesleyan Conference held at Bristol and other towns' obtainable at 1s to 2s a dozen - 1d or 2d each - clearly aiming to undercut the official medal on price. Ibid., 16 October 1839.

Another centenary medal was by Messrs Myers, Sparrow, & Co of Cannon Street, London. Theirs was described as 'a Splendid Medallion Engraving on Steel, of the late Rev John Wesley, from the celebrated Bust of that eminent man, in the possession of Henry Longden, Esq'. Ibid., 23 October 1839.

[144] Ibid., 25 September, 16, 23 October 1839.

scope for expressions of secondary-level control and insubordination. It was not unusual by the early 1830s for distinguished Wesleyan clergymen to be drawn and painted and the portraits engraved for publication. It was one sign of the growing size and social respectability of the Wesleyans.[145] However, during the run-up to the Centenary, in the four years 1836-39 inclusive, Rev Dr Jabez Bunting received an unusual amount of visual publicity, with four public images in three media. While he was President of Conference (for the third time) in 1836, Bunting's portrait was painted by John Bostock (1808-72), a fashionable painter of aristocratic personages, and was exhibited by Agnew & Zanetti in their gallery in Manchester. High-quality engravings were promised ranging in price from a guinea to three guineas.[146] That same year James Heeley & Sons, craftsmen in metal working of Birmingham where Conference was then held, announced to fellow Wesleyans that on 15 December 1836 (no doubt to catch the Christmas market) they would publish a 'splendid medal' struck in white metal, bronze, and silver. On the obverse was a likeness of 'the Reverend Jabez Bunting DD, President of the Wesleyan Methodist Conference', on the reverse a likeness of the Rev Robert Newton, Conference Secretary (and twice previously President).[147] Newton, a popular and prominent preacher, was also painted by Bostock ca. 1838.[148]

In readiness for the Centenary year itself, 1839-40, a high-quality engraving of the Bostock oil portrait of Bunting was

---

[145] John Jackson RA (1778-1831) began producing portraits of eminent Methodists for the *Wesleyan Magazine* in 1813 but other artists of lesser ability offered likenesses of popular pulpit characters. The 'Hubard Profile and Portrait Gallery' in Birmingham sold portraits 'taken from life' of eminent Wesleyan ministers, like Adam Clarke, Richard Watson, and Valentine Ward, in July 1836, just before the Conference met in that city. Felicity Owen, 'John Jackson', *ODNB*; *The Watchman*, 27 July 1836

[146] Ibid., 30 November 1836.

[147] Ibid., 14 December 1836.

[148] Ibid., 14 November 1838.

announced by Thomas Agnew the Manchester art dealer and gallery owner (now operating by himself). The engraver was S.W. Reynolds Jr, (already noted) and his highly-praised work was published early in 1839.[149] Its description suggests it was a mezzotint; if so, anywhere between 50 and 300 copies could be printed from a single plate.[150] The initiative for the new Bunting engraving probably came from the enterprising Agnew who in March 1840 advertised it in a trilogy of engraved portraits of Wesleyan leaders: the late Rev Richard Watson, unknown engraver after the portrait by John Jackson RA; the Rev Jabez Bunting, by Reynolds after Bostock; and the Rev Robert Newton, again by Reynolds after Bostock. By March 1840 only a few impressions of the Bunting engraving remained with Agnew.[151]

By this time Agnew, spotting another golden opportunity after the three day preparatory meetings in Manchester were held in November 1838, set his artist contact Duval to work on the great group portrait of a hundred of the 250 Wesleyan ministers and leading layman who then assembled. The result was 'The Wesleyan Centenary Meeting'.[152] Forty years later George Stevenson pronounced this painting, 'one of the most interesting pictures of Methodist history which has ever been produced.' Not drawing attention to the fact that Thom-

---

[149] *Manchester Times*, 9 February 1839. In the National Portrait Gallery, Index, its ref no. is NPG D32389.
[150] Ellen G. D'Oench, *'Copper into Gold': Prints by John Raphael Smith, 1751-1812* (New Haven CT: Yale University Press, 1999), p. 8.
[151] *The Watchman*, 4 March 1840.
[152] The painting apparently hung in Salford Art Gallery in the 1930s. It has since disappeared, possibly destroyed during the Second World War. An engraving of the painting, made by C. E. Wagstaff, was published by Thomas Agnew of Manchester and Messrs Ackermann & Co of London in 1843. Copies of this engraving (measuring 76.7 x 93.7 cms) are rare. Two have survived in the Frank Baker Collection of Wesleyana and British Methodism in the David M. Rubenstein Rare Book & Manuscript Library at Duke University, NC, USA. See Illustration 2.4.

as Jackson was the President of Conference that year, he observed that 'Dr Bunting is the central figure, standing on the platform in the attitude of addressing his brethren'.[153] Clearly the placing of a standing speaker on the platform made a more interesting pictorial composition than a row of seated platform figures. Yet why was Jackson not the central figure? Was it an attempt by the artist and promoter to pander to pro-Bunting supporters? Or did it reflect Bunting's clumsy attempt at self-promotion?

Yet there was also subversion of Bunting's influence in the Centenary paintings. In Perlee Parker's painting of the five-year-old John Wesley being rescued from the Epworth rectory fire in 1709, the face of the figure standing lower down than John Brown the rescuer but ready to receive from Brown's hands the young Wesley was none other than James Everett: the well-known Wesleyan minister and erstwhile Manchester bookseller, increasingly disenchanted with Bunting's authoritarian rule.[154]

NEXT PAGE

Illustration 2.8
Detail from Wagstaff engraving after Duval of the Wesleyan Centenary meeting, 1838 (see Illustration 2.4); courtesy of the David M. Rubenstein Rare Book and Manuscript Library, Duke Unversity. Noticeably, most eyes among the platform party look towards Bunting, standing on the right.

---

[153] Stevenson, *Methodist Worthies*, vol. 2, pp. 258-9. Stevenson noted that not all likenesses were equally true to life. James Everett was not happy with his. Richard Chew, *James Everett: A Biography* (London: Hodder & Stoughton, 1875), p. 314

[154] David A. Gowland, *Methodist Secessions. The Origins of Free Methodism in Three Lancashire Towns: Manchester, Rochdale, Liverpool* (Manchester: Chetham Society, 1979), pp. 17, 33, 36, 38, 39, 44.

Compared to the intriguing relationship between Bunting and Agnew (and hence Bostock and Reynolds,) the artist and sitter connection in the case of Parker and Everett is much clearer. When Agnew advertised a private viewing of Parker's 'Grand Centenary Picture' in his Repository of Arts on Exchange Street, Manchester, in August 1839, he promised those subscribing to prints 'a pamphlet descriptive of the picture, with historical references by the Rev J. Everett'.[155]

It is known that Everett, while he was in the Newcastle District, was friendly with Perlee Parker; Parker and his family had 'for many years been in connexion with the Wesleyans as hearers or members'[156]; Everett was a skilled draughtsman who could appreciate Parker's skill;[157] Parker consulted Everett when he was looking for an appropriate subject to paint to commemorate the Centenary of Methodism; and Everett took a keen interest in the progress of the painting. Everett's account is worth quoting:

> I told him [Parker] that, independently of the occasion, he could not have a finer subject for the display of artistic skill, and suggested to him the main object, with a few of its surroundings, hurriedly throwing before his imagination the house in flames, the child at the window, one person on the shoulder of another to effect a rescue, the father engaged in prayer, the distressed family grouped together in

---

[155] *Manchester Times*, 17 August 1839. Chew, *James Everett*, p. 314. In writing *Faces in the Firelight: on Henry Perlee Parker, Painter of the Epworth Parsonage Fire, 1709, and on the Wesley Family* (London: Epworth Press, 1934), Sir (Richard) Walter Essex had access to the pamphlet (p. 9), repeated some of Everett's identifications, but missed the symbolism. A copy of this pamphlet, which might have been revealing, would probably have been in the archive of Agnew's, the distinguished London art dealers; unfortunately they went out of business early in 2013.

[156] *The Watchman*, 12 August 1840.

[157] See his sketch of Dr Adam Clarke reproduced in *Wesley Historical Society Proceedings*, vol. 38 (1972), 144a.

front of the building from which they had just es-
caped; neighbours, half dressed, coming to lend
their aid; the poultry on the wing, in fright; the cat-
tle, let out of the fold, fleeing for safety; snow on the
ground, with footprints, to denote the season; the
moon in the heavens, giving the advantage of a double light, one from the heavens for more distant objects, with the church in the background, and the
other from the house in flames, vividly flickering
over every immediate object in commotion, etc. Mr
Parker said 'It will do'.

The next day Parker brought a rough oil sketch for Everett's comment. Thereafter Everett watched the picture's progress with interest. He goes on to say,

I furnished the artist with the attitudes of the various
personages introduced, by throwing myself in different postures. .... In this picture Parker took a profile likeness of myself, and placed my figure towards the place of rescue, between the dog and the
group below the window, with outstretched arms
ready to receive the child second-hand from his first
deliverer. The part I took in this picture afforded me
much amusement.[158]

NEXT PAGE

Illustration 2.8
Detail from Henry Perlee Parker's, 'Is not this a brand plucked out of the
fire?' (See Illustration 2.5). Courtesy of the Minister (Rev Eden Fletcher)
and Trustees of Brunswick Methodist Church. Photographer: David J. Jeremy. James Everett is the figure on the lower right. See back cover of this
book.

---

[158] Chew, *James Everett*, pp. 313-14, passim.

Everett suggests that although he modelled for Parker, he was surprised to see his face in the painting. In all likelihood Parker in their conversations over the months and years had learned, perhaps shared, Everett's attitudes towards Bunting and thought he would give some prominence in paint to Everett: Victorian artists dealt in symbols and multi-layered images; if this was not subversive, it was mischievous.[159] At any rate it caused no harm to Parker. His painting was gratefully accepted by Conference for hanging in the new Centenary Hall and within months he was appointed Professor of Painting at the new Sheffield Wesleyan College.[160]

If the Perlee Parker painting contained an element of subversion, why did Conference readily accept it for hanging in the Centenary Hall, the Wesleyan Methodist Missionary Society's headquarters? Several reasons may be advanced. First, though partly known and sometimes suspected, the depth of Everett's intense hostility towards Bunting's centralising and clerical policies, and Bunting himself, did not always surface at this time.[161] Second, the episode John Wesley perceived as the first sign of his divinely ordained mission, the perilous moment on which the existence of Methodism turned, was captured in a stunning record that readily burrowed into the viewer's visual memory. Third, the realism with which the

---

[159] Other layers of interpretation have been projected into the picture: Amy Green (quoted by Peter Forsaith) sees the divide between the women on the right and the men on the left of Parker's picture as symbols of the gender/power divide in nineteenth century Methodism. Peter Forsaith perceives the widening gap between Wesleyan Methodism and the Established Church, lifeless in the shadows of the picture, but in 1839 newly invigorated by the Oxford movement. Forsaith, *John Wesley: Religious Hero?*, pp. 9-10.

[160] *The Watchman,* 12 August 1840; *Newcastle Courant*, 13 November, 11 December 1840.

[161] Gowland, *Methodist Secessions*, pp. 17, 33, 36, 38; Chew, *James Everett*, pp. 309-10; Stevenson, *Methodist Worthies,* vol. 6, pp. 913-21.

artist caught the epochal moment evidently subdued Methodists' avowed suspicion of images of the divine and of pictures
in general.[162] Above all, displaying the painting helped to
energise faith and diffuse Wesleyan Methodist identity.

Early in 1840 both Parker's 'Epworth fire' and Duval's
'Hundred Wesleyans' were being separately exhibited in English cities. Thus, in the spring while the former was moving
through venues in other Wesleyan Conference cities and London (including City Road Chapel) on its way to Newcastle
upon Tyne prior to presentation to the annual Conference in
August, the latter was exhibited in the Exeter Hall, London, a
major public hall opened in 1831 in the Strand.[163]

Side by side, in the mind of the viewer, the two paintings
projected startling contrasts. One (Parker's) conjured up a
terrifying scene, the pastoral night illuminated by a dreaded
house fire, yet focused on heroism amidst panic. The other
(Duval's) in contrived manner presented a sedate congregation
in a commodious Wesleyan chapel. One captured a rudely-
awoken, coatless rural crowd, the other a well-dressed, afflu-
ent urban gathering. One spoke of social obscurity, the other
of social self-satisfaction, prominence, and respectability.
One epitomised the old order, the other the new and coming
one of merchants and industrialists. To the initiated, one related beginnings, the other arrivals. Here was destiny
glimpsed and destiny fulfilled. To the spiritually minded,
here was Providence promised and Providence proven.

---

[162] John Wesley, in his Sermon on 'The Use of Money' in the volume containing the denomination's official teaching, excoriated 'costly pictures,
painting, gilding, books' as gratifying the desire of the eye. Yet as Kenton
Stiles, quoted by Peter Forsaith, showed, John Wesley's attitude to art was
in fact ambivalent. Wesley, *Sermons on Several Occasions*, p. 622 (see
above footnote 117 for full citation); Forsaith, 'Methodism and Its Images',
pp. 365-66.
[163] *The Watchman,* 13 November 1839, 29 April 1840. It was exhibited in
Exeter Hall 'for friends attending the Missionary meetings'.

In terms of ecclesiastical polity, the Church of England loomed in the background of Parker's dramatic canvas, suggesting where religious power lay in the old order. In Duval's group portrait of the new order, New Dissent sat in comfortable, assured independence. To insiders, sensible of issues of Wesleyan polity, contrasts between the two pictures carried pointed meaning. Everett's profile and position, placed by Parker as a key link in the chain of rescuers, suggested that Everett's ideology (radical, working class) rightly belonged in the Wesleyan legacy: that democratic governance ought to be inherent in the Wesleyan Conference. In the other painting, Duval portrayed a privileged, hierarchical assemblage: rich, tail-coated laymen in the foreground; prospering ministers similarly garbed in the middle- and backgrounds; bonneted women and the occasional child in the balconies; and dominating the platform, his head symbolically near and claiming the authority of Bible and pulpit, addressing the assembly, stood Rev Dr Jabez Bunting. To many he was the helmsman guiding the connexion through storms of schism, to others he was Wesleyan clerical tyranny personified.

In the long run it was the Parker painting that won the day, with its message of providential design remembered and its disruptive subtext forgotten: leaving untouched for decades male, clerical supremacy in Wesleyan governance.

Because the painting had such a powerful effect upon the Wesleyan Methodist imagination in sustaining the denomination's providential creation myth, the Everett-Parker friendship had a greater impact than they might have expected. Copies would initially have been confined to the middle classes: prints were variously priced at 31s 6d, proofs for three guineas, and 'proofs before letters' five guineas.[164] Later the image percolated more widely.[165] Wesley's understanding of

---

[164] *Manchester Times*, 17 August 1839.
[165] See Frontispiece 2.

himself as a brand providentially plucked from the burning, an interpretation of a memory that shaped his identity and empowered his mission,[166] supported the Wesleyan assertion that 'Methodism is a revival of apostolical Christianity'.[167]

5 LONG TERM PATTERNS IN WESLEYAN MEMORIALISATION?

What can be deduced about long-term patterns of memorialisation within Victorian Methodism? There was the possibility that Wesleyans, following John Wesley's woollen shroud example, might reject entirely the secular funereal norms. This did not happen. Indeed only the Quakers, and then only those remaining 'plain', totally rejected the elaborate, costly funerals and memorials of Victorian society.

Wesleyans (if they were like the New Connexion Methodists of Rochdale) might sometimes exceed the funeral norms of the upper middle classes. More work needs to be done to discover whether the funerals of the Wesley brothers, Adam Clarke, Jabez Bunting, and Thomas Farmer, described above, were typical of wealthier Wesleyans throughout the nineteenth century.

What seems clear is the intensification in the production of Wesleyan artefacts during and for decades after the Methodist Centenary celebrations of 1839. In England and Wales John Wesley was recalled in large numbers of busts, medals, ceramic tableware, and engravings. These far exceeded those memorialising either his brother Charles, the great hymn writ-

---

[166] From about 1737, Wesley saw himself mirrored in this biblical metaphor (Zechariah 3: 2). Rack, *Reasonable Enthusiast*, p. 57.
[167] *General Report of the Wesleyan Centenary Fund*, p. iii. While this report (evidently written by Thomas Jackson) is shot through with a sense of providential leading in the rise of Methodism, no reference was made to the rescue of Wesley from the Epworth fire. Jackson, *Recollections*, pp. 299-300.

er, or Adam Clarke the hugely erudite Biblical scholar and popular preacher of the early nineteenth century. Yet Wesleyans were slow to erect public monuments to John Wesley: only one before 1850, only three more before 1914, and a total of seven to the present. This may be compared to 30 plus for Queen Victoria and about 20 each for Nelson and Wellington.[168]

The inscription evidence hints at contrary trends. The most widespread opportunity for moderately wealthy Wesleyans to express their true feelings towards John Wesley came on the occasion of two great fundraising projects, the Centenary Fund of 1839-44 and the Thanksgiving Fund of 1878-83. Among several hundred published dedications were few indeed for John Wesley for his own sake. And while the output of Methodist biographies seems to have increased markedly after 1840, attention focused on many more individuals than Wesley, though his biographies outnumbered those of rivals like Adam Clarke.

Of course the denomination was growing and maturing but in doing so, in general, Wesleyan memorialisation followed society's practices. Throughout the Victorian period Wesleyans echoed the secular preoccupation with heroes. Their hero, however, was singular. John Wesley was the founder and the impressions he left as a result of his numerous publications and his ubiquitous travels across the British Isles, and the visual reminders handed down through the generations, cut deeply into the collective chapel consciousness. These impressions were reinforced by fashions in art and advances in technology, both sometimes driven by alert entrepreneurs from within or outside the Methodist community of faith.

---

[168] Jo Darke, *The Monument Guide to England and Wales: a National Portrait in Bronze and Stone* (London: Macdonald, 1991).

6 HOW DID MEMORIALISATION SHAPE WESLEYAN METHODIST IDENTITY?

Before the 1870s a variety of rival Methodist groupings lured Wesleyans with opportunities for more democratic governance or lay representation in their ruling bodies, or the promise of revivalist practices. Consequently the Wesleyans, as the main but least democratic body of Methodists, were vulnerable to internal dissent and schism.[169] Memorialisation therefore offered a social bonding mechanism of some significance. Facing inwards, it could help reinforce internal cohesion and unity; facing outwards it offered possibilities for building a distinctive identity.

Exactly these possibilities were perceived by those ministers and laymen who organised the Centenary celebration of Wesleyan Methodism in 1839. The occasion and its preparation in fact became an arena in which the highest purposes of memorialisation were expressed but at times were sullied by the means adopted.

The highest purposes were voiced by two distinguished ministers, Rev Dr John Hannah and Rev Richard Waddy, in one of the last resolutions, No XXIII, which they respectively moved and seconded, at the Centenary preparation meetings in Oldham Street Chapel, Manchester in November 1838. Inspired by 'the peace and amity which now happily prevail throughout the Connexion' they were filled with hope that the Societies, walking more closely than ever 'in the fear of the Lord, in the comfort of the Holy Ghost' will be abundantly 'multiplied' and that the approaching Centenary 'will obtain a permanent memorial from heaven - the memorial of a great and extensive revival of pure and primitive Christianity'. The resolution (together with 23 more specifying the objectives of the fundraising effort accompanying the Centenary celebra-

---

[169] Gowland, *Methodist Secessions*.

tion) was unanimously adopted by the 250 ministers and laymen then present.[170]

Remembering the ways in which the founder John Wesley
had been blessed and the manner in which his vision of the
Christian gospel for the whole world was being realised likewise confirmed the sense that the Wesleyans were on a di-
vinely-directed apostolic mission. Memorabilia of John Wesley therefore became valuable aids in sharing this sense of
mission with the ordinary members of the local Wesleyan societies. These items -- medals, busts, engravings -- served to
recall John Wesley's heroic, divinely-honoured life and work,
and to inspire Wesleyans to greater efforts in maintaining
their unity and in advancing their cause in local communities
and overseas.

In their contribution to the Wesleyan Centenary, sympa-
thetic artists spying a commercial opportunity incidentally
contributed images of John Wesley which, taken with all the
other visual memorabilia available before 1850, portrayed him
as the man with whom the ordinary Wesleyan at every stage
in life to some extent could identify. Always he was engaged
in heroic action, daring, pioneering, persisting against the
odds: in the Perlee Parker painting, as the child rescued for
great purposes in later life; in the Wood and other busts and
the medals, wearing the clerical bands of his sacred vocation;
in the Manning statue, as the Gospel proclaimer on worldwide
mission; and, in the Edinburgh portrait, as the frail old
preacher adhering to his pulpit appointment. Marshall Claxton's painting of Wesley on his deathbed, 'Holy Triumph'
(1844), and William Overend Geller's paintings of Wesley
preaching at Gwenap Pit (1845) and at Oxford with his friends
(ca 1850),[171] though not considered here, similarly trans-
formed John Wesley into a hero for all stages of life. Young,

---

[170] *The Watchman*, 14, 21 November 1838.
[171] See Forsaith, *John Wesley: Religious Hero?*, pp. 11-12.

adult, old, and dying in the Methodist societies would find in these images much with which to identify and to aspire. Rev Thomas Jackson's response to the Manning statue typified this effect. Taken together, and not always under the absolute control of Conference, the Centenary memorialisation of the 1830s and early 1840s sought and produced a solidarity of identity among Wesleyan Methodists which the rest of society might admire.

A local example illustrated how memorialisation helped to create identity in a competitive religious environment. The *Manchester Times* in summer 1840 reported,

> on Sunday last the Wesleyan Methodists of New Mills held the anniversary of their Sabbath and day schools. The officers, teachers, and scholars assembled in the school and proceeded from thence through some of the principal streets to the Wesleyan Chapel, wearing their Centenary medals.

Despite many other school and public sermons in the neighbourhood and unfavourable weather, two sermons delivered by Rev J. Strawe of York 'raised the liberal sum of £41 7s 2d'.[172] A clearer example of the Sunday School medal so swiftly promoting a distinctive collective identity could not be found. Such distinctiveness of course did not always induce desirable rivalries in local communities.

There were dangers in memorialisation. It could be an opportunity to vent old antagonisms or petty jealousies. Jabez Bunting's manoeuvring of Clarke's memorial in the City Road Chapel, as seen in the early 1830s, typified this kind of hazard. It might also be an occasion for the proud display in death of the social distinctions of life - the middle-class funerals of Wesleyans, clerical and lay, could be viewed as this by their social inferiors. Likewise memorialisation could

---

[172] *Manchester Times*, 18 July 1840. Oddly, *The Watchman*, 22 July 1840 report of the same item made no mention of the medals.

tempt the proud to fall. Bunting's visual dominance in memorabilia during the years 1836-39 and above all in Duval's group portrait of the Wesleyan clergy and laity, smacked of self-regard if not overweening pride. In turn that triggered the mischievous intrusion of Rev James Everett's visage in the Perlee Parker painting of John Wesley, 'a brand plucked out of the fire'.[173] The legitimating inscriptions accompanying some donations to the Centenary and Thanksgiving Funds revealed those donors as blue blooded Methodists of the second, third &c generation - as if faith were inherited, rather than the gift of God's grace.

Wesleyans' glorification of their founder ran parallel to the heroic status accorded to Nelson or Wellington. Unlike them, however, John Wesley was engaged in an unending spiritual battle for the souls of the lost. Carlyle's great man theory of history lent respectability to the apotheosis of Wesley which in turn was fed by the Victorian taste for the heroic. Two decades after the Centenary, Edward Corderoy's veneration of John Wesley verged on the idolatrous. By the 1890s, as Dr Lloyd shows below,[174] the exaltation of John Wesley had lost touch with the historical evidence, to say nothing of Christian orthodoxy. By that time, as seen, many more heroes besides John Wesley populated the late Victorian reading public's imagination, like Livingstone, General Gordon, Gladstone, Queen Victoria, Methodist 'worthies', and missionary martyrs. Yet John Wesley remained the ubiquitous, if not the super-, hero.

Can it be said that, overall, Wesleyan forms of memorialisation helped to create a particular Methodist identity? The main evidence of this aspect of the phenomenon must be the

---

[173] John Wesley altered the AV noun 'fire' to the present participle 'burning', arguably widening the application of the text.
[174] Gareth Lloyd, 'In the Shadow of the Founder; Methodist Memorialisation of John Wesley' (Below, Chapter 4).

combination of Wesleyana mementoes with the other distinctive features of Methodism - their emphasis on Arminian theology (believing that Christ died for all[175]), the hymns of Charles Wesley, an accent on religious experience, their pursuit of Christian perfection, and the chapel-based social life of a multitude of local societies and circuits - on top of their more widely shared Protestant evangelical religion with its emphasis on personal conversion, the Bible, a Christ-centred Gospel, and social action.[176] For Wesleyan clergy, the tangible array of artefacts elevating Wesley as a founder-hero had special meaning because it reminded them of their claims, through John Wesley as well as through his teaching, to their apostolic inheritance and mission. For the middle class chapel-goer, artefacts like an engraving of the Perlee Parker painting hanging in the drawing room at home, a bust or a medal in the display cabinet, or John Wesley-decorated tableware at chapel social functions - when poorer members could view the engravings - were all reminders of their shared mission, their shared sameness, their social belonging. After the 1890s new technologies widened forms of memorialisation, as for example photographic postcards or cigarette cards,[177] but the functions of creating internal cohesion and differentiating identity persisted. Whether they energised Christian vocation in the twentieth century in the same way as early Victorian memorabilia is very doubtful.

---

[175] Ironically the Wesleyan Conference excluded laymen until 1878 and women until 1911.

[176] David Bebbington's definition of an evangelical in his *Evangelicalism in Modern Britain: a History from the 1730s to the 1980s* (London: Routledge, 1989), pp. 4-17.

[177] See Tom Norgate, *From Pedagogy to Photography: the Life and Work of John William Righton* (Petersfield, Hampshire: 613 Books, 2008); Donald H. Ryan, 'John Wesley, Cigarette Cards and His Advice on Tobacco', *Wesley Historical Society Proceedings*, vol. 58 (2011).

CONCLUSION

Like other historical experiences of memorialisation, the phenomenon among Wesleyan Methodists pre-1860s was complex and contradictory. Largely disdained by John Wesley, the middle class funereal rituals and pictorial memorials of secular society were embraced by his followers. Aiming to glorify God, Wesleyan memorialisation wildly extolled the founder-hero and to a lesser extent his successors. Intended to promote a revival of Christian faith, it provoked commercial competition. Shaped by a new middle class elite, it muted up-and-coming democratic voices. Controlled by a clerical party guarding their own London pantheon, it failed to remember very much about the laity, the human source of their financial support. Designed to bring peace and amity throughout the connexion, it stirred division.

Despite all these drawbacks Wesleyan memorialisation preserved the essential elements of the Christian faith. Prompted by their memorabilia, Wesleyans could look back on their life stories and see the redemptive hand of Providence bringing them to conversion, directing their collective fellowship and Gospel mission, supporting them in their struggles to reach Christian perfection, comforting them in grief, and giving them hope beyond the grave: experiences they shared in common, the foundation on which their social identity ultimately rested.

The problem with religious artefacts is that they tend to become ends in themselves - collectors' items prized for their aesthetic or economic value. Their original human and religious meaning has departed, whether we are considering a country chapel, a bust of John Wesley, a Methodist tombstone, or a subscription list. Private or public, the memorial might mark a new beginning (like a chapel foundation stone); invariably it was an expression of human sorrow. The artefact represented a loss, whether of the denomination's founder, or a congregation's loss of a respected preacher and pastor, or the nigh-inconsolable loss of a spouse, parent, or child. Any triumphalism, any sense of victory, related to the cross of Christ, victory over sin and death, and to hopes of a new heaven and a new earth where sorrow and sighing have passed away and the church triumphant is 'Lost in wonder, love, and praise', to quote the vision of St John the Divine and Charles Wesley's immortal hymn.[178]

Religious memorials are only partly understood unless they are informed by the circumstances, intentions, and faith of the people who invested them with meaning. In an age of unbelief, the challenge for those engaged in any aspect of exploring Methodist heritage is to work at lifting the veil shrouding memorialising objects and practices to reveal both their humanity and their core religious dimension of faith.

---

[178] Revelation 21:1-4 (AV); Charles Wesley, 'Love Divine, all loves excelling' first published in 1747. Richard Watson and Kenneth Trickett (eds.), *Companion to Hymns & Psalms* (Peterborough: Methodist Publishing House, 1988), Hymn 267.

2.3 Appendix
Memorial tablets inside City Road Chapel, as existing in 1872

Six tablets fixed to walls within the communion rails

Person	Occupation or role	Death date	Tablet date	Place of burial
Rev John Wesley	founder	1791	1800	City Road graveyard, vault
Rev John Fletcher	exponent of Arminian theology	1785	1822	Madeley, Shropshire
Rev Joseph Benson	apologist and editor	1828		
Rev Charles Wesley	hymn writer	1788		Old Marylebone Churchyard
Rev Dr Thomas Coke	missionary pioneer	1814	1822	died at sea
Rev Dr Adam Clarke	linguist and polymath	1832		

Fifteen tablets fixed to walls outside the communion rails

Joseph Woolley	scale maker; original trustee	1803		
Mrs Elizabeth Mortimore	widow of Harvey Walklate Mortimer	1835		
HarveyWalklate Mortimer	gunmaker; trustee	1819		

Rev Dr Robert Newton	popular preacher	1854		Easingwold, Yorkshire
Rev Edmund Grindrod	church governance specialist	1842		
Rev Theophilus Lessey	centenary year (1839) President	1841		
Rev Joseph Fowler	Conference opponent of Bunting	1851		
Rev John Murlin	early itinerant (minister)	1799		
Lady Mary Fitzgerald	aunt of Prime Minister, Lord Liverpool	1815		John Wesley's vault
Joseph Butterworth MP	law publisher	1826		vault under CRC
Mrs Anne Butterworth	widow of Joseph Butterworth	1820		vault under CRC
Lancelot Haslope	merchant	1838		
James Hamilton MD	doctor	1827	1860?	
Rev John Mason	denominational book steward (editor)	1864		
Jacob Jones	surgeon	1830		City Road graveyard, vault

Two monumental pillars

Rev Dr Jabez Bunting	denominational administrator	1858	City Road graveyard, vault
Rev Richard Watson	systematic theologian	1833	City Road graveyard, vault

Missing

Rev Duncan Wright	preacher under John Wesley	1791	John Wesley's vault

Source
Stevenson, *City Road Chapel*, pp. 250-51, 341-58.

ACKNOWLEDGEMENTS
Without the resources of the Methodist Archives in the John Rylands Library, Manchester, and the helpfulness of the staff there, the research necessary to write this chapter could not have been done. To them I am most grateful. I am also indebted to Dr Clive Field, and Professors Edward Royle and Geoffrey Tweedale for reading an earlier draft, correcting some points, and extending some of my thoughts. Christian Dettlaff, Curator of Wesley's Chapel, City Road, London, kindly provided images from their collections. Dr Peter Forsaith answered queries about the whereabouts of the Parker paintings of 1840; and David Stabler, one of the Trustees of Brunswick Methodist Church, Newcastle upon Tyne, kindly showed me the half-size copy of the Parker painting in their custody. Geoff Tweedale's expertise in web browsing allowed me to locate engravings of the Parker and Duval paintings; his experience with self-publishing also eased my own continuing ascent along that learning curve. David Pavelich, Curator in the David M. Rubenstein Rare Book & Manuscript Library at Duke University, North Carolina, USA, has kindly facilitated the reproduction of two engravings in this volume. Peter Farrant resolved a tricky graphics problem. Martin L. Bower generously and swiftly provided me with images from his unrivalled collection of Methodist medallions, medals, and tokens. Jean, my wife, not only tolerated my preoccupation with this topic but also read the final draft, catching some slips. Remaining defects lie at my door.

3

The Transformation of the *Arminian Magazine* from John Wesley's Theological Instrument of Control to His Vehicle for Expressing and Preserving the Evocative Voices of Early Methodism

Barbara Prosser

John Wesley drew up proposals for what would become his *Arminian Magazine* on 14 August 1777 at the age of seventy-four. On 1 November he completed the introduction to the first issue, and in doing so clearly stated that his motive for beginning the venture was to offer 'open, avowed opposition' to both the Calvinist *Gospel Magazine* and *Spiritual Magazine* which, he believed, propagated indefensible decrees with 'arguments worthy of *Bedlam*, and with Language worthy of *Billingsgate.*'[1] As the first issue of the *Arminian Magazine* reached the movement, he explained to Thomas Taylor: 'Whatever is designed for an antidote to this poison must be spread in the same manner', and, in order to 'guard those who are not poisoned yet (not to get money), I fight them at their own weapons. I oppose magazine to magazine, though of a totally different kind.'[2]

The reason why he felt so strongly about the Calvinist publications is clear. In the issue for March 1779, the second year of the *Magazine*, he referred to the unparalleled persecution and criticism that he and his brother had been subject to over

---

[1] *Arminian Magazine,* vol. 1, p. iv, 'To the Reader'. [Hereafter *AM*]
[2] John Telford (ed.), *The Letters of John Wesley* (8 vols., London: Epworth Press, 1960), vol. 6, p. 295. [Hereafter *JWL*]

the years. 'In sermons, newspapers, and pamphlets of all kinds', he lamented, 'we were painted as unheard–of monsters.'[3] Although there was much anti-Methodist literature circulating in the wider publishing arena prior to 1778 ,[4] there were in fact only mild references to Wesley in the early pro-Calvinist periodicals, the *Christian's Amusement* and the later *Weekly History (or The Account),* under the editorship of John Lewis. The vitriolic criticism came from the later Calvinistic magazines and primarily from the editorship of the *Gospel Magazine*, which had been opposing Wesley on religious grounds since its inception in 1766.[5] Editor Augustus Toplady recognised the damaging nature of the harassment and acknowledged in the *Gospel Magazine* in 1776 that the Methodist leader had been so 'severely peppered and salted of late years' that he must have been made to ' smart and wince like an eel dispossessed of its skin '.[6]

---

[3] *AM*, vol., 2, p. 119, 'Thoughts on Salvation by Faith'.

[4] George Lavington (1684-1762) Bishop of Exeter 1747-62, published *The Enthusiasm of the Methodists and Papists Compared* in 1749 and 1751 in which he brought charges of immorality against the Methodists, and denied the presence of the Holy Spirit in their conversions. Written reactions to this came from George Whitefield (1749), Vincent Perronet (1749), and John Wesley (1750, 1751 and 1752). See Thomas Jackson (ed.), *The Works of John Wesley, A.M.* (14 vols., London: Mason, 1829-31) vol., 9, pp. 1- 64 [hereafter *JWW*] and Frank Baker, 'Bishop Lavington and the Methodists', *Wesley Historical Society Proceedings,* 34 (1963), 17-41; Clive D. Field, 'Anti-Methodist Publications of the Eighteenth Century: A Revised Bibliography', *Bulletin of the John Rylands University Library of Manchester*, vol. 73 (1991), 159-280.

[5] The editorship comprised John Gurney (1766-74), William Mason (1774-75, 1776), Augustus Toplady (December 1775–June 1776) and Erasmus Middleton (1776-83). Contributors who used pseudonyms included Augustus Toplady (Minimus and Concionator); John Newton (Omicron and Vigil); John Berridge (Old Everton), and John Ryland (Elachistoteros). William Cowper, Lady Huntingdon and Rev. Henry Venn also contributed.

[6] *The Gospel Magazine,* 1776, p. 475: http://www.gospelmagazine.org.uk/. [accessed 2007]

Wesley clearly read and was affected by the critical Calvinistic press but he did not expect the Calvinists to read his magazine which he saw as an innovative venture, referring to it as, 'a new thing in the land . . . quite another thing and published upon other motives.'[7] His intention was quite clear as can be seen in this explanation to Thomas Taylor in January 1778: 'I do not desire any Calvinist to read it. I publish it not to convince but preserve.' The *Arminian Magazine* would, unlike the Calvinist press, contain 'no railing, but (properly speaking), *no controversy*.'....'It goes straight forward taking notice of no opponent, but invariably pursuing the one point.'[8] That one point was universal salvation.

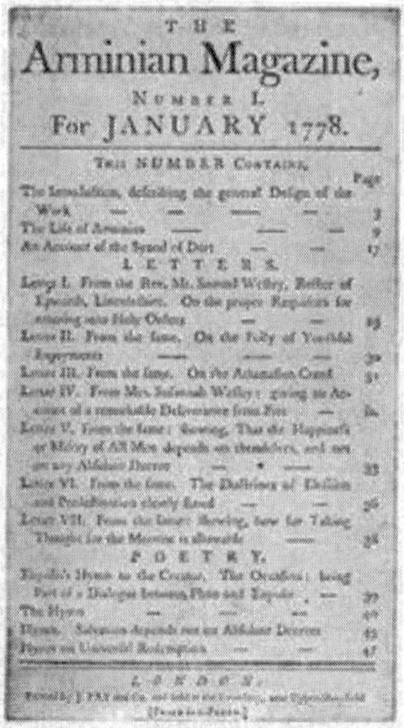
THE
Arminian Magazine,
NUMBER I.
For JANUARY 1778.

LETTERS.

POETRY.

Illustration 3.1
The first page of the Contents from the first issue of the *Arminian Magazine* in January 1778 which contained twenty pages of historical theological treatises, seven early theologically themed letters belonging to the Wesley family, and four heavily theological poems all defending Arminianism.

---

[7] *JWL,* 6, p. 295.
[8] *Ibid.*

It is evident that in his magazine Wesley underplayed Calvinistic influences upon the Methodist movement. In the accounts of Methodist lives, Calvinism was portrayed as inconsequential in conversions, especially any influence in the early lives of many of the first preachers such as Thomas Olivers, Thomas Rankin, Thomas Tennant, John Murlin, John Haime, and John Mason.[9] This was also the case in the exemplar deathbed accounts.[10] He published indifferent comments from John Pawson,[11] Thomas Olivers, Thomas Lee,[12] Thomas Taylor, and Christopher Hopper'[13] in relation to the longstanding Arminian/Calvinist dispute and the first of his own personal correspondence which he chose to include in his *Arminian Magazine* were from the leaders of the Calvinist movement namely James Harvey, George Whitfield,[14] John Cennick,[15] and Augustus Toplady.[16] These letters portrayed a mutual respect and friendship rather than rivalry and contention. This Wesley noted in an aside in relation to James Har-

---

[9] See *AM,* vol. 2, pp. 77ff, for Thomas Olivers; *AM,* vol. 2, pp. 182ff, Thomas Rankin (1738-1810); *AM,* vol. 2, pp. 358ff, Benjamin Rhodes (1743-1815); *AM,* vol. 2, pp. 469ff, Thomas Tennant (1741-93); *AM,* vol. 2, pp. 530ff, John Murlin (1722–99); *AM,* vol. 3, pp. 207ff, John Haime (1710-84); *AM,* vol. 3, pp. 650ff, John Mason (1733- 1810); *AM,* vol. 3, pp. 367ff, Thomas Taylor (1738-1816); *AM,* vol. 4, pp. 25ff, Christopher Hopper (1722-1802); *AM,* vol. 4, pp. 580ff, Thomas Payne (b. 1741); *AM,* vol. 5, pp. 14ff, George Story (1738 – 1818).

[10] See *AM* vol. 7, p. 554, 'The Dying Speech of Andreas Zekerman, who (with three others) were executed at Dublin, a few years ago, for the murder of Captain Glass', and *AM,* vol. 10, p. 629, 'A Short Account of Robert Calverley'.

[11] *AM,* vol. 2, pp. 25ff.

[12] *AM,* vol. 3, pp. 145ff.

[13] *AM,* vol. 4, pp. 23ff.

[14] *AM,* vol. 1, p. 178 (XXII), 8 November 1739; *AM,* vol. 2, p. 318 (LXXV), 3 December 1753; *AM,* vol. 1, p. 478 (XLIX), 11 September 1747; *AM,* vol. 5, p. 439 (CCL), 25 September 1764; *AM,* vol. 6, p. 273 (CCXCVI), 12 September 1769; *AM,* vol. 6, p. 684 (CCCXV), 28 December 1768.

[15] *AM,* vol. 1, p. 179 (XXIII), 12 September 1739.

[16] *AM,* vol. 3, pp. 54-55 (XCVII), 13 September 1758.

vey's letter to him of September 1736 which he produced in the *Magazine* in March 1778 with the following aside: 'The candid reader will learn hence, in what light he viewed me, before he was thoroughly tinctured with Calvinism.'[17]

Wesley's aim for his *Magazine* was to *preserve* the Arminian character of the widely expanding Methodist movement as it grew at home and abroad in an increasingly enlightened context, and amid the mounting awareness of his own mortality. Right from the outset Wesley announced that his magazine, under its full title of *"The Arminian Magazine, Consisting of Extracts and Treatises on Universal Redemption"* would include 'some of the most remarkable tracts on the Universal Love of God.'[18] Some of the excerpts would be rare, some would be first translations, and others would be written specifically for the Methodists reading his *Magazine.*

The majority of these overtly theological treatises were printed in the first two years of the *Magazine*, substantiating the view that Wesley believed it would be a short-lived venture: 'My time is short', he remarked to Christopher Hopper on 18 October 1777, 'so I publish as much as I can at once; if haply I may live to finish it.'[19] However, the first explicitly theological extracts chosen by Wesley for the early Methodists were, overall, unsuitable even for an increasingly literate readership. They were scholarly, not practical texts; historical rather than contemporary; the language was complex; the doctrines taxing and repetitive, with many having little scriptural authority; and were printed mainly without introduction or comment. In spite of Wesley's initial claim of a focused remit, there were also pieces which concentrated on opposing Calvinistic 'controversial' doctrines.

This first collection, however, did form a library of texts upon which the first Methodists could reliably call, and, in

---

[17] *AM,* vol. 1, p. 130.
[18] *AM,* vol. 1, p. v 'To the Reader'.
[19] *JWL,* vol. 6, p. 284.

this respect, the *Magazine* came to be an extension or conclusion to Wesley's ambitious *Christian Library,* one of his principal works which comprised fifty volumes of practical divinity, issued at intervals between 1749 and 1755. Indeed an overlap between the two projects is apparent with some biographies being repeated with only a few moderations such as those of Bernard Gilpin, Bishop Bedell, John Donne and Archbishop Usher. Other repetitions involved works especially of a 'Puritan' nature including those of Joseph Allein, John Bunyan, Isaac Barrow, Dr. Goodwin, Bishop Joseph Hall, Samuel Annesley, Ralph Cudworth, and Richard Baxter.[20] The aim of the *Christian Library* had been to select a manageable and trustworthy collection of Christian Divinity, edited and abridged in order, according to Wesley's Preface to the work, to 'extract the gold out of these baser mixtures.'[21] However, the project met with criticism over its size, cost and content, and it appears that Wesley intended to revise it as late as May 1771.[22] In spite of enforcing the reading of it amongst the itinerancy and within the societies, Wesley lost money on the venture, and noted in his *Journal* for 6 November 1753 with some regret, 'Perhaps the next generation may know the value of it.'[23] This next generation had his *Arminian Magazine.*

Wesley initially justified the academic character of the theological content of his *Magazine* noting that some of the religious treatises may not, as he prefaced one particularly difficult article, 'be understood by inattentive Readers, nor by

---

[20] See Robert C Monk, *John Wesley, His Puritan Heritage* (London: Epworth Press, 1966), pp. 31-63.

[21] *JWW,* vol.14, p. 237.

[22] *JWL,* vol. 5, p. 241. John Wesley to Christopher Hopper, 5 May 1771. For evidence of Wesley answering criticism regarding the venture via the *London Magazine,* (1760) see *JWL,* vol. 4, p. 119; and 'Some Remarks on Mr. Hill's "Ferrago Double-Distilled" *JWW,* vol.10, pp. 418ff.

[23] *JWW,* vol. 2, p. 278.

any that are not accustomed to close thinking.'[24] He continued to defend works like those by Jacob Bryant, and John Locke, which some members argued were 'not intelligible to common Readers'.[25] Wesley protested as late as 1784: 'Did I ever say this was intended for common Readers only? By no means', he continued. 'I publish it for the sake of the learned as well as the unlearned Readers. But as the latter are the greater number, nine parts in ten of the Work are generally suited to their capacity. What they do not understand let them leave to others, and endeavour to profit by what they do understand.'[26]

However, even by the time the *Arminian Magazine* was published in 1778, early Methodism had acquired forty years of disciplined training and the acquisition of reading practices both intensive, via disciplined study, and extensive, through reading outside purely scriptural texts, and all within a growing print culture. Throughout his ministry Wesley saw the significance of literacy for both evangelism and individual conversion and saw to it that schooling, study and a disciplined reading pattern were followed within the movement. With increased literacy came increased confidence and self-belief so, consequently, it was not surprising that some members found the assurance to have their say regarding the con-

---

[24] *AM*, vol. 3, p. 33. 'On the Eternity of God'.

[25] *AM*, vol. 7, *Preface,* par., 8. Such texts included *AM*, vol. 5, pp. 27ff, 'Remarks upon Mr Locke's Essay on Human Understanding'. In August 1784 when asked to recommend books for children he advised Miss Bishop to use Locke, '….with the Remarks in the *Arminian Magazine'* for the older ones. (*JWL*, vol. 7, p. 228). See also *AM*, vol. 6, p. 36, 'Of the Sybills' on literary techniques; *AM*, vol. 6, pp. 138ff, 'Extracts from Mr Bryant's Analysis of Ancient Mythology' taken from *A New System or an Analysis of Ancient Mythology,* (1774); *AM*, vol. 12, pp. 150-55, 'Of Hebrew Points'; and *AM*, vol. 3, p. 552 (CXXXII), John Wesley to Dr Robertson, 24 September 1753.

[26] *AM*, vol. 7, *Preface,* A similar sentiment was given by Wesley in correspondence to Captain Richard Williams, 9 November 1783. *JWL*, vol. 7, p.195.

tents of what would be their own *Magazine*. Such was the demand for change from the original theologically academic slant that Wesley was uncharacteristically compelled to include six *Prefaces* of explanation and justification in the early years of its publication.[27] Evidence from an analysis of the first nine months of the very first volume justifies the audible censure from elements of the readership who were assailed with 201 pages of historical and theological discussion averaging out at over 22 pages per issue, the intensity lightened only by nine pages of the life of Arminius, 49 pages of the life of Martin Luther, and 31 of clergyman and educator Bernard Gilpin.

The first criticisms came from an unidentified spokesman, given in what Wesley believed was a 'friendly' manner. The critic complained that there were not as many lines per page as in other magazines to which, via his *Preface* to the October 1778 edition, Wesley replied: 'I spare both my reader's time and my own by couching my sense in as few words as I can.'[28] Other complaints concerned the lack of variety in the material and the unattractiveness of the work. In June 1778, Wesley re-justified his choice of theological content but in January 1779 he conceded and agreed to insert the more relevant and inspiring spiritual accounts of the lives of the first Methodist preachers, to improve the engravings, to have less demanding theological commentaries, and to include poetry written specifically for the *Magazine.*

He, however, took issue with the claim from some readers that they had no need for devout articles which reinforced what they had already accepted and had in fact been examined

---

[27] *AM* , vol. 1, 'To the Reader' January 1778; *AM,* vol. 1, preceding p. 433, 'An Answer to Several Objections against This Work in a Letter to a Friend'; *AM,* vol. 2, 'To the Reader', Preface to *Arminian Magazine* 1779; *AM,* vol. 3, 'The Preface' 1780; *AM,* vol. 4, 'The Preface' 1781; *AM,* vol. 7,'To the Reader, The Preface' 1784.
[28] *AM,* vol.1, part 2, preceding p. 433.

on before becoming members of the movement. Although he reduced the amount of theological material Wesley was adamant that such material was still needed, noting with regard to the Calvinist *Gospel Magazine*, that 'the poison is still spreading on every side,' therefore, 'is there not need to spread the antidote too?'[29]

In his *Preface* of 1780, Wesley finally conceded that pages promoting Universal Redemption would 'not take up so large a compass as it has done in some of the preceding numbers.' This would leave more room for the more practical exemplar accounts of 'Lives', especially those of preachers that revealed providential protection, and again he agreed to include more poetry. Wesley also agreed to 'occasionally insert several little pieces, that are not immediately connected with my main design.'[30] This was a rare occasion where Wesley was not to be in absolute control of his *Magazine* and his vacillation could be seen in his continuing statement: 'Only let it be remembered', he told the readership, 'that if I wander a little from my subject, it is in compliance with the judgement of my friends.'[31] This hesitant decision began the transformation of his *Magazine* and ensured its survival.

Further changes began to take hold. In his *Preface* to the 1781 edition Wesley explained that: 'in order to [further] comply with those who desire a little more variety,'[32] he had agreed to write sermons especially for his *Arminian Magazine*. He had hoped that some younger members would do this but these were not forthcoming, hence he agreed to undertake to write 'practical Discourses, on those which I judge to be the most necessary of the subjects I have not yet treated of.'[33] The relative ease at which he agreed to write what

---

[29] Preface to *AM*, vol.2.
[30] Preface to *AM*, vol. 3.
[31] Preface to *AM*, vol. 3, p. vii, 1780.
[32] Preface to *AM*, vol. 4, p. v.
[33] Ibid.

turned out to be sixty-four original sermons supports the con-tention that at the age of seventy-eight he not only still had the passion to write but saw his *Magazine* as the new vehicle for communication with the movement.

These sermons were 'little pieces' in both size and content. Each was approximately just five to six pages per issue and given in two, monthly instalments; they were not theological-ly challenging nor did they attempt to standardise doctrine as this had been accomplished in previously published ser-mons.[34] They were written to guide converted Methodists, already in the societies and already working out their salva-tion. A personal analysis of the sermons has presented five general themes confirming the spirit of Arminianism, namely those written to give confirmation of the characteristics of God,[35] those written to confirm assurance,[36] sermons of en-couragement,[37] sermons advocating vigilance,[38] and those which offered practical teachings.[39] Wesley's practice of in-cluding the exact date and place of composition in the *Maga-zine*, led to these sermons being 'hot off the press', and were

---

[34] *JWW*, vol. 4, p. 135, 1 September 1778. Volumes of Wesley's *Sermons* were published in 1746, 1748, 1750 (each of twelve sermons), 1760 (seven sermons and tracts), and the *Works* in 1771-74 which included all the previous sermons with minor changes and nine additional sermons. In 1787-88, eight volumes of *Sermons* appeared, the latter four being those written for the *Arminian Magazine*.

[35] See Sermons (VII), (X), (XXI), (XXX), (XXXVI), (XXXXV), (LII), (LIII), (LVI) and (LXIV).

[36] See Sermons (IV), (IX), (XI), (XXXXVIII), (LXII) and (XXXXIV).

[37] See Sermons (XIII), (XVI), (XX), (XXVI), (XXVIIII), (XXXII), (XXXXII), (XXXXVIIII), (LI) and (LXIII).

[38] See Sermons (1), (II), (III), (XII), (XIIII), (XV), (XVIIII), (XXII), (XXIIII), (XXXIV), (XXXVII), (XXXXVII), (L), (LIV), (LV), (LVIII), (LX) and (LXI).

[39] See Sermons (V), (VI), (VIII), (XVII), (XVIII), (XXIII), (XXV), (XXVII), (XXVIII), (XXXI), (XXXIII), (XXXV), (XXXVIII), (XXXIX), (XXXX), (XXXXI), (XXXXIII, (XXXXVI), (LVII) and (LVIIII).

evidence that he was still alive and well, still travelling amongst his people and still speaking directly to them.

In 1781, only three years into the *Magazine's* life, two further adaptations were instigated by Wesley. 'Little pieces' recording the lives of recently deceased members and an abridgement, in manageable size portions (104 monthly issues), of his own lengthy work on natural history, *A Survey of the Wisdom of God in Creation.*[40]

By 1784 the subscriptions for the *Magazine* were increasing yearly, 600 extra copies having to be published in 1783 and the same extra number at the start of 1784.[41] It would seem that the *Magazine* was now being read out of interest and desire not pressure from Wesley to do so. However, no matter how popular, some readers were still not satisfied with the religious content and asked Wesley the unthinkable: *'Is it not now high time to drop the Controversial part?'*[42] Wesley argued that what he was really being asked to do was finish with his *Arminian Magazine* and start a new venture and claimed, *'It is too late for me to begin a new work.'*[43] However, he admitted that the title of the *Magazine* was now no longer valid: *'Therefore I will order it to run thus for the time to come: "The Arminian Magazine, consisting chiefly of Extracts and Treatises on Universal Redemption"'*. The mere addition of 'chiefly' to the title was still inaccurate, but it was recognition of a much greater transformation.[44]

The 'little pieces' which had been reluctantly agreed to by Wesley increased year by year and gave the *Magazine* its rel-

---

[40] There was a criticism of this policy, which Wesley answered in the 'Preface' in 1784, justifying his actions on the grounds of scarcity of ownership of the 'five little volumes' of the work.

[41] *AM,* vol. 7, 'To the Reader', Preface, par. 2, 1784.

[42] Ibid., par. 4.

[43] Ibid.

[44] In 1784, controversial writings accounted for 86 pages as did the sermons; Methodist lives and deathbed accounts 148; *Survey* instalments 55; and 'little pieces' 144.

evance, colour, veracity and enthusiasm which supported the growing movement. The monthly editions came to include educative material on such issues as travel in Europe and beyond; accounts of shipwrecks; articles concerning music; prisoners' welfare and justice; penal reform; historical anecdotes; comments on Catholicism; examples of admirable and detestable historical characters; teachings on right living; sobriety; manners; the Sabbath; suicide; hymn singing; generosity; frugality; educational methodology; meteorology; Kingswood school; the relationship with the Church of England; arguments against slavery; involvement in political issues; humorous anecdotes; medical reports and remedies; scientific advances; horticultural advice; accounts of witchcraft; apparitions; dreams and visions; curious and inexplicable medical facts; fascinating facts from home and abroad; healing accounts; examples of providential protection at sea, from the elements and through hardship; comments on wise judgment; Methodist news and information from around the societies in Great Britain and America; 651 poems which supported and confirmed the various prose inclusions; 64 original sermons; 557 letters; 240 spiritual accounts; 172 death bed scenes and much, much more.

The *Magazine* was originally costed on 80 pages for a princely one shilling.[45] Within less than two months Wesley had reduced this to a more accessible price. 'Certainly there are larger magazines than ours' he told Joseph Benson, 'but it does not follow that they are better. Ours is reduced to half the price, and will contain forty-eight pages, which is the usual number for sixpence.'[46] There were in reality, on average, 65 pages per issue. The monthly amount charged for the *Magazine* may have seemed prohibitive for many of the ordi-

---

[45] *JWL*, vol. 6, p. 284. John Wesley to Christopher Hopper, 18 October 1777: 'Other Magazines give forty pages for sixpence; this gives eighty for a shilling'.
[46] *JWL*, vol. 6, p. 291, 8 December 1777.

nary Methodists, which may have encouraged the practice of shared reading irrespective of literacy demands.

Delivery was taken on the first day of each month and subscriptions were taken in at the Foundery (later at the City Road Chapel) and booksellers throughout the country. Annual volumes were also published from single copies, thus forming an encyclopaedic collection for future reference. Unlike the monthly copies, which would have been passed around, the volumes were more likely to be used as reference or for private consultation, and would have been easy to transport abroad if this was ever necessary. Volumes were certainly in existence by the end of Wesley's life as a contemporary book inventory illustrates,[47] and the volumes seem to have been valued within early Methodism. In February 1788, for example, Wesley informed Ann Bolton that 'A copy of the *Magazine* is not now to be had, but you may have abundance of single ones',[48] and Thomas Jackson records that his father resolved that each of his children should have one volume of the *Magazine* bound in calf, presumably to keep for posterity following Wesley's death.[49]

Unlike contemporary newspapers, distribution was purely in the hands of Methodist members. The Book Room took orders on the first Monday of each month and, if collected at City Road, collectors received a one shilling allowance. Named distributors had an allowance of 10 per cent of the sales. Outside London, stewards received the copies together with 10 per cent of the cost for selling them, 25 per cent discount off the cost of the magazine, and 10 per cent off all oth-

---

[47] *John Wesley's Book Inventory,* 1791, JRULM Special Collections, Loc2bNUG.
[48] *JWL,* vol. 8, p. 39, 23 February 1788.
[49] Thomas Jackson, *Recollections of My Own Life and Times* (London: Wesleyan Conference Office, 1873), pp. 25-26. Cited in H. F. Mathews, *Methodism and the Education of the People* (London: Epworth Press, 1949), p. 170.

er books.[50] Wesley placed responsibility for gaining subscriptions and for distribution purely upon the itinerant preachers,[51] criticising those who would not comply.[52] 'Take a little pains in recommending the *Magazine*' he told Samuel Bardsley in January 1780, '*Urge* it from love to me and to the preachers; and whatever you do, do it with your might.'[53]

There must have been no doubt within the movement that the *Magazine* was there to be read, as evidenced by Wesley's directions to Joseph Benson in January 1782:

> DEAR JOSEPH. It gives me pleasure to hear that you are not weary in well doing, but are diligent in advancing the cause of religion. There is one means of doing this in which it will be worth your while to take some pains; I mean in recommending the Magazines. If you say of them in every Society what you may say with truth, and say it with an air of earnestness, you will produce several new subscribers. - I am, dear Joseph, Your affectionate friend and brother.[54]

---

[50] *Minutes of the Book Room Committee,* 1797-1817, JRULM Special Collections.

[51] See *JWL,* vol. 6, p. 296, John Wesley to Thomas Carlill, 23 January 1778; *JWL,* vol. 6, p. 374, John Wesley to Lancelot Harrison, 16 January 1780; *JWL,* vol. 6, p. 378, John Wesley to Samuel Bardsley, 30 January 1780; *JWL,* vol. 7, p. 40, John Wesley to Zachariah Yewdall, 3 December 1780; *JWL,* vol. 7, p. 45, John Wesley to John Valton, 31 December 1780; *JWL,* vol. 7, p. 97, John Wesley to Joseph Benson, 5 January 1782; *JWL,* vol. 7, p. 138, John Wesley to Richard Rodda, 9 September 1782; *JWL,* vol. 7, p. 138, John Wesley to Joseph Taylor, 9 September 1782; *JWL,* vol. 7, p. 143, 24 September 1782; *JWL,* vol. 7, p. 205, John Wesley to Thomas Carlill, 12 January 1784; and *JWL,* vol. 8, p. 120, John Wesley to George Holder, 28 February 1789.

[52] *JWL,* vol. 7, p. 140, John Wesley to William Roberts, 12 September 1782; *JWL,* vol. 7, p. 143, John Wesley to Joseph Taylor, 24 September 1782.

[53] *JWL,* vol. 6, p. 378. See also Ibid., John Wesley to William Tunney, 29 January 1780.

[54] *JWL,* vol. 7, p. 97.

Methodists were expected to read their *Magazine* either individually or collectively and taking into account the level of literacy of the first generation of Methodists it is more than likely societies and families shared copies. It was a prized possession with an estimated 100,000 readership. The evolution of the *Arminian Magazine* was testimony to the fervour, dedication and loyalty of a membership who were spurred on by the discipline and instruction within Wesleyan Methodism. Through the tenacity of the members, the theological *Magazine* became the instructional miscellany which guided the movement into the new century.

Wesley used the *Arminian Magazine* to preserve not only the Arminian flavour of the movement but also the personal interaction with which his evangelism had come to be associated. As he aged, the energetic interaction became less easy and was replaced by a different relationship with the readers of his *Magazine*. As Methodism spread, his customary personal way of relating to the adherents would inevitably have to be adapted. He could neither write nor speak personally to the growing number, although he continued to follow his lifestyle of rising at four a.m., preaching, travelling and writing. The congregation that he could reach through his *Magazine* was now far greater and more diverse than he could ever have hoped for, and could bring into reality the notion that the world was indeed his parish. Through the *Magazine* format, subscribed to and delivered regularly month by month and read within homes and societies, interaction with the leader of Methodism continued in the public eye as well as on a personal level throughout the final thirteen years of his life.

John Wesley was autocratic by nature and it was unusual for him to concede to the request of others in relation to the content of his magazine. However, this did not mean he had lost control. It should not be any surprise to note that he did not follow the contemporary practice of using a pseudonym in relation to his editorship; in fact, by 1789 it is clear that he saw himself as *author* of the *Magazine* as opposed to its *editor*.[55] It was at this time that the distribution also moved from the booksellers to the preaching houses, emphasising that this was indeed a magazine for the Methodists under Wesleyan control.

Although Wesley admitted that he turned to his brother Charles for help in deciding some inclusions particularly in relation to the poetry, it is obvious that his ultimate control over the magazine was non-negotiable – including the character and content of those 'little pieces'.[56] Sole control meant making time within his own busy schedule for the production and selection of all its content; abridging and extracting material; eliciting material from members; choosing from his own personal material of many decades and also of that sent to him; correcting publication mistakes and so on. It was an enormous task but as the *Magazine* started to evolve naturally into a miscellany, Wesley confidently informed the readership in 1781 that he was sure that he could easily supply all that was needed.[57]

The *Arminian Magazine* in its transformation became in fact a tool of control within the movement. Wesley's personal control over the content and therefore over the reading material which potentially reached all of Methodism is evident in two complementary strategies. The first was an obvious and direct censorship of material including the 'little pieces' in which he incorporated only works supporting Arminian beliefs and considered by him to be useful to the readership. A large number of the unaccredited prose inclusions were unquestionably his own work, as can be identified from the style, content, repetition of favoured phrases, and his identifi-

---

[55] From 1791 the inscription changes to 'Printed for the EDITOR...'
[56] *JWL*, vol. 7, p. 20, John Wesley to Charles Wesley, 8 June 1780.
[57] *AM*, vol. 4, Preface, p. iv.

able practice of dating and placing his work.[58] This control included adding evangelistic comments to contributions if applicable,[59] and giving warnings about ignoring instruction.[60]

Wesley's practice of not acknowledging the work of other authors published in the *Magazine* in fact reinforced his control. This meant that the members were not distracted from Wesleyan authority over reading matter, but rather directed to focus on the chosen instructional content alone. His declaration in correspondence to the *London Magazine* in December 1760, 'for I mind not who speaks, but what is spoken',[61] supports this intent. Wesley spent little time and energy on attributing authorship. The accepted work of some familiar writers and poets was acknowledged, regardless of the denomination of the author,[62] and this policy gave the *Magazine*

---

[58] See *AM*, vol. 12, p. 46, 'Thoughts upon a late Phenomenon', dated Nottingham, 13 July 1788; *AM* vol. 13, p. 545, 'Thoughts on a Late Publication', dated Peckham, 30 December 1789.

[59] *AM*, vol. 7, p. 162, 'A Strange Account'; *AM* vol. 10, p. 434, 'Superstition and Religion'.

[60] See Sermons XII, XIV, XXXVII, XLIV and LIV. See also *AM* vol. 5, p. 654, 'A Sermon Preached by an Old Minister to Three Highwaymen'.

[61] *JWL*, vol. 4, p. 119, John Wesley to the Editor of the *London Magazine*, 12 December 1760, in which Wesley defended the inclusions in his *Christian Library*. This letter was also sent to the *London Chronicle* on the 26 December.

[62] *AM*, vol. 1, p. 201,'An Account of Sebastian Castellio and Michael Servetus. Transcribed from Dr. Chandler's History of Persecution'; *AM*, vol. 1, pp., 250ff, 'A Discourse Concerning the Necessity and Contingency of Events in the World: in Respect of God's Eternal Decrees. Written about the Year 1620', by Thomas Goad; *AM*, vol. 4, p. 604, 'Of the Right Method of Meeting Classes and Bands in the Methodist Societies' by Charles Perronet; *AM*, vol. 4, pp. 606ff, 'Necessity Considered as Influencing Practice; Extracted from Bishop Butler's Analogy of Religion'; *AM*, vol. 5, pp. 27ff, Remarks upon Mr. Locke's Essay on Human Understanding, with Short Remarks'; *AM*, vol. 5, pp. 200ff, 'An Account of the Passions: Extracted from Dr. Watts'; *AM*, vol. 5, p. 257, 'Sermon on John ii. 3,4. by Dr. Cudworth; *AM*, vol. 6, pp. 33ff, 'Free Thoughts upon the Brute Creation' by

a wider, and perhaps more reputable appeal, but a large number of the articles were attributed merely as '[By a Late Author]'or '[Extracted from a Late Author]'.

Wesley also had a more subtle editorial policy which consummated his ultimate control. Contributions of 'little pieces' from the membership gave the appearance that individuals were allowed into a partial ownership of the *Magazine,* For example 249 (over 47 per cent) of the Wesleyan letters included in the *Magazine* were either sent, or received by females thus highlighting the feminine role within Methodism and the special protective relationship which Wesley had with many of these women. His decision to reprint the personal introductory comments in such correspondence reinforced the subtlety of the above strategy. The letters illustrated an enviable relationship between correspondent and editor which would be evident to all the membership reading the *Magazine.* However, all the material was more likely being used by Wesley as a further instrument to gain conformity of belief and behaviour. This can be seen especially in relation to the evangelical narratives and death bed scenes – the most personal and sensitive of the 'little pieces'.

By the era of the *Magazine,* the genre of evangelical narratives was not just concerned with the conversion process itself but had evolved into recording life-long, self-questioning narrative accounts. Methodism, within the context of the Enlightenment, encouraged self-analysis, so autobiographical

---

John Hilldrop; *AM*, vol. 6, pp. 37ff 'An Answer to Mr Madan's Treatise on Polygamy and Marriage' by Joseph Benson; *AM,* vol. 6, pp. 138ff 'Extracts from Mr Bryant's Analysis of Ancient Mythology'; *AM,* 6; 212ff 'An Extract from Mr Baxter's Certainty of the World of Spirits; Fully Evinced by Unquestionable Histories of Apparitions and Witchcraft'; *AM,* vol. 8, pp. 3ff, 'An Extract from Dr Whitby's Discourses on the Five Points'; *AM,* vol. 8, pp. 44ff, An Extract from a Journey from Aleppo to Jerusalem at Easter A.D. 1697' by Henry Maundrell; *AM,* vol. 11, pp. 33ff, 'An Extract from a Volume Entitled "A Review of Dr Priestley's Doctrine of Philosophical Necessity"'.

writing was cathartic and constructive for the individual but, more importantly, educative for the movement. Each step along the sanctification journey for Arminian Methodists was accountable; they were in a sense, as Bruce D. Hindmarsh suggests, 'reborn' repeatedly.[63] Hindmarsh also argues that the early evangelical accounts were structured as microcosms of the Biblical story of the creation, fall, redemption, and the new creation. Each story, he argues, 'was *the story* in miniature', illustrating the struggles and victories of each stage of the conversion process.[64] Keith Haartman maintains that the conversion narratives often reveal psychological wounding through the converts having witnessed deaths of siblings or parental repression, and displayed a preoccupation with divine judgement which disallowed self-assertion and led to the expression of guilt. He also argues that Methodists could tolerate intense introspection as they were free from the notion of predestination and possible exclusion from the saved elect.[65]

Ninety-seven of the 240 spiritual accounts in the *Magazine* were of women, 18 being of children from the age of eighteen down to three years and five months. Accounts of dissenters were also included, although, as Henry Rack observes Wesley tended to take note of those who had been ejected from the Church rather than any who became dissenters voluntarily.[66] To guarantee the precise format, Wesley wrote ten of the accounts in the early editions himself, six of these being of

---

[63] Bruce D. Hindmarsh, *The Evangelical Conversion Narrative: Spiritual Autobiography in Early Modern England* (Oxford University Press, 2005), p. 229.

[64] Idem, '"My Chains Fell off, My Heart Was Free": Early Methodist Conversion Narrative in England', *Church History*, vol. 68 (1999), 910-29.

[65] Keith Haartman, *Watching and Praying* as reviewed by Richard T. Vann, *Journal of the American Psychoanalytic Association*, vol. 53 (2005), 1375-81.

[66] Henry D Rack, *Reasonable Enthusiast: John Wesley and the Rise of Methodism* (3rd edn., London: Epworth, 2002), p. 307. See *AM*, vol. 8, p. 461; Thomas Wadsworth, *AM*, vol. 8, p. 465; Richard Wavel,

women.[67] Although he may have decided not to write accredited male biographies to alleviate any accusations of favoritism, this does not preclude him having written unaccredited accounts. In February 1789 Wesley, in correspondence to George Holder, commented upon the significance of the popular accounts as he saw it for not only managing the movement but for the existence of his precious *Magazine:*

> There is something very remarkable in the relation which you give of the life and death of Mr. Charles Laco. 'Right precious in the sight of the Lord is the death of His saints.' And every Assistant should take all possible care to procure the best account of them that can be had. These accounts are frequently means of awakening men of the world as well as of encouraging the children of God. In every place the subscribers to the Magazines will fall off unless great care be taken.[68]

Wesley's control over the personal content of the *Magazine* seemed to include avoiding contemporary accounts published elsewhere. There seemed little point in repeating material in the movement. Evidence for this comes from his letter to Thomas Rutherford in December 1789: 'I thank you for your account of Jane Newland, which I trust will be of use to many. A short extract from it I shall probably send you in a day or two. A larger will be inserted in the *Magazine.* There is no great probability that her brother will be so foolish as to print anything on the occasion.'[69]

---

[67] Namely, Jane Muncey (March 1781); Sarah Whiskin (April 1781); Mrs. Susannah Wesley (June 1781); Mrs. S. (July 1781); Elizabeth Marsh (December 1781) and Sarah Peters (March 1782). The remaining were not itinerants: a child (February 1782); the deathbed account of Francis Coxon (February 1782); Dr. Dodd (July 1783) and 'An Eminent Man' (May 1784).

[68] *JWL,* vol. 8, p. 120. Wesley did not publish the account of Laco in the *Magazine.*

[69] *JWL,* vol. 8, p. 191.

Wesley in fact decided not to include this in his *Magazine* but rather published it himself as a tract in 1790 without accrediting Rutherford. His actions here raise the questions as to how much material originally collected for the *Magazine* appeared independently (and without crediting the original contributor) and to what extent decisions to include material were based upon the practicalities of available space within the monthly periodical.

The itinerancy was a central and precious feature of Methodism hence Wesley made the editorial decision early in his original proposals (before his decision to include the little pieces), to incorporate accounts of the exemplary lives of those he referred in the Magazine as his 'children of many mercies'. Sixty-two autobiographical responses were published, mainly from itinerants, which were not historical and complete, but animate, recorded experiences of people still undergoing sanctification. This factor was important to his management and the future of the movement because the readers, by relating to those still on their journey like themselves, could consequently emulate such experiences and be encouraged into the itinerancy.

It would have been difficult for many of the less literate members to respond to the editorial decree to submit an autobiographical account which, potentially, could be distributed throughout England and beyond. As editor, Wesley would have chosen those capable of doing just that; in fact some of the individuals had already written autobiographical texts prior to their appearance in the *Magazine,* and some were spurred on to write publicly following the publication of their efforts. Wesley encouraged this by selling both autobiographies and biographies throughout the association, an action which again reinforced his control.[70] As Bruce Hindmarsh

---

[70] See *An Account of the Life, and Dealings of God with Silas Told* (1786); James Morgan, *The Life and Death of Mr. Thomas Walsh, Composed in Great Part from the Accounts Left by Himself* (1762 -1763); *The Case of*

observes, 'The lives of the early Methodist preachers thus represented a progression of conversion narrative from the oral and manuscript culture of lay autobiography to the public culture of the printed page. '[71]

Of the male autobiographical responses, 17 out of the 28 which materialised in the first four years had been sent to Wesley in correspondence, suggesting, as the following evidence from itinerants shows, that Wesley, as editor, had insisted upon them. Thomas Taylor sent his account to Wesley in November 1779. It appeared in the July 1780 edition with the following introduction:

> The profit which I have found in reading the lives of experienced Christians, makes me the readier comply with your request, of selecting a few Memoirs of my own unworthy Life; hoping it may be of as great use to some simple souls, as things of a like nature have been to me.
>
> I am aware how hard it is for anyone to write his own history; as there are many things, which would have a far better grace, were they to come from another hand; which, never- the- less, are needful to be related. Again, there are several things which one would wish to be buried in oblivion; and, yet, an ingenuous mind cannot pass them over. As this is really my case, it made me the more reluctant in publishing my own folly. [72]

John Nelson, Written by Himself (1745); *An Extract of J. Nelson's Journal* (Bristol, 1767); Thomas Taylor, *Redeeming Grace Displayed to the Chief of Sinners* (York, 1780); *A Short Account of the Life of Mr. Thomas Mitchell* (1781); *Short Account of God's Dealings with Mr. John Haime* (1785). Wesley also advertised these in the 1789 booklist in the *Magazine* itself eg. *Mr. John Nelson's Journal* and *Life &c. of Tho. Walsh*, price one shilling; *Life of John Haime* , 4d.

[71] Hindmarsh, *Evangelical Conversion Narrative*, p. 233.

[72] *AM*, vol. 3, pp. 367ff, 'An Account of the Life of Mr. Thomas Taylor'. Taylor forwarded a supplement the following year as he felt he had not dealt with his salvation in the required depth. See also *AM*, vol. 3, p. 477

A similar reluctance on the basis of apparent unworthiness, failure to cope with the demands of the itinerancy, issues regarding age and ill health, or the more practical reason of actually not having any written evidence on which to base an accurate account could also be seen in the accounts of Thomas Hanson,[73] William McCornock,[74] Peter Jaco,[75] Sampson Staniforth,[76] and William Hunter.[77]

Hunter's conclusion to the account of his life is typical of many in that he contemplates what being an itinerant preacher meant to him personally. Writing the requested accounts was in fact a perfect opportunity to reflect upon their contribution to the movement; their total reliance upon God to do this work; and their own spiritual journey during their ministry. There is no doubt that Wesley anticipated such accounts could well enable others to identify with the same emotions and would be of encouragement to others who might choose to take the same path: A similar reflection was seen in the accounts by Thomas Olivers, John Murlin, John Allen,[78] and Thomas Payne.

An analysis of the early autobiographical responses of the itinerants from 1778-80 reveals that 13 out of 20 male accounts were dated, the average time between writing and inclusion in the *Magazine* being just over four months, with five of the accounts being seen by the readership within two months of writing. As so many itinerants submitted accounts within the second year of publication, it can also be assumed that pressure was put upon them to do this. Wesley pestered

---

for the response from Thomas Hanson, and *AM,* vol. 8, p. 16 from William McCornock.

[73] *AM,* vol. 3, p. 477.
[74] *AM,* vol. 8, p. 16.
[75] *AM,* vol. 1, p. 541.
[76] *AM,* vol. 6, p. 78.
[77] *AM,* vol. 2, p. 589.
[78] *AM,* vol. 2, p. 635.

his correspondents: to Christopher Hopper he exclaimed: 'Why should not you write an account of your life?'[79] To John Bredin: 'Whatever you judge would be proper for the Magazine, send. You can comprise much in a sheet.'[80] It is also clear that Wesley edited the material sent to him prior to publication as can be seen by his continual urging to John Valton: 'I have received the first two sheets of your *Life*. Be not afraid of writing too much; I can easily leave out what can be spared.'[81]

The spiritual accounts of the itinerants had a common Wesleyan template to follow. They mainly began by describing the place of birth, childhood, and schooling where appropriate. The writers then turned to describe their character before conversion; the recognition of their need to change; the part (influential or not) played by the Methodist preachers in their awakening; their spiritual state prior to conversion with the broken soul, anxiety, and doubts, the overcoming of the devil and temptation. Much was given concerning the description and effect of their conversion process and the effect of their conversion upon others. The accounts then turned to record a history of the author's work in the movement showing progression from exhorting to preaching and the impact of such work upon others. If Wesley had a hand in this it is accredited to him. In biographies the final illness and concluding days are described with specific dates. An exhortation to emulate the spiritual state of the subject completed the accounts.

Some of the narratives were testimonies not to just spiritual attributes and service to Christ but also confirmed Wesleyan teachings on right living. *An Account of Mr.* THOMAS EDEN. *[By the Rev. Mr. B.]* illustrates how one spiritual account could confirm the teachings of many 'little pieces'

---

[79] *JWL,* vol. 6, p. 380, 16 February 1780.
[80] *JWL,* vol. 7, p. 301, 16 November 1785.
[81] *JWL,* vol. 7, pp. 100-101, 18 January 1782.

which had recommended such traits as frugality, temperance, and restraint with regard to self but generosity towards others. The readers were able to see the teachings personified in the account of an ordinary Methodist, one of their own, who died on 27 April 1781 and whose account reached the movement in the December issue of their *Magazine*:

> The Writer of this Account has often found fault with him; but now retracts the censure. Reader, he was in reality one of the only true economists. He sent most of his money before him to that country, to which his soul aspired, and in which he now rests from his cares and labours. Let us copy such devotedness to God, in our own lives: and not be content, (as is too frequent) with only admiring it in others.

The spiritual accounts became extended and more detailed as the *Magazine* emerged month by month, departing from the focused remit of exemplar spiritual experience into more narrative and factual content of individual lives. It is clear that Wesley became frustrated with this – it was a missed opportunity to ensure compliance. After a long three month narrative from February to April 1780 Alexander Mather was asked by Wesley to concentrate on a fuller account of the more spiritual nature of his life. He explained his reason for doing this in the magazine: 'After reading and considering the foregoing Account, I observed to *Mr Mather*, That he had wholly omitted one considerable branch of his Experience, touching what is properly termed, *the Great Salvation*. He wrote me a full and particular Answer, the substance of which I have subjoined.' Following the requested revised account Wesley commented to the readers; 'I earnestly desire, that all our Preachers would seriously consider the preceding Account. And let them not be content, never to speak against *the Great Salvation*, either in public or private; and never to discourage either by word or deed, any that think they have attained it.'[82]

Other accounts frustrated Wesley in relation to the length and lack of focus. Following a three month account from John Haime in which he concentrated on his life as a preacher - especially the negative issues, Wesley added the following comment: 'We intended to conclude MR HAIME'S Life this Month, but the Copy containing more Matter than was expected, we are obliged to put it off a Month longer.'[83]

Eight autobiographical narratives in the *Magazine* were written by females[84] who were, as far as Wesley was concerned, role models for Methodist women. That of Sarah Ryan, written in March 1760 (eight years prior to her death) appeared hastily in 1779 in place of an account of 'Dr. C.' which Wesley felt was 'not thought advisable to insert' at the time.[85] As the engraving for that month is of Thomas Coke it can be assumed that this is the Dr C. to whom he referred. John Vickers notes the friction that was then being stirred by Wesley's 'favourite' amongst the older Methodist itinerants which may have caused Wesley to have 'reservations about Coke's spiritual maturity' at this time, hence the withdrawal of the account.[86] This is in stark contrast to the introduction to the account for Sarah Ryan: 'The following account of a woman of long and deep experience will be deemed a good substitute by all lovers of real religion.' Wesley astutely used

---

[82] *AM,* vol. 3, p. 207.

[83] *AM,* vol. 3, p. 273.

[84] Sarah Ryan (June 1779); Ruth Hall (September 1781); Martha Thompson (September - October 1783) and Sarah Clay (October – December 1783) who do not appear in the index; Rachel Bruff of Maryland (March – May 1787); Mrs. A. B. (August – September 1789); Mrs. S. N. (October – November 1789) and Phebe Blood (December 1790).

[85] *AM,* vol. 2, p. 296.

[86] John Vickers, *Thomas Coke: Apostle of Methodism* (London: Epworth Press, 1969), p. 47.

this occasion to make the point to those who, like his own wife criticised his questionable relationship with Sarah Ryan.

There were also other accounts of exemplar female lives. An account of Sarah Mallitt [Mallet] was recorded, no doubt due to her noted extraordinary calling to preach, but the first instalment was written not by her but by her uncle, the following three being an account of her experience sent to him, not Wesley, in correspondence.[87] Margaret Jenkins' spiritual account is also included but as an historic account written in 1743 and inserted in the *Magazine* in 1778 via correspondence to Wesley.[88] 'An account of Puritan Margaret Baxter, [Wrote by her husband, Mr. Richard Baxter]' was printed in the 1784 editions of the *Magazine* over eleven monthly instalments.[89] It is significant that Wesley did not include an account of Hester Ann Roe's mystical experiences as confided to him and recorded in her own *Journal*. Just prior to his own death, he persuaded her to revise this for publication but, as Vicki Collins notes, Roe's *Journal* was problematic in that although it would have been exemplar material for the Methodists, it did not promote feminine filial loyalty, marriage, or motherhood.[90] This would weaken control of the focused readership.

When the *Arminian Magazine* was taken over to America, Thomas Coke and Francis Asbury continued much of Wes-

---

[87] *AM,* vol. 11, pp. 91ff, 'An Account of Sarah Mallitt [By William Mallitt]'.

[88] *AM,* vol. 1, p. 228, Margaret Jenkins to John Wesley, 8 October 1743.

[89] See *AM,* vol. 7, pp. 85ff.

[90] Vicki T. Collins, 'Account of the Experience of Hester Ann Rogers: Rhetorical Functions of a Methodist Mystic's Journal', in Christine Mason Sutherland and Rebecca Jane Sutcliffe (eds.), *The Changing Tradition: Women in the History of Rhetoric* (Calgary: University of Calgary Press, 1999), pp. 109-18. After Wesley's death, the movement published the *Journal* (1793), but with texts by male authors appended, and portrayed her as a good and holy woman who did not preach. It became the best selling female text in a century of Methodism.

ley's format. In the first edition of April 1789 'A *Short Account of the Life and Death of William Adams, a Youth in Virginia. Drawn up by a Friend, Personally Acquainted with the Deceased.'* appeared. The account, first written in 1782, is referred to as 'A little history of a human heart' and such a portrayal really sums up the spiritual accounts in the *Arminian Magazine* under Wesleyan editorship and control. The introduction to this first account in the New World accurately expressed the remit and value of such exemplar accounts for Methodists and Methodism throughout its expanding world.

> It pleaseth the Lord sometimes to raise the simple out of the dust; to take knowledge of an individual here and there, even in the lowliest walks of life; to endue them with more than common graces, and call them forth to distinguished usefulness; that the Excellency of the treasure enriching their souls, and withal committed to their trust for the benefit of others, may evidently appear to be, as it invariably is, not of man, but of GOD.
>
> Friendly reader, thou hast now before thee an instance of this kind. The following pages give thee, in artless, unadorned particulars, a little history of a human heart—a heart, as carnal once, and insensible as thine hath been; nay, probably, as thine is yet;—they contain the narrative of a mind and conversation, in the beginning estranged from, but afterwards assimilated unto the heavenly mind and life of Christ Jesus.
>
> Thou seest the deep exercise, the conflicts, the many troubles of a young soul, panting after redemption, and finding it: thou viewest a mere stripling, through the operation of free grace, brought unto a perfect man, unto the measure of the stature of the fulness of Christ: thou canst observe his life-rendered eminently meek, self-denied, zealous, and intent on doing good; and then closing with uncommon illumination and blessedness.
>
> It may be, *thou* art yet a youth: The character here simply represented, speaks with a persuasive force, particularly to thee: it bids thee shun the flat-

> tering snare of worldly pleasure: it bids thee never to
> think of any real enjoyment without having the Al-
> mighty for thy friend: it bids thee, not to hazard thy
> salvation and eternal peace upon the Render chance
> of living long: it bids thee, very early to give up
> thine heart to GOD; to cry, under the weight of in-
> expressible unworthiness, for the renewing opera-
> tions of a Saviour, through the Spirit;—never to rest,
> until thou hast a knowledge, an abiding perception
> of pardon and reconciliation, by faith in the blood of
> the covenant; and then, incessantly to walk in purity
> and love, as the ransomed of the Lord,—as one of
> the children of the light and of the day.

Just as the spiritual accounts educated and motivated the
early Methodists under the Wesleyan eye so did the exemplar
accounts of death bed scenes, the practice having been active
prior to the *Magazine* as evidenced by Wesley's comment to
Joseph Benson in October 1777: 'I have no objection to your
printing a thousand or two of the account of Mrs. Hutton's
death.'[91]

As editor, Wesley started to include accounts of deathbed
scenes in 1780.[92] His reason for doing this was to 'animate'
the readership into recognising the value of a Christian death
in an enlightened age which increasingly demystified death,
and promoted a quiet, dignified ending with the use of opiates
if necessary.[93] In the March edition of 1781 Wesley, preceding his own account of the death of Jane Muncy, originally
written in 1741, justified the practice of recording such
deaths: '[As nothing is more animating to serious people, than
the dying Words and Behaviour of the Children of God, I

---

[91] *JWL,* vol. 6, p. 285, 22 October 1777.

[92] *AM*, vol. 3, p. 592, 'Some Account of the Life and Death of Mrs. Sarah
Brough, by Barnabas Brough, of Clinton, near Whitehaven'.

[93] Roy Porter, *Enlightenment: Britain and the Creation of the Modern
World* (London: Penguin, 2000), p. 210.

purpose inserting, in each of the following Magazines, one (at least) of these Accounts, and the rather, because the Tracts from which most of them are extracted, are not in many hands.]'[94]

Evidence suggests that the *Magazine* was seen by late eighteenth-century Methodists as the natural receptacle for reports of deaths to be shared amongst the movement. 'Among many instances of happy deaths, which occurred during the two last years I was at *Halifax*', wrote Joseph Benson in December 1785, 'perhaps an account of the following, which happened in July last, may not be unworthy of a place in your Magazine.'[95] Wesley certainly depended upon readers sending him exemplar accounts – on 1 October 1782 he praised Hester Ann Roe for doing just that: 'You did exceedingly well to send me so circumstantial an account of Robert Roe's last illness and happy death. It may incite many to run the race that is set before them with more courage and patience.'[96]

The accounts were published primarily as examples to the rest of the membership, and wherever possible were used by Wesley as editor for evangelistic comment.[97] He wrote to Mrs Crosby on 30 November 1788 'MY DEAR SISTER, I thank you for your account of the death of Miss Corkle, which is highly remarkable. It ought not to be hid under a bushel; so I shall order it to be inserted in the *Magazine*.'[98] There is no record of this happy death in the *Magazine* but the intention is clear – others needed to read the account.

---

[94] *AM,* vol. 4, p. 153, 'An Account of Jane Muncy' by John Wesley.

[95] *AM,* vol. 8, p. 309, 'Some Account of Robert Dennis' by Joseph Benson, dated December 1785, inserted in the *Magazine* June 1785 (misplaced).

[96] *JWL,* vol. 7, p. 143, 1 October 1782. This account appeared in the *Magazine* in December 1784.

[97] *AM,* vol. 11, p. 632, 'A Short Account of the Death of Ann Ritson'.

[98] *JW,* vol. 8, p. 105, 13 November 1788.

The 172 happy deaths, or deathbed accounts,[99] recorded in the *Arminian Magazine* invigorated the readership with a sense of the dramatic, stressing the experience of those dying and those witnessing the privilege. They emphasized the assurance of salvation, as this was the climax of the dying person's life, seen as an achievement of a goal, and an assurance which gave encouragement to those witnessing the event and those reading about it. As David Morris notes 'The death bed held a semi-public status. Death was, ideally, a performance, an event, subject to the same artful preparations as any serious action performed on the stage, and like any stage performance it also held the power to move and to edify its audience.'[100] Through publication the reader was given the privilege of being part of that audience of death and salvation.

The language used in these death-bed accounts was the same language which Wesley encouraged in the Methodist pulpit, plain and to the point without embellishments for the benefit of the ordinary witnesses.[101] It was the language of certainty of going to rest, journeying onto safety, freedom from pain and suffering, and a guarantee of better things to come. The date of death was normally commented on in the accounts, and in many cases the exact hour and minute were noted. In some of the narratives, one gets the strong impression that how the person died was more important than how they lived, the final passing equal to the original conversion experience. Happy deaths were also evidence that the Arminian Methodist message of holiness, discipline and piety was right after all.

---

[99] Richard J. Bell notes that there were 152 deathbed scenes but upon analysis there are twenty further ones which do not appear in the Index.

[100] David B. Morris, 'A Poetry of Absence' in John Sitter (ed.), *The Cambridge Companion to Eighteenth-Century Poetry* (Cambridge University Press, 2001), p. 232.

[101] *An Address to the Clergy* (1756).

> His weakness increasing towards the night, he
> could speak but little; but he lay quiet with a heav-
> enly smile upon his countenance: he whispered, 'O,
> I hear that heavenly music again! Do you not hear it
> also?' When one answered, 'No'; he replied, 'The
> angels are waiting to conduct me to the heavenly
> mansions. O! come Lord Jesus! I shall soon sup with
> him in paradise.' The last words he was heard to
> speak were, 'Come, Lord Jesus, my heavenly Physi-
> cian.' A few minutes after, he fell asleep in Jesus
> about eight o'clock at night the 25th of January,
> 1789, in the 28th year of his age.[102]

As editor, Wesley shrewdly made use of the accounts to
investigate the possibility of using additional material for his
Magazine. Following a moving account of the death of Elizabeth Waller in March 1790, he commented, 'Her Diary will
probably be inserted in some future Magazine, if we can find
room.'[103] There is no evidence of this during his editorship.
He did follow the death bed scene of Mary Mahony with ten
pages of extracts from her personal journal with a characteristic aside, 'We could not give the particular dates of the days,
as they were not specified in the Manuscript.'[104] Wesley also
placed the emotional records in a more rational setting by including diaries, wills and articles in further 'little pieces' relating to the wider topic of death.[105]

---

[102] *AM,* vol. 13, p. 475.

[103] *AM,* vol. 13, p. 138.

[104] *AM,* vol. 13, pp. 356ff.

[105] *AM,* vol. 5, p. 298, 'Journal of Mr. G. C.'; *AM,* vol. 4, pp. 35ff, 'An
Extract from the Diary of Mrs. Bathsheba Hall'; *AM,* vol. 7, p. 102, 'A
Remarkable Will'; *AM,* vol. 8, p. 371, 'The Will of the Late Lady Palmerston, Endorsed for the Lord Palmerston'; *AM,* vol. 9, p. 672, ' A Copy of
the Will of the Rev. Dr. Annesley'; *AM,* vol. 9, p. 671, 'An Extract from
the Will of Mr. R. Baxter; *AM,* vol. 9, p. 281, 'A Remarkable Will'; *AM,*
vol. 13, p. 265, 'Thoughts on Making Wills'; *AM,* vol. 9, p. 39 ff, 'An
Extract from Three Dialogues' Extracted from Long Account; *AM,* vol. 10,
p. 26, 'A Short Account of the Death of a Daring Sinner: by Mr. J. F. of
Leeds; *AM,* vol. 10, p. 652, 'On Despising Death'; *AM ,* vol. 12, p. 663,

By regularly inserting accounts of happy deaths Wesley was, in fact, reinforcing a repetitive message across Methodism. The number of deathbed scenes rose more than any other type of inclusion during his editorship as nature took its toll on the aging preachers and first generation members including his own brother,[106] John Walsh argues that the recording of early persecution and struggles within Methodism 'gave the movement its equivalent of a martyrology and built up the image of heroic, primitive Methodism which, like the image of primitive Christianity itself, stimulated and reproved the piety of later, more comfortable generations.'[107] The deathbed accounts, as recorded in the *Magazine* had a similar function.

The impact of the death bed scenes was not confined to the spiritual state of the dying believer. Their salvation was celebrated by those looking on and assurance enabled death to be a happy occasion. [108] A crucial part of the death bed scenes constituted prayer by the dying for those left behind as evidenced by the account of the death of Jane Nancarrow by John Moon given in the *Magazine* in May 1790:

'The Translation of an Inscription on the Monument of the Duke of Wirtemberg'; *AM,* vol. 13, p. 384, 'Epitaph on John Viscomti, an Italian Prince'.

[106] *AM,* vol. 11, p. 407. Charles Wesley died on the 29 March1788. The letter from Miss S Wesley describing his last days was sent on 4 April and later shared with the readers in the August edition.

[107] John Walsh, 'Methodism and the Mob in the Eighteenth Century', *Studies in Church History,* vol. 8 (1972), 213.

[108] Examples of responses by mothers (of John Hattan, two Dutch children); by sons (of Hannah Wood, Mrs. Vaughan); by husbands (of Sarah Brough, Mrs. Martha Rogers, Mrs. Bunsted, Elizabeth Murlin, Mrs. Spencer, Mrs. Elisabeth Shacklock, Dorothy Wright, Elizabeth Mather, Mrs. Boardman, _____, William Blake); by a brother (of C Middleton); by a brother in law (of Henry Tarboton); by a widow (of Jonathan Simpson); by a daughter (of Elizabeth Henson; of Mr. C. Wesley); by a cousin (of Robert Roe); by a father (of Abisha Mayo); by a sister (of Mrs. Trimnell); by a grandfather (John Nelson) and by an uncle (of Sarah Mallitt, not account of death).

About twelve her brother- in-law coming in and asking how she was, she said, 'I am just going home to
Jesus. But let me entreat you once more, (it is the
last time) to turn and seek the Lord; call upon him,
and he will abundantly bless you; for his blessings
are free for all. Prepare to meet thy God. The Lord
grant that you and I may meet him with joy; then
shall we sing his praises in the courts of endless
bliss'.

On her friends taking their leave of her, giving
them her hand, she exhorted them to keep close to
God: crying out 'O my heart doth rejoice at leaving
you! Farewell here.' Then, turning to her sister, she
said. 'How joyfully can I give up them and *you* my
dear sister, into the hands of Him, who is able to
keep you in the right way!'

Her speech now altering, she could no longer be
understood. However, when some friends afterwards
came in, she would shake hands with them; and
when she failed to do this, she still beheld them with
apparent satisfaction: having in this her desire granted, viz. That they might be around her at her last
hour. . .

A little after, her sister desired she would speak
to her; but she could not answer. She then asked if
she wanted to take her flight above? She immediately lifted up her hands as high as she could; and
about eight o'clock, after a struggle with the cough,
resigned her soul to Him who give it on the the 29th
of June 1788.

The eye witnesses to the celebratory dying process of an
assured believer were often left contemplating their own spiritual welfare as can be seen in the account of *The Death of*
MARY THOMAS, first sent in correspondence to Wesley in
1745 and inserted in the *Magazine* in January 1782: The
writer Sarah Colston reflected after the death upon her own
situation no doubt echoed by the readers of the periodical:

> O Lord, my God! Glory be to thee for all things. I
> feel such desires in my soul after God, that my
> strength goes away. I feel there is not a moment's
> time to spare: and yet how many do I lose? Lord Je-
> sus, give me to be more and more diligent in all
> things. It is no matter to me, how I was an hour ago.
> Is my soul now waiting upon God? O that I may in
> all things, and through all things, see nothing but
> Christ! O that when he comes, he may find me
> watching!

The death bed scenes, like the spiritual accounts became longer and more detailed as the years passed and the writers became more confident. The accounts grew to include an account of the lives of the deceased as well as their death. Wesley chose accounts which were pertinent to the growing movement such as 'An account of the death of a Mr D' who died in April 1789 and whose account appeared in the *Magazine* in January 1790 which highlighted the conversion of a lifetime sinner – again confirming the readership in their faith and in the necessity for evangelism.

> I asked him was he happy *now*? He replied in a low
> voice, but so as all around the bed could hear, 'very
> happy'. His senses continued to the last moment. He
> was going on saying something, but we could not
> understand him; his face being full of smiles of
> transport, when his breath just stopt without any
> struggle or pain; and his happy spirit took its flight
> to behold that Jesus, whom he so lately knew, and
> yet had so much longed to see! Surely this was a
> brand plucked from the burning! And is another in-
> stance of the willingness of God to receive every re-
> turning prodigal; and that Christ is able to save to
> the uttermost all that come to God through him. To
> whom be all the glory! Amen!

Illustration 3.2
Alexander Mather (1733-1800), converted 1754, early itinerant preacher
and later close adviser to Wesley. An earlier engraving of him aged forty-
five can be found in the February 1780 volume of the *Arminian Magazine* together with his autobiographical spiritual account given
over February, March, and April of that year.

During the Wesleyan editorship deaths began to occur not
only of first generation itinerants but of members of their families. Alexander Mather's account of the death of his wife in
November 1789 reached the membership in July 1790. To-

gether the membership could grieve with one of their own and
unite in the certainty of salvation.

> Being truly sensible of her approaching dissolution,
> she gave directions concerning her funeral, and the
> week before she died laid out everything that might
> be wanting at her death. When her daughter, who
> was now with her, was much affected at this; she
> said, 'Why do you weep? I am preparing for my
> wedding day: It will be my happiest day' She then
> took to her bed, from which she was moved only
> once or twice afterwards. During the last week she
> suffered much; but was more patient, and more re-
> signed than ever; still confident in God and wholly
> disengaged from all things below, till she shook off
> the earthly tabernacle and went to taste of the joys
> prepared in the mansions above.

The Methodist family was allowed a privileged, rare insight into the personal sorrow of one of its first itinerants
through being allowed to read the whole of the original correspondence from Mather. This included the very personal conclusion where he reveals to Wesley his own vulnerability:

> I now enter upon a state of probation, to which I am
> practically a stranger; therefore I know not how I
> shall act; but my design and desire is so to act as
> may tend most to the glory of God, for which end I
> ought only to live. I remain, as ever,
> Your very affectionate, and dutiful Son in the Gos-
> pel,
> Alexander Mather.

Reports relating to the final moments of women by sisters in
the faith were particularly emotional:

> I returned to her, armed with divine power, and
> with the most intrepid courage said, 'My dear sister,
> do not fear; the Lord will be with you all the way
> through. There a convoy of angels stands ready, to
> conduct your soul into Abraham's bosom.' She said

'Yes' repeatedly, with the appearance of much delight. The mucus that fell on her throat was removed, and she lay quite calm, frequently saying I
am Christ's; I am dying in Christ, &c. till her power
of utterance quite failed, and she only breathed
shorter and shorter, till she breathed no more. And
on Tuesday the 12th of May 1789, at three in the
morning, her happy soul was sweetly dislodged
from its tenement of clay.[109]

The last death bed account chosen by Wesley was published
in the *Magazine* in February 1791, a month before his own
death:

At a few minutes past eight, a sudden rapture of joy
diffused new life over her dying countenance; - her
eyes beamed with unusual vivacity and pleasure; -
she strongly attempted to express the sentiments of
admiration and bliss, which she appeared to feel; but
her exertions were in vain; - the silver cord was
loosed – the golden bowl broken – the vapour of life
vanishing away! – In a moment, the effort was over!
– she calmly closed her eyes!- gave a slight struggle! – and the spring of life stood still![110]

In his *Memoirs of the Late Rev. John Wesley A. M.* (1791),
John Hampson stated: 'During the last ten or fifteen years of
his supremacy, he [Wesley] was the most absolute of monarchs.'[111] This period coincided with the publication of the
first 157 monthly instalments of the *Arminian Magazine*
which, as has been illustrated, was subject to unyielding editorial control. However, it is also during this period that Wesley, perhaps uncharacteristically, listened to the needs of the
membership regarding the content of what would be their pe-

---

[109] *AM*, vol. 13, p. 86. 'The Account of the Death of Mrs Trimnell Recorded
by Her Sister Anne Bolton'.
[110] *AM*, vol. 14, p. 83, 'An Account of Mrs. Langridge'.
[111] *Monthly Review*, vol. 6, p. 392.

riodical. This resolution to allow what was originally a theological retort to become a relevant, practical, interesting, supportive, thought provoking and adaptable miscellany not only led to the survival of his precious *Magazine*[112] but also ensured that the voices of early Methodism would safely echo from its pages to tell their own inimitable story.

Postscript

An analysis of the spiritual accounts in the *Arminian Magazine* can be obtained from the author at barbaraprosser3@gmail.com.

---

[112] The *Magazine* became one of the longest running Christian magazines under its future names of, *Methodist Magazine,* (1798-1821), *Wesleyan-Methodist Magazine* (1822-1913); *Magazine of the Wesleyan Methodist Church* (1914-1926) and *Methodist Magazine* (1927-1970).

4

In the Shadow of the Founder: Methodist Memorialisation of John Wesley

Gareth Lloyd

In 1891, as part of the commemoration of the centenary of John Wesley's death, a collection of sermons and essays was published by the Wesleyan Methodist Church based, with one exception, on addresses delivered during the course of that year at City Road Chapel in London. The tone of the collection is summed up by the following passage written by the former president of Conference, Rev Charles Garrett:

> John Wesley was the Morning Star of the Second Reformation; the herald and Inbringer of a new era of blessing for the Church and the world. To look beyond him is to look into the dark ages, where men had no rights and God no honour. All the great religious and social movements, which are the glory of the nineteenth century, were in John Wesley's mind, and he attempted to carry them out. As to foreign missions, he made the Methodist Church a foreign missionary society ... while the Home Missionary system he established was such as the world had never seen since the early days of Christianity. Sunday schools were started by Wesley ... He founded a bible society before the Bible Society had come into existence; and wrote tracts ... long before the era of the Religious Tract Society. He established schools for poor children before the British and Foreign School Society ...he was a temperance advocate long before the time of the Seven men of Preston ... he visited the prisons before John Howard ...

an energetic enemy of the slave trade before Wilberforce ...[1]

Garrett's claim for Wesley of superhuman qualities are reiter-
ated elsewhere in the collection – for Frederick William Macdonald, Wesley was the 'most influential of theologians';[2] as
an evangelist, he is compared to St Paul – 'Like the angel fly-
ing in the midst of heaven, [Wesley] had a message to all nations, peoples, kindreds and tongues'.[3] Rev Dr John Clifford,
leading Baptist minister, placed Wesley in the company of the
Prophets, with whom he is compared very favourably:

> Like Abraham, he early catches a glimpse of the far-
> off issues of his life ... Like Samuel, he is the
> founder and head of a band of prophets ... he has
> the intrepidity but not the crushing fierceness of Eli-
> jah ... he attains at length the Isaiah passion for ho-
> liness ... he repeats the experience of Jeremiah and
> he follows John the Baptist in the total subordination
> of all his life and work to the glory of Christ the Re-
> deemer ...[4]

Nor was the Methodist founder devoid of human qualities –
he was for example 'a great lover of children' and was loved
in turn by them.[5]

Extravagant praise of John Wesley and unquestioning ac-
ceptance of his dominant role in the Methodist story has not

---

[1] 'Address by the Rev. Charles Garrett', in *Wesley: The Man, His Teaching
and His Work. Being Sermons and Addresses Delivered in City Road Chapel at the Centenary Commemoration of John Wesley's Death*. (London,
1891), pp. 172-73. [hereafter, *Wesley: the Man*]

[2] F. W. Macdonald, 'Divine Service' in *Wesley: the Man*, p. 127.

[3] 'Address by the Rev. Richard Roberts', in *Wesley: the Man*, p. 169.

[4] John Clifford, 'The Prophet of the Eighteenth Century', in *Wesley: the
Man*, p. 114.

[5] Frederick J. Murrell, 'Wesley and the Children' in *Wesley: The Man*, pp.
140-141.

been confined to the great and the good or limited to significant anniversaries. Since Wesley's lifetime, his name has appeared on chapels, mission stations, insurance companies,
schools and hospitals, not just in Britain and the United States
but in many other countries. Wesley has become a popular
choice of first name, even in families and communities that
have experienced no significant Methodist or evangelical in-
fluence.Wesley's influence on Methodism and the broader
evangelical movement has been enormous. His example is
routinely cited by Church leaders; his writings have formed
the starting point for polity and doctrine, and the essential
building blocks of structure that he introduced, have survived
into the twenty-first century. It is true that the resonance that
Wesley's name once evoked is no longer strong with ordinary
Methodists, but the large number of biographies and theological studies that continue to appear, is testimony to an enduring
influence.

Analysis of this central place poses a peculiar challenge for
historians and theologians alike. It is peculiar in the sense that
Wesley's role has rarely been subjected to critical examination from within the discipline. John Wesley has been dead
for two hundred and twenty years, yet he is still regarded
without question as both the starting point and terminus for
discussions of the origin and character of Methodism in many
of its aspects. If one compares this treatment to some of his
contemporaries, such as the Duke of Wellington in military
affairs or William Pitt in politics, then it is clear that Wesley's
reputation has not been subject to the usual trends in scholarship that have buffeted the reputation of even the most eminent of individuals. He has certainly been discussed and his
contribution examined, but always with the assumption that
he remains a man and a leader apart.

This essay does not seek to challenge the legitimacy of
Wesley's claim to primacy within the Methodist tradition, but
will instead look at three specific areas connected to the birth

and evolution of the legend. First, it will examine how John Wesley consciously laid the foundations of this personal primacy; second, it will look at how his legacy was consolidated and shaped after the Methodist founder's death. Finally, the essay will consider some of the positive and negative effects of the movement's preoccupation with this one extraordinary man.

One of the things that can be said about John Wesley with little fear of contradiction is that he was convinced of his special place in God's plan. From a relatively early stage in Wesley's ministry after the conversion of 1738, he was referring explicitly to a divinely appointed personal mission. In a letter of 23 June 1739 to his brother Charles, John made the following statement:

> I have both an ordinary call and an extraordinary.
> My ordinary call is my ordination by the bishop ...
> My extraordinary call is witnessed by the works
> God doth by my ministry ... Perhaps this might be
> better expressed in another way. God bears witness
> in an <u>extraordinary manner</u> that my <u>thus exercising</u>
> my <u>ordinary call</u> is well-pleasing in his sight.[6]

Wesley's claim is noteworthy when one considers that he was writing at an early stage in the revival, before Wesleyan Methodism had emerged as a distinctive movement.[7] When this letter was written, most people would have regarded George Whitefield, not Wesley, as the Revival's pre-eminent

---

[6] John Wesley, *The Works of John Wesley*, vol. 25, ed. Frank Baker (Oxford: Clarendon Press, 1980), p.660 [hereafter *JWW*].

[7] For another illustration of Wesley's use of the term 'extraordinary call' to refer to special divine favour, one can cite his justification of Mary Bosanquet preaching in 1771. Methodist Archive, John Rylands Library [hereafter, MARC], MAM JW 1.101, John Wesley to Mary Bosanquet, 13 June 1771.

leader.[8] John Wesley's sense of being a man set apart was reinforced by every challenge that Wesleyan Methodism overcame in its rise to pre-eminence within the evangelical movement. Throughout this long and sometimes faltering process, Wesley's stance was simple and consistent - if Methodism was of God, then it would succeed and if it was not, then it would not. When Wesley applied this litmus test to his management of the Methodist societies, he felt vindicated by the result and by God's validation of his leadership. The intimate connection between God's work and Wesley's authority was the platform on which Methodism was built and remembered.

Such was the weight of legend and story-telling that accumulated around John Wesley's name that it can be difficult to tease out the reality of how the foundations for his enduring legacy were laid. In the first place, there can be no doubt that Wesley possessed exceptional moral stature and spiritual gifts and these qualities underpinned everything that he did. He shared these talents with other gifted evangelists of his generation; what set Wesley apart were his powers of leadership combined with a pre-disposition towards independent action. Contemporary accounts refer to Wesley's calmness under pressure and refusal to give way to anger.[9] This serenity was combined with an iron will and extreme reluctance to bow to any authority, other than that of the divine. The Methodist archives contain many first-hand testimonies to Wesley's authoritarian instincts. In 1776, Ann Chapman complained that 'the people here are discouraged and say its of no use for them to speak: I believe they think of Mr W. [John Wesley] as some do of our K. [King] that he will not hearken to any re-

---

[8] Henry D. Rack, *Reasonable Enthusiast: John Wesley and the Rise of Methodism* (3rd edn., London: Epworth Press, 2002), p. 191.
[9] 'Wesley's emotional detachment ... seemed to be a miracle of calm controlled serenity.' Rack, *Reasonable Enthusiast*, p. 540.

monstrance'.[10] This reluctance to share power can be seen from Wesley's earliest days as a public figure. In 1741, Charles Wesley asked a pointed question concerning his brother's rejection of the Moravians: 'Are you not afraid lest they should eclipse your own glory, or lessen your own praise?'[11] From the very birth of Wesleyan Methodism, there was never any doubt that it would bear John Wesley's personal stamp. Wesley's placid temperament could never be confused with softness; any who crossed the leader's will tended to feel the effects of his anger, expressed not in a rage, but in a dispassionate rejection of the offending party, which was all the more effective for its emotional detachment.[12]

Yet at the same time, like all great leaders, Wesley was an outstanding manager of people. He knew instinctively how far to exert his authority without suppressing the rugged individualism that was a vital aspect of the movement's success. Wesley was tolerant of the idiosyncrasies of his followers as long as they were compliant to his direction. One colourful character, in a movement that was not short of them, was a man called George Escrick of Bolton in Lancashire, whose obituary appeared in the *Arminian Magazine* in 1808. Escrick was a devoted Wesleyan for over fifty years, acting as a local preacher, class leader, and Sunday School teacher. According to his obituary, Escrick was

> rough in his manners, apt to be angry at times, and a
> little too positive in his way. It was well-known that
> he almost adored Mr Wesley, yet he would be warm

---

[10] MARC, DDCW 2/13, Ann Chapman to Charles Wesley, 21 August 1776.
[11] *JWW*, vol. 26, p. 53. Charles Wesley to John Wesley, 10 March 1741.
[12] '[John Wesley] never doubted, that the plans he had formed, were the best that could be devised, so, when any of the preachers were of a different opinion ... he treated them as the mariners treated Jonah. He threw them overboard with the most perfect indifference.' John Hampson (junior), *Memoirs of the Late Rev. John Wesley, A. M., with a Review of His Life and Writings* ... (Sunderland: 1791), pp. 199-200.

and rough with him upon occasions. For instance; on a certain occasion when Mr Wesley was going Northward, George was informed that he had not Bolton in his plan; and as he was then at Liverpool, 31 miles from Bolton, our dear departed friend set out in the evening for that town, saying ... 'I will neither eat nor sleep till I see him'. He arrived in Liverpool, by the time of service at five in the morning, and after the preaching was ended, and the congregation dismissed, he followed Mr Wesley to his lodgings, and being admitted to his apartment, said, 'So the devil may take Bolton for you', repeated the words and then withdrew ....[13]

The fact that Escrick was not disciplined for taking his leader to task, illustrates Wesley's skilful handling of his followers. On the one hand, he was a demanding patriarch, but he was also surprisingly tolerant, as long as his leadership was not threatened. This was a delicate balancing act, which Wesley performed with finesse, exercising supreme authority, but sparingly and ruthlessly. It was a lesson in the art of management that his successors failed to master, contributing to the divisions that plagued Methodism after his death.

Virtually every aspect of Wesley's life as the leader of the Methodists provides evidence for the deliberate construction of a movement that was devoted to God, but centred on the authority of one man. Attention can be usefully drawn to two aspects of Wesley's practical management as having particular relevance for memorialisation. The first is his activities as an editor, author and publisher.

Wesley issued his first publication as early as 1733,[14] while

---

[13] Thomas Taylor, 'Memoir of George Escrick', *The Methodist Magazine for 1808: Being a Continuation of the Arminian Magazine...,* vol. XXXI (March, 1808), 129-130.
[14] In his bibliography of Wesley publications, Green lists: *A Collection of Forms of Prayer for Every Day in the Week* as having been issued by John Wesley in 1733, although no copy of this 1st edition survives. Richard

he was still at Oxford. In the decades that followed, he became nothing short of a publishing phenomenon with approximately five hundred separate titles issued under his name or from his press, placing him among the most prolific writers and publishers of the eighteenth century. An inventory of the contents of the Book Room carried out as part of the administration of Wesley's estate, listed over 250,000 volumes awaiting nationwide distribution.[15] John Wesley was a visionary, who saw limitless potential in a printing industry that expanded rapidly during his lifetime. As one might expect, many Methodist works were religious in nature, covering a range of material from sermons to biographies and theological treatises. These comprised Wesley's own writings, together with works by other authors, which he edited to suit his own doctrinal views. However, not all of the publishing output was religious: Wesley realised the importance of appealing to as many tastes as possible, while still pursuing a long-term spiritual agenda and this also suited his own broad interests. The Book Room inventory[16] included works on history, natural philosophy, medicine and current affairs, which were again often authored or edited by the ubiquitous Mr Wesley.

Wesley's publishing activities served a number of purposes. In the first place, they promoted and consolidated revival. The principal market was among the poor and dispossessed, so great stress was placed on making the majority of the publications affordable. A number of mechanisms were employed to maximise circulation and minimise cost including the use of cheap materials and employing preachers to distribute cop-

---

Green, *The Works of John and Charles Wesley. A Bibliography* ... (London: Methodist Publishing House, 1906), p. 9.

[15] Vicki Tolar Burton, "Something for the People to Read": John Wesley's Book Inventory (1791)', *Bulletin of the John Rylands University Library of Manchester*, vol. 85 (2003), 230.

[16] MARC, MAW Ms 695, Inventory of the contents of the Methodist Book Room, 1791.

ies and aggressively promote their use. Wesley regarded himself as the primary mouthpiece for God's message of salvation to his followers – he did his best to carry out this task in person, but in his physical absence, he relied on print to maintain a presence in every household. This process also served to keep Wesley's name and guidance in the forefront of Methodist minds; he was closely engaged in the editing or writing of publications and his name was often prominent on the final published copy. His cavalier attitude towards putting his name on other people's work sometimes landed him in hot water, even in an age where such matters were loosely regulated. In 1745, Wesley paid £50 compensation for breach of copyright,[17] and he was in trouble again in 1775, for plagiarising a work by Samuel Johnson.[18]

An illustration of Wesley's unshakeable self-belief can be found in the foreword to his *Complete English Dictionary* published in 1753:

> This little dictionary is not only the shortest, and the cheapest, but likewise, by many degrees the most correct, which is extant to this day. Many are the mistakes in all the other English Dictionaries, which I have yet seen. Whereas I can truly say, I know of none in this ... for if I had, I should not have left it there.[19]

Wesley's control of Methodist publishing ensured delivery of his message, and that has been tremendously influential. It was Wesley's doctrine, opinions and version of the birth and early struggles of Methodism that was propagated. The pub-

---

[17] MARC, JWV 14, Bond by John Wesley to pay £50 to Robert Dodsley, 8 February 1745.
[18] Rack, *Reasonable Enthusiast*, pp. 346, 376.
[19] John Wesley, *The Complete English Dictionary, Explaining Most of Those Hard Words, Which Are Found in the Best English Writers* (London: printed by W. Strahan, 1753).

lished works have provided the single most important source of information about Wesley's life and ministry ever since. This is true of course for many historic figures, but it has been enhanced in Wesley's case by the sheer volume of material that he left for scholarship, and the fact that much of it has been continuously in print for over two hundred years. Wesley's collected works have shaped and defined early Methodist studies for successive generations and have significantly impacted on how the wider revival has been viewed.

Itinerancy was another aspect of Wesley's ministry and leadership that made a substantial contribution to his enduring reputation. There must be few circuits, certainly in England that cannot be linked to the physical presence of the founder – a building or location where Wesley preached or a road along which he travelled. Because Wesley documented and published his travels with painstaking precision, his daily progress can be charted with unusual accuracy and in often colourful detail. The places that Wesley visited often became local landmarks and continue to this day as focal points for commemorations of the early Methodist story.

If one probes beneath the surface of the often superficial way in which the itinerancy has been viewed, then it becomes clear that there was a gifted organisational talent at work. Wesley's itinerancy did not simply happen, but was carefully planned and publicised in advance through the issue of 'preaching plans'

The letters of Wesley and his assistants often contain references to revisions to Wesley's schedule and to the necessity for giving public notice of where and when he would be preaching, as for example with the following passage from a letter written by John Pawson in Leeds to a colleague in Glasgow:

> I saw Mr Wesley at Manchester a fortnight ago …
> We expect him here next Sunday but he only intends
> staying two nights … his plan when I saw him was

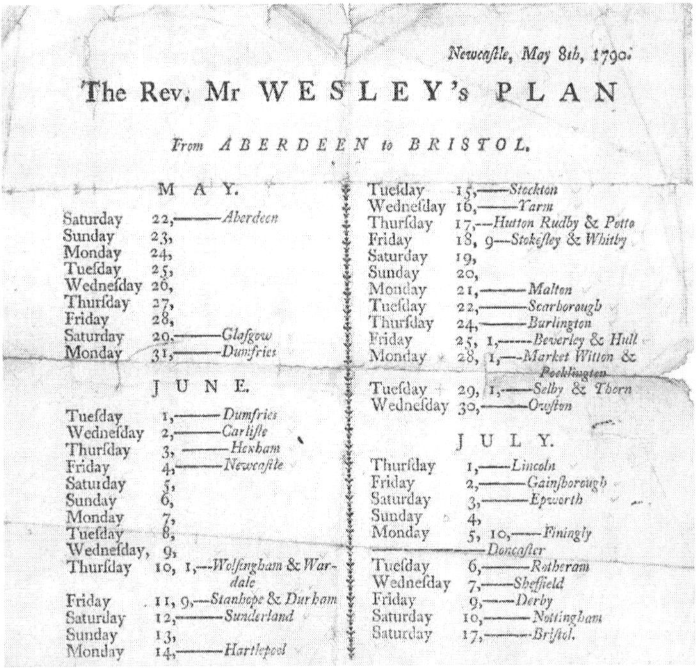

Newcaſtle, May 8th, 1790.

The Rev. Mr WESLEY's PLAN

From ABERDEEN to BRISTOL.

MAY.

Saturday 22,——*Aberdeen*
Sunday 23,
Monday 24,
Tueſday 25,
Wedneſday 26,
Thurſday 27,
Friday 28,
Saturday 29,——*Glaſgow*
Monday 31,——*Dumfries*

JUNE.

Tueſday 1,——*Dumfries*
Wedneſday 2,——*Carliſle*
Thurſday 3,——*Hexham*
Friday 4,——*Newcaſtle*
Saturday 5,
Sunday 6,
Monday 7,
Tueſday 8,
Wedneſday, 9,
Thurſday 10, 1,--*Wolſingham & Wardale*
Friday 11, 9,—*Stanhope & Durham*
Saturday 12,——*Sunderland*
Sunday 13,
Monday 14,——*Hartlepool*
Tueſday 15,——*Stockton*
Wedneſday 16,——*Yarm*
Thurſday 17,--*Hutton Rudby & Potto*
Friday 18, 9—*Stokeſley & Whitby*
Saturday 19,
Sunday 20,
Monday 21,——*Malton*
Tueſday 22,——*Scarborough*
Thurſday 24,——*Burlington*
Friday 25, 1,-----*Beverley & Hull*
Monday 28, 1,—-*Market Witton & Pocklington*
Tueſday 29, 1,——*Selby & Thorn*
Wedneſday 30,——*Owſton*

JULY.

Thurſday 1,——*Lincoln*
Friday 2,——*Gainſborough*
Saturday 3,——*Epworth*
Sunday 4,
Monday 5, 10,——*Finingly* ——*Doncaſter*
Tueſday 6,——*Rotheram*
Wedneſday 7,——*Sheffield*
Friday 9,——*Derby*
Saturday 10,——*Nottingham*
Saturday 17,——*Briſtol.*

Illustration 4.1
John Wesley's Preaching Plan, May to July 1790. MARC, Call number JRL 023007bw.

to be at Dumfries, May 13, Edinburgh 16 and Glasgow 17. But I expect he will change again before he reaches you and will come to Glasgow before Edinburgh. If he should spend a Sunday at Glasgow, I would advise you to desire him that as he dislikes the form of Scotch service, to stay at home till 11 o'clock and so you give the lecture and he come and preach.[20]

[20]MARC, PLP 82.4.4, John Pawson to Charles Atmore, 28 April 1788.

Works of Methodist history, particularly those written during the nineteenth century, preferred accounts of demanding journeys and pictorial representations of persecution to the reality of a ministry, which was planned and relatively uneventful, once the anti-Methodist riots of the early years faded away.

Illustration 4.2
John Wesley being attacked in Wednesbury in 1743; nineteenth century engraving. MARC, Image call number JRL061080

It is certainly the heroic incidents that made the deepest impression on the Methodist imagination – there are no picture engravings of Wesley examining the circuit financial accounts or perusing the membership lists, but it was these activities that guaranteed the movement's future prosperity and underpinned the legend.

Wesley's pattern of well-publicised annual or biennial visits to major centres of population and favoured places in-between made a cumulative impression, not just on his followers, but on society at large. Other revivalists of the time,

154

such as Whitefield and Benjamin Ingham, also travelled and evangelised with conspicuous success, but their personal impact was felt for shorter periods and was not accompanied by Wesley's organisational flair and eye for detail. The fact that Wesley out-lived his contemporaries and was still travelling in his late eighties increased the popular fascination – the secular *Gentleman's Magazine* referred to Wesley as one of the most remarkable men of the age.[21] John Wesley's itinerancy made a significant personal contribution to the consolidation of Methodism throughout the British Isles. It is noticeable when reading obituaries in the *Arminian Magazine*, how many Methodists across the country and from every social class claimed a personal connection with their leader. Wesley was not a remote figure positioned exclusively at a central location, but someone who was a part of their life and community – his visits were infrequent, but they were significant events and were recalled as such. Folk memories of Wesley's personality and ministry, no doubt often embellished, were passed down for generations.

The death of John Wesley in March 1791 marked the end of physical ministry and the beginning of memorialisation, although this dividing line is not as distinct as one might assume. For years before he died, Wesley was already a legend and a process of apotheosis was under way. This had its most evocative representation just after Wesley died, in an illustration of the Methodist leader being carried by angels to paradise. Wesley's personal ministry also continued after 1791 through his published sermons and other devotional works.

---

[21] Anonymous, 'Obituary of John Wesley', *Gentleman's Magazine*, vol. 69 (1791), 282–84.

Illustration 4.3
John Wesley being carried to heaven by the angels, 1791. MARC, Image
call number JRL022522tr.

The one thing that could not continue indefinitely was Wesley's physical presence. His death presented the preachers and people with a problematic transition from one man rule to collective government. In 1784, Wesley appointed Conference as the body that would assume oversight of Methodism in the event of his death, subject to the chairmanship of a president. This measure did not prevent manoeuvrings behind the scenes as certain senior preachers attempted to manipulate the situation, or were suspected of doing so. In 1794, a clandestine meeting of senior figures was held at Lichfield to consider the future government of the Connexion. The gathering did not attempt to reverse the Wesleyan settlement, but did propose certain reforms with regard to ordination and the creation of districts, each under a superintendent. The proposals were emphatically rejected by Conference as creating 'invidious and unhallowed distinctions among brethren'.[22] The frosty response to the "Lichfield Plan" illustrates the deep abhorrence felt by the preachers to the possibility that one man could step into Wesley's shoes: the fact that the Lichfield proposers nominated all but one of their own number as 'Superintendents' did little to sell the idea. This was an early manifestation of what became a common Methodist phenomenon during the nineteenth century – if a minister started to acquire too much power or influence, a counter-reaction would set in.

Aversion to one man rule did not prevent individuals from trying to claim a privileged place as one of the heirs to Wesley. For ambitious preachers, this involved emphasising personal connections with the Methodist leader. One of the bitterest disputes in this period had its origins in control of Wesley's personal papers as a prelude to writing the first official life. This struggle was not simply about money, but was also connected with the prestige of being Wesley's official biog-

---

[22] John A. Vickers (ed.), *A Dictionary of Methodism in Britain and Ireland* (Peterborough: Epworth Press, 2000), p. 205.

rapher. Inevitably, the dispute escalated, resulting in suspensions from membership, battles between trustees and itinerants, and a legal bill of over £2,000. In keeping with the confused nature of the affair, the City Road society ended up paying the court costs for both sides.[23] Unseemly public bickering did little to persuade the Methodist people that there was anyone who had the authority and judgement to be Wesley's successor. The fact that Wesley had avoided making such a nomination reinforced this impression. For Methodism, there would never be another "King in Israel" and this elevated John Wesley to a position that could never be challenged.

One might have expected that the dramatic expansion of Methodism during the first half of the nineteenth century would have consigned Wesley to the background. At the time of his death there were 72,476 members in the British Isles.[24] By 1800 this figure had reached 109,911[25] and by 1825 it was a quarter of a million.[26] By 1850 Wesleyan Methodism was the most important Protestant denomination in England and Wales after the Anglican Church. By the time of this highwater mark in British Methodist fortunes, Wesley had been dead for many years, but he was still seen as the architect of success and was actively promoted as such. The institutional response to disharmony and other challenges within the Wesleyan movement was to cling to the founder's coat tails. In its essentials, the system that he imposed remained in place: chapels and circuits functioned as well in Victoria's reign as they had a hundred years previously; Conference continued as the policy-making body with the representative structure be-

---

[23] George J. Stevenson, *City Road Chapel London and Its Associations Historical, Biographical and Memorial* (London: George J. Stevenson, 1872), pp. 131-39.

[24] *Minutes of the Methodist Conferences from the first, held in London ...*, vol.1 (London: Conference Office, 1812), 244 [hereafter, *Conference Minutes*]

[25] Ibid., vol. 2, pp. 53–54.

[26] Ibid., vol. 6, p. 42.

queathed by Wesley; the liturgy of the Church until 1882 was an abridged form of the Book of Common Prayer (abridged of course by Wesley); and the overwhelming majority of hymns sung in chapels were Wesley compositions; written almost exclusively by Charles, but edited by his older brother.

It was accepted by Wesleyan Methodist leaders that they were caretakers of Wesley's movement. In their professed strict adherence to Wesley, the nineteenth century leadership found the source and justification for their own closely guarded authority. Jonathan Crowther in the influential *Methodist Manual* of 1810 stated 'The rules of the Society, drawn up, and signed by Messrs John and Charles Wesley, May 1 1743 ... still remain in force'.[27] In 1829 a Conference committee overturned an exclusion from society membership on the grounds that the original decision was not 'in conformity ... to the original plan of Mr Wesley, whose example in London, we deem binding as a precedent in all similar cases'.[28] The secretary of this committee was Jabez Bunting, the dominant Wesleyan Methodist of the nineteenth century. Bunting was no shrinking violet where exercise of personal authority was concerned, but even he doffed his cap in the founder's direction. This is one of the striking aspects of the memorialisation of Wesley within the Wesleyan movement. For generations after he died, Wesley's direct influence over policy, governance, ethos and doctrine remained intact. He was not a symbol, but a living and vital aspect of the Church that bore his name; not in his honour, but because it was his. What he meant for other Methodist traditions will be covered later

This is not to say that Wesleyan Methodism was frozen in time; there were many changes in response to the shifting challenges facing the Church. The district system was intro-

---

[27] Jonathan Crowther, *The Methodist Manual: or, a Short History of the Wesleyan Methodists* ... (Halifax: J. Walker, 1810), p. 129.
[28] W. R. Ward (ed.), *The Early Correspondence of Jabez Bunting, 1820-29* (London: Royal Historical Society, 1972), p. 122.

duced in the late 1790s, sacraments were administered in increasing numbers of chapels, and the ever-expanding business of Conference gave birth to committees and sub-committees; but these reforms could be seen as a natural process of evolution and often had a Wesley precedent. More radical innovations tended to be controversial, often on the grounds that they were not in accordance with Mr Wesley's plan. One example was the controversy surrounding the introduction of college training for ministers. The proposers of the scheme in 1834 were very aware of this potential objection when they published their proposals:

> Some may, not improbably, indulge an unfriendly feeling towards the projected [training] institution, from a suspicion that it is 'at variance with the plans and proceedings of the venerable founder of Methodism.'[29]

They went on to argue:

> ... in pleading for such a system of tuition ... [the proposers] are not acting at variance with Mr Wesley's original purposes, but are only attempting to revive and perfect one of his early and favorite plans.[30]

Needless to say, many disagreed with this interpretation.[31] After a bitter public row, several thousand society members seceded to join the Wesleyan Methodist Association.

---

[29] *Proposals for the Formation of a Literary and Theological Institution ...* (London: J. Mason, 1834) p. 9 [hereafter, *Proposals*]
[30] Ibid., pp. 11-12.
[31] For example, ' ... the projected Institution ... would be found in fact, and in working, to be a very considerable distance from the original and uniform practice of Methodism'. Samuel Warren, *Remarks on the Wesleyan Theological Institution* (3rd edn., London: Simpkin & Marshall, 1834), p. 16.

The wish to stick rigidly to Wesley's arrangements was not the only factor in such controversies, but the question 'Is this in accordance with the old plan?' was never far from people's minds. The different factions tended to look to the Methodist leader for support, as shown in this illustration from a tract of 1846 showing Wesley's ghost castigating his modern day followers.

Illustration 4.4
John Wesley accusing his modern-day followers, engraving from 'Vetus', *Wesley Ghost* (Manchester and London, 1846). MARC, Image call number RL023005bw.

During his lifetime, Wesley was notoriously difficult to pin down on a range of doctrinal and ecclesial issues often changing stance to suit the needs of the moment. This fancy footwork served early Methodism well, but after Wesley's death, gave rise to endless debate and produced fuel for controversy. Factions interpreted Wesley to support very different viewpoints and found supporting material in Wesley's voluminous works. For some nineteenth century policy-makers, interpreting Wesley assumed an importance akin to interpreting scripture.

The original body that was in 'connexion' with Wesley in 1791 split over the next half century in several directions. The secessions were damaging in some respects, but had the effect of spreading Wesley's name and influence further afield. It is no coincidence that there are currently over 40 denominations around the world that claim descent from the eighteenth century Wesleyan movement.

In Britain, Wesleyan Methodism was the denomination that was most associated with its founder. Break-aways and other independent groups tended to have greater distance; and for such bodies, the adjective Wesleyan became associated with ministerial monopoly of power and abuse of privilege. The Wesleyan leadership's view of their right, indeed their obligation, as the heirs of Wesley to exercise his authority, was summarized by the following extract from *The Polity of Methodism*, published in 1869: 'no inference can be drawn that Mr Wesley ever intended that the laity should share in the Conference power, and need we say such a step taken after Mr Wesley's decease would have shivered the entire fabric of Methodism'.[32] Lay participation in the Wesleyan Conference

---

[32] Joseph Henry Skewes, *A Complete and Popular Digest of the Polity of Methodism* (London: Elliot Stock, 1869), p. 53.

was not introduced until 1878 and even then, was subject to considerable restrictions.[33]

For non-Wesleyan Methodists, the fact that Wesley was used as justification for what was often viewed as oppressive practices affected his reputation. Churches like the Primitive Methodists and Bible Christians adopted the fundamental structure that Wesley pioneered and acknowledged him in an often vague manner as the father of Methodism, but did not use his name or image to any significant degree.[34] This reserve did comparatively little to dilute Wesley's iconic status; the Wesleyan Church was the only Methodist denomination to have a considerable presence throughout England and Wales and their membership exceeded all the other Methodist denominations combined. For non-Methodists, Wesley and Methodism became almost synonymous.

The negative legacy of Wesley's high view of the ministry lingered into the twentieth century, acting as a brake on moves towards union as the various denominations tried to reconcile differing views of what it was to be a Methodist. In 1933 shortly after unification was finally achieved, the ex-Wesleyan missionary Harold Burgoyne Rattenbury wrote to his wife that his new colleagues in the China mission, former United Methodists, 'have one thing in common with you. They think J. Wesley over-exaggerated & have heard quite enough about him ...'.[35] Over the years, John Wesley has been a source of unity and division, strength and weakness, but always a talking point.

---

[33] For a list of the subjects that remained a ministerial preserve, see *Conference Minutes 1877*, p. 422.

[34] For example, the official history of the Primitive Methodist Church dates the origins of the Connexion to 1812 and barely acknowledges Wesley at all. Holliday B. Kendall, *History of the Primitive Methodist Connexion* (London: Primitive Methodist Publishing House, 1902).

[35] MARC, DDHB 7/50, Harold Burgoyne Rattenbury to Emily Rattenbury, 8 October 1933.

Illustration 4.5
Commemorative mug showing the head of John Wesley. MARC, image call
number JRL030500tr

This process of continuing influence is easy to chart where
the leadership is concerned, but is less straightforward with
regard to the membership. One indication of what Wesley
meant to ordinary chapel goers is provided by the sizeable

memorabilia industry that sprang up around his name. Busts, figurines, and other ceramics bearing Wesley's likeness were manufactured for the Victorian mass market.[36]

Even today Wesley's name and face can be found on a range of products from book markers to baseball caps, and key rings. Wesley's image and name provided the brand for Methodism not just in Britain, but around the world. Wesley-an Methodism needed a distinctive identity to set it apart from other denominations, particularly the Church of England. The movement inherited in John Wesley a charismatic and acces-sible figure, ideally suited to become the face of a new and exciting religious movement; the colourful wrapper on the Methodist product. From chapels to t-shirts and all points in-between, Wesley remains the father of the Methodist family more than two hundred years after he died.

The continuing focus on Wesley is particularly marked with regard to reporting of early Methodist history and theol-ogy. One negative result of this pre-occupation with Wesley is 'diversion of historical attention from the study of the Revival as a whole'.[37] The significant contribution made by a large number of early revival pioneers have fallen victim to what at times has come close to an obsession with Wesley. This dis-proportional emphasis has also affected works of local histo-ry; coverage of eighteenth century grassroots Methodism has often focused on visits made to a particular locality by Wes-ley, underplaying the significant contribution made by preachers and lay people. The field is now starting to broaden, with excellent research being done on non-Wesley aspects of the Revival, but there is still much ground to be made up.

---

[36] See David J. Jeremy, '"What Mean Ye by These Stones? Aspects of Me-morialising and Remembering in Wesleyan Methodism' (Chapter 2 above).

[37] John D. Walsh, 'Origins of the Evangelical Revival', in G. V. Bennett and John D. Walsh (eds.), *Essays in Modern Church History, in Memory of Norman Sykes* (London: Adam & Charles Black, 1966), p. 132.

The intimate bond between Methodism and Wesley has served the movement well. He was an exciting figure, whose mix of conservative theology, charismatic practices, and organisational grasp, provided the launch pad for a wave of expansion. These aspects alone would have guaranteed the survival of his name, but when you add his heroic persona and endless stock of pithy quotations one can understand why John Wesley has been a marketing man's dream.

Not everyone felt comfortable with the adulation accorded to Wesley, even within the Wesleyan tradition. John's brother Charles for example found much to criticize - in August 1783 he wrote to his wife that John was preaching three times in two days, before adding: 'I never knew a wise, good man, so FOND OF BEING heard as he is'.[38] Some nineteenth century Wesleyans were equally irritated by their Wesley-centred environment: Alice Macdonald, mother of Rudyard Kipling, was a daughter of the Manse. As a teenager, Alice 'made a bold gesture of defiance: during one of the regular house-packing operations, she discovered a yellowing envelope containing a carefully wrapped lock of John Wesley's hair. Scornfully, she held it before her sisters, then, with the words, "See! A hair of the dog that bit us!" tossed it in the fire ... her sisters awaited awestruck, expecting the hand of God to strike'.[39]

Methodism continues to wrestle with Wesley and his significance for today's Church. Is he purely an historic figure or does he have contemporary relevance? This debate is conducted against the background of a declining membership and an uncertain future. Looking to the past for inspiration, identity, and organisational models benefitted the nineteenth century movement, but today there is an uncomfortable realization that an institution, rooted in the past, often has little future to look forward to. At the same time, many still look to Wesley

---

[38] MARC, DDCW 7/86: Charles Wesley to Sarah Wesley, August 1783.
[39] Ina Taylor, *Victorian Sisters: the Remarkable Macdonalds and the Four Great Men They Inspired* (London: Weidenfeld & Nicolson, 1987), p. 23.

as a source of practical guidance in such matters as church growth or re-discovered worship models, regarding him as a contemporary spiritual and organisational resource. American Methodism is particularly active in this respect, founded in part on the close relationship between Wesley and the holiness tradition. It is somewhat ironic that despite the decline of mainstream Methodist Churches, interest in Wesley himself has never been greater.

Since his death, John Wesley has been an enduring source of fascination, inspiration and irritation. This has formed part of a constant process of re-interpretation of his message and the importance of his contribution. The term memorialisation does not in fact do justice to what Wesley signifies for a Methodism that is still influenced by him in matters of doctrine, structure, and identity. One of the contemporary challenges for Methodism is how to engage with a man, who is both an historic figure and a continuing presence across substantial areas of Church life and mission. In the 1891 collection, Charles Henry Kelly wrote that John Wesley 'towers not only above the other great men of early Methodism, but above the greatest in all the other Churches in Christendom'.[40] This assessment of Wesley's importance is perhaps exaggerated, but the fact that he is still being discussed and analysed around the world is achievement enough - although John Wesley himself would probably not have been too surprised.

Acknowledgement
Permission to publish the images used in this article was granted by The John Rylands Library, The University of Manchester, and the Trustees for Methodist Church Purposes.

---

[40] Charles H. Kelly, 'The Man: His Teaching and Work', in *Wesley: the Man*, p. 6.

5

Men Who Left the Wesleyan Methodist Ministry, 1791-1932: a Database in Progress

John Lenton

The period 1791 to 1932, which I want to call the ' Methodist long nineteenth century', spans the period from the death of Wesley, when Wesleyanism began to live independently of its founder, until Methodist Union, when the Wesleyan Methodist Church became a part of the Methodist Church. This was a time when the Wesleyan Methodist Church grew rapidly, survived the schisms of the early nineteenth century, and settled in middle age into a mixed Methodist economy after the admission of laymen to Conference in 1878 and laywomen to Conference in 1911. The ministry grew from around 320 ministers on Wesley's death in 1791 to 2,518 in 1932.[1] This exploratory essay is confined to the ministry of the Wesleyan Methodist Church, by 1914 the largest of the bodies of profes-

---

[1] Estimates for the figure at Wesley's death are based on the 1790 figure in John Lenton, *John Wesley's Preachers: a Social and Statistical Analysis of the British and Irish Preachers Who Entered the Methodist Itinerancy before 1791* (Milton Keynes: Paternoster, 2009), p. 438, Table 22 and Appendix 2. The 1790 figure includes Irish preachers, missionaries and supernumeraries. Cf. John M. Turner, *Wesleyan Methodism* (Peterborough: Methodist Publishing House, 2005), p. 7: '300 active in 1791'. For the 1932 figure see Rupert E. Davies et al. (eds,), *History of Methodism in Great Britain* (4 vols., London: Epworth, 1965-88), vol. 3, p. 339 and Turner, *Wesleyan Methodism,* p.70. Many historians work in terms of 'active' ministers, in which case the 1932 figure is significantly lower.

sional Nonconformist clergy apart from the Congregational-ists.[2]

Studying the ministry in that long period throws up many problems, such as the different concepts of ministry in 1791 and 1932. One of the most challenging questions surrounds those who left the ministry. Studying such men is difficult since often they have no obituary. Frequently we know little about where they came from. Their departure is often not described. They can simply 'disappear' from the *Minutes*. Historians have looked at individual leavers like James Everett, Richard Watson, or Samuel Warren,[3] but well known individuals are rarely typical of the majority. Some historians have attempted sampling.[4] However, the only satisfying answer is collective biography or prosopography. Prosopography involves studying a group of individuals with one or more common characteristics, not just a sample, which is what historians and sociologists, including Methodist ones, have tended to do in the past. Sir Lewis Namier's study of eighteenth century parliamentarians was based on this principle, as was my study of Wesley's preachers. The latter used a database which included *every* itinerant preacher who entered in Wesley's lifetime.[5] Since then I have been re-embarking on a bigger and much more difficult project concerning those men,

---

[2] Robert Currie, Alan Gilbert, and Lee Horsley, *Churches and Churchgoers: Patterns of Church Growth in the British Isles since 1700* (Oxford: Clarendon Press, 1977), Appendix D, which gives 2,518 ministers for 1932.

[3] For all these see John A. Vickers (ed,), *Dictionary of Methodism in Britain and Ireland* (Peterborough: Epworth Press, 2000) or the online version at http://wesleyhistoricalsociety.org.uk/dmbi/ (accessed 23 July 2012), [hereafter *DOMBI*].

[4] Kenneth D. Brown, *A Social History of the Nonconformist Ministry in England and Wales, 1800-1930* (Oxford: Clarendon Press, 1988).

[5] Lewis B. Namier, *The Structure of Politics at the Accession of George III* (London: Macmillan, 1929); http://www.gcah.org/site/c.ghKJI0PHIoE/ (accessed 10 June 2011) for the complete list, some of the fields and a description. Lenton, *John Wesley's Preachers*.

and more recently women, who left the British and Irish Methodist ministries. Both Beckerlegge and Leary, in their work on the United Methodist and Primitive ministries,[6] endeavoured to include all those who left their denominations. Nobody has done this for the Wesleyans (except in my *John Wesley's Preachers* for those who entered before 1791) or for the Methodist Church since 1932. My databases will hopefully fill these gaps.[7] The inclusion of Irish ministers follows on from my study of *John Wesley's Preachers* where, as is explained in my Chapter 11, the ministry under Wesley was interchangeable between Great Britain and Ireland. Certainly very few have belonged to both ministries since, but there have been some individuals and it is interesting to compare how the two ministries, starting from a common source, have moved in similar but different ways.[8]

1 WHY STUDY THOSE WHO LEFT?

Knowing more about those who left the Wesleyan ministry has several purposes. It is useful to the genealogist in that it helps to fill a gap. Trying to explain to enquirers from all over the world what happened to 'those who left', the lack of an obituary, and why it is so difficult to discover their history, is always a problem. Another reason has been to attempt to learn

---

[6] Oliver A. Beckerlegge, *United Methodist Ministers* (London: Epworth Press,1968); William Leary, *Primitive Methodist Ministers* (Loughborough: Teamprint, 1990).

[7] The late Ken Garlick prepared a series of file cards for men who left between the 1740s and shortly before Ken's own death in 1993. These cards give the stations of about half of the total number. I am still using them.

[8] See also John Lenton 'British Preachers in Ireland and Irish Preachers in Britain; the Importance of the Irish Dimension', *Bulletin of the Wesley Historical Society of Ireland,* vol. 16 (2011), 5-38. Again this inclusion complicates the figures. Currie et al, *Churches and Churchgoers,* for example, though their sub-title is *Patterns of Growth in the British Isles since 1700,* do not appear to cite Irish figures.

from what happened. Historians usually believe we can learn lessons from the past, though they may disagree about choosing the right lesson. The Methodist way of allowing men (and now women) to 'disappear' from the ministry, though very understandable, is not instructive for either the Methodist community or for the historian. In 1912 the *Methodist Recorder* commented 'the numbers of ministers and probationers who have disappeared from the roll in this year's *Minutes of Conference* is so large as to be symptomatic of some serious disorder'.[9] Often such losses were hidden, passed over and not discussed, nor any lessons learned for the future. For almost two hundred years Methodism has spent much money, time, and energy on training its ministers, and when rising numbers leave, then clearly resources of money, energy, and time are wasted. Reduction of such wastage would provide more ministers for the connexion as well as reduce costs.

For the Methodist historian this sheds a new light on the ministry and its problems, showing, for example, that throughout the nineteenth century health or its lack was a major problem and that doctrinal questions were rarely of importance. The study of those who left also affirms the work they did while in the ministry: as in the case of David Mace, admirable founder of the Marriage Guidance Council.[10]

Almost all those who entered the Wesleyan Methodist ministry in this period and then left have been put onto a database. The total number at the moment is 1,733, but this will change. A few will need to be added. Some of those at present in the database are likely to be excluded because they were

---

[9] *Methodist Recorder*, 24 October 1912. *Minutes of Several Conversations at the One Hundred and Sixty-ninth Yearly Conference of the People Called Methodists....* (London: Wesleyan Conference Office, 1912), p. 172; [hereafter *Minutes,* and date]. Here the usual message is given: 'their names are recorded in our Journals,' a statement from which the historian or concerned lay leader learns nothing.

[10] *DOMBI;* Mace left in 1948.

never British or Irish ministers on station, but either students who never were in active ministry in this country because they went abroad as missionaries; or because they left while they were students and never served as pre-collegiates. Much information, however, can still be gathered about most of these people, especially about what they did once they left, and in many cases about their early lives. There is no intention to publish information about individuals who entered after 1932 for reasons of confidentiality.

From the point of view of Methodist history in this period the numbers and proportion of ministers leaving have reduced over time from the rather large 30 per cent among the last cohort who entered under Wesley. It is also worth noting that many of those who left were missionaries who transferred to newly established Conferences in Australasia, Africa, Canada and elsewhere, and can therefore be difficult to trace. After 1932, in the late twentieth century there was a large increase of leavers which is beyond the scope of this paper.[11]

2 KENNETH BROWN'S GROUNDBREAKING STUDY OF THE NONCONFORMIST MINISTRY AND HIS FINDINGS

In 1988 Kenneth Brown, then a Reader in Economic and Social History at Queen's University Belfast, later a professor there, published an important study of the Nonconformist ministry in England and Wales between 1800 and 1930.[12] His period is very similar to that of this paper. Undoubtedly the Nonconformist ministry was far wider than the comparatively narrow field of Wesleyan Methodism. Brown dealt not only

---

[11] For a discussion of some of the reasons behind this see George Thompson Brake, *Policy and Politics in British Methodism 1932-1982* (London: Edsell, 1984), pp. 289-314. Brake himself left in order to enter the Baptist ministry but later returned.

[12] Brown, *Nonconformist Ministry.*

with the other Methodist churches, but also with Baptists and Congregationalists. (He excluded the Presbyterians on the grounds that their main strength lay outside England and Wales.) It is therefore not surprising that he used sampling rather than trying to examine all the ministers of the period. He was also dealing with all ministers including those who never left and so died in the work. My work includes those who died in the work, but only those who returned, a relatively small proportion of those who left.[13] The aim here is to assess his methodology and findings and see how they compare with what my database shows so far.

Brown's work was rightly celebrated at the time as the first real attempt to analyse the Nonconformist ministry in the nineteenth century using modern social and economic criteria. His samples were relatively large. His main sample for the whole book consisted of the 2,554 individuals whose deaths were recorded by their denomination in any of the years 1851-55, 1871-75, 1891-95, 1911-15, 1931-35, 1951-55, and 1971-75. However, the chapter which is most pertinent to why ministers left is Chapter 4. This is based on a different and smaller career line sample, consisting of those who entered every tenth year between 1831 and 1911. He never stated what his numbers were from this. Chapters 4 and 5 provided a thought provoking study of the Nonconformist ministry in the nineteenth century. I am most grateful to Professor Brown for trying to remember more detail behind his sampling techniques, but in his own words 'all of my working notes and records on the ministerial project were discarded when I retired some years ago. I would not really trust my memory as far as the composition of the samples is concerned'.[14]

---

[13] Less than 6 per cent: 100 out of 1,733.
[14] Email from Professor Brown, 31/07/2012. 'All of my working notes and records on the ministerial project were discarded when I retired some years ago. I would not really trust my memory as far as the composition of the samples is concerned. For example, I think, but cannot now be certain, that I

The technique used by Brown for a smaller sample in his Chapter 4 is logical and should produce slightly under a tenth of the total ministry, allowing for losses especially in the first few years of ministry. However, since he only used the 'information given in the annual *Minutes*, supplemented and perhaps corrected from material in the Rylands Library archives',[15] he will have missed some of those who entered the Wesleyan ministry. See Table 5.1, below.[16]

---

excluded men who spent their entire careers overseas. Any who served in a domestic pastorate, no matter how short the period or at what stage in his career, were included. I'm also pretty sure that the dates of ministry and entry thereto relied simply on the information given in the annual minutes, supplemented and perhaps corrected from material in the Rylands Library archives. More than this I wouldn't like to say and even then I can't be certain'.

[15] Ibid.

[16] In 1831 the *Minutes* list 21 names ROT (Received On Trial). In 1832 there were 36 who were continued On Trial having travelled one year. The years 1849 and 1850 saw a major crisis and this might have made the situation different. In fact it was very similar. In 1849 eight British ministers were Received On Trial, with another one in the Foreign Missions and three in Ireland. In 1850 the list of those continued after one years' travelling is quite different. Some 52 were continued On Trial in Britain, three in 'our Foreign Missions' and still the same three in Ireland. Finally for 1872 and 1873: in 1872 ten were Received On Trial in England with a further two in the Missions and five in Ireland. In 1873 those continued having travelled one year numbered 43, in the Missions there were 11 names, and the five in Ireland had become six. *Minutes* 1831, p. 6; 1832, p. 5; 1849, pp.7-8; 1850, p. 6.

Table 5.1
Numbers entering the Wesleyan ministry, 1831-73

1831 total ROT (Received On Trial)	21
1832 travelled 1 year	36
Increase	15
1849 total ROT	12
1850 travelled 1 year	58
Increase	46
1872 total ROT	17
1873 total travelled 1 year	59
Increase	42

Source
Minutes of Conference; see footnote 16.

Each year there was a list of men in the *Minutes* who were Received On Trial into the ministry. The list of those who were continued On Trial having travelled one year the *next* year should also be considered and compared with the previous year's list of Received On Trial. For most of the century the two lists are not the same, not because some who began are no longer there (which could be the case), but rather because other names, usually several more and sometimes a very large number more, have been added during the year. [17]

It is obvious therefore that a list based only on those officially Received On Trial named every tenth year is not going to be a tenth of the ministry, because each year many more were accepted during the year and then shown as having trav-

---

[17] *Minutes of Conference.*

elled one year already.[18] Professor Brown's sample was therefore smaller than he thought and his conclusions become less certain than he expected.[19] However, it is important to examine them in detail and see how they compare with those from the database.

3 REASONS WHY WESLEYAN MINISTERS LEFT

Reasons for ministerial departures are often complex and deeply personal. The evidence so far shows most have been multi-causal, and that ranking their importance will always be subjective. Complete figures on why ministers left are unlikely ever to be available, but it is also clear that in all periods some left to join the ministries of other churches in this country, particularly the largest of those churches, the Church of England. The main reasons can be illustrated by examples of their life stories. The examples quoted are all from the 99 with surnames beginning with the letters K and L, since their names were being entered in the database at the time this article was started. Otherwise the fifteen which follow are chosen at random.[20]

(A) HEALTH

As with Wesley's preachers in the eighteenth century, one of the most important reasons for leaving was ill health, a less frequent and important cause in the twentieth century with

---

[18] Note also that these figures are taken from the *Annual Minutes* printed at the time, rather than the collected minutes printed later, which are often more usually used for this period.

[19] I think that what Brown thought was 10 per cent was actually less than 4 per cent. This is an argument against sampling. If the sample is taken from those listed the second year as having travelled one year, then the sample misses those who leave during the first year.

[20] Lenton, *John Wesley's Preachers*, p. 292 and Appendix 1, Table 15.

improvements in general health and increasing life expectancy. Brown did not classify anyone under this heading, because he subsumed them under those who retired early or those for whom the reason was unknown. Brown spent much time on financial rewards and explained how these improved, thus raising their standard of living. Rising prosperity had an effect on health so that losses to the Wesleyan ministry by ill health became fewer as the nineteenth century progressed. However, as Brown also pointed out, the Wesleyans were better paid and more secure than other Nonconformist and Methodist ministers throughout the nineteenth century. Consequently the problem of money was less keenly felt by them than others even at the beginning of this period.[21] It also explains why few joined other Methodist denominations. Of the 1,733 at present in the database, 462 have no recorded reason why they left. For the remaining 1,271, health problems were found in 216 cases (around 17 per cent). The following illustrate the point:

Pierre Le Sueur, e .m. 1812, left 1823.[22]
This man was atypical in several ways.[23]. In 1798 he went to represent Jersey Methodists before the Privy Council about the question of the militia drilling on Sundays. He was able to state to the Councillors and the King that they were not refusing to serve. George III turned to the Duke of Portland and

---

[21] Brown, *Nonconformist Ministry,* Chapter 4 especially pp. 141-43, Table 4.4 and pp. 147-55. See also Lenton, *John Wesley's Preachers,* Chapter 15.
[22] *The Report of the Jubilee Fund of the Wesleyan Methodist Missionary Society, 1863-68* (London: Wesleyan Methodist Missionary Society, 1869); William Hill, *An Alphabetical Arrangement of All the Wesleyan Methodist Preachers, and Missionaries, Who Are now Travelling in Great Britain, and in Different Parts of the Globe* (Bradford: Inkersley, 1819); [hereafter Hills, plus date of publication]; *Minutes,* 1872, p. 43.
[23] His father of the same name was a Jersey fisherman converted in Newfoundland who returned to Jersey and became one of the key early leaders who founded Methodism in the Channel Islands.

said his subjects must not be oppressed in this way.[24] In 1812, then a farmer and local preacher almost in his forties, Le Sueur answered the call to leave his farm and preach to the French prisoners in Dartmoor Prison, and thereby entered the ministry. Peace meant the prisoners went home and so in 1815 he left for a year, receiving £50 from the Preachers' Fund so that he could set up in farming again.[25] In 1816 he was a minister once more in his own Jersey where they were short of French speaking ministers. In 1818 as an itinerant Le Sueur had to move on and was attracted by the the the challenge of missioning France where Wesleyanism was attempting to preach under the restored monarchy. After a year in Beauville, Périere, and Condé in the Norman countryside, Le Sueur came back to the Channel Islands, retiring again from the ministry in 1821 for 'want of health', and aged just fifty.[26] He remained a local preacher and, because he went back to his farm (he received £60 the second time), his ill-health cannot be regarded as debilitating.[27]

Matthew Lee, e. m. 1880, left 1888.

If historians depended always and only on the *Minutes*, Matthew Lee would be described as having entered in 1881. However, the Census that year shows him already a Wesleyan minister doing a pre-collegiate period in Bishop Auckland before attending Headingley College.[28] All Wesleyan ministers before the 1830s were trained on the job and many were

---

[24] R. D. Moore, *Methodism in the Channel Islands* (London: Epworth Press, 1960), pp. 62-64.
[25] Manchester, John Rylands University Library, Methodist Church Archives, MSS, Conference Journal, 1815; [hereafter CJ].
[26] *Minutes* 1821; Moore, *Channel Islands*, p. 79.
[27] CJ, 1823.
[28] Census 1881, via https://www.familysearch.org/search/ (accessed 23/5/2011), then living at South Road, Bishop Auckland. 'Pre-collegiate ministers' was the name for those who were in circuit before going to theological college.

prepared in the same way for most of the nineteenth century. In the 1887 *Minutes* Lee is described as 'retired out of health'. He then disappears from the 1888 *Minutes*.[29]

William Lavers, e.m. 1824, left 1828.

Lavers is another example of men leaving for health reasons and not returning. There were many like him. He was born in 1797 at Blackawton, Devon, the youngest son of a 'small but respectable farmer'. He served first in Dartmouth and then in Maidstone and Dover before he retired to Honiton, Devon, where he died in 1831.[30]

(B) UNKNOWN

There are many for whom no reason is certain, though sometimes it is possible to suggest one. Brown dealt with these men under column C in his Table 4.1. They comprised around 23 per cent of Wesleyans in his figures for the first part of the nineteenth century, though this reduces to 15 per cent for the sample 1881-1901 and to only 11 per cent by his final sample for 1891-1911. My numbers are greater: 462 with no reason given (27 per cent), but this will reduce with further work. The two following are examples:

John Kirby, e.m. 1862, left 1872.[31]

John Kirby is typical of many entries, an example of the lack of information and the problems of this kind of research. Little about him is known apart from his time in the ministry. He

---

[29] *Minutes*, 1887-88.

[30] Oxford Brookes University, Wesley Historical Society Library has a copy of John S. Elliott, *Memoirs of the Life and Correspondence of the Rev William Lavers* (London: Simpkin & Marshall, 1833). This clearly reveals his health problems.

[31] The year he left is the year his departure was reported to Conference. The 'leaving' might have taken place in the previous calendar year. Similarly the year of entry to the ministry is the year Conference agreed to that, when they might have started on a circuit before Conference.

spent ten years in rural circuits in the south (Melksham, Sherborne, Monmouth, and interestingly returned to Melksham for his final circuit), but it is not known where or when he was born, who he married (if he did), why he departed or what he then did. When he left, the *Minutes* simply recorded 'also retired'. He appeared in a donation list, but this gave little new information. From the genealogist's point of view unless the minister returned, which some did in every period, they did not receive an obituary and are, like Kirby, difficult to trace. The frequency of appearance of the name is also important. In tracing ministers who left, 'John Jones' or 'William Smith', can be very elusive unless there is a clear and proven trail. A name like John Kirby's is too common.

John D. Lamb, e. m. 1899, left 1904.

This minister served an unusual variety of circuits in only five years, from Devonport to Shetland, via Pontypridd, Crewe, and Liverpool (Waterloo). Another puzzle is his MA, still rare among Methodist ministers around 1900. As with others who only travelled for a brief period in circuit there is little else known of him.[32]

(C) BECAME MINISTERS FOR OTHER CHURCHES

Large numbers come into this category, though often it cannot be ascertained whether it mingled with other reasons or was the real reason for their departure. Sometimes (rarely) doctrinal differences are cited (this is true for only 24 ministers). Again most is known of those who went to the Church of England, partly because the evidence is clearer. For those who joined another Methodist church, or more rarely founded one (like Samuel Warren or James Everett), similarly the evidence is not always clear. Some 171 are known to have joined the Church of England or the Church of Ireland. In all 93 became

---

[32] Hill, 1900; *Minutes*, 1899-1904.

Congregational ministers (like James Knight below), eight became Baptists, six Presbyterians, and six Unitarian ministers such as Herbert King (see below). The relatively high number gleaned for Unitarians may well be the result of the hard and careful work of Unitarian historian Alan Ruston who has spent much time chasing the origins of Unitarian ministers and has provided most of their data here. Multiple entries can result in the same minister being a minister for different churches at different times. An example of this was John Joyce who after his British ministry was variously a minister of the Methodist Episcopal Church, the Congregational Church, and the Presbyterians in the USA, so occurs in these figures on several occasions. The total going into Nonconformist ministries (non-Methodist) is therefore 110, probably an underestimate. The total for other Methodist ministries is 167 who transferred to Methodist churches (mostly Wesleyan) abroad. Of these 30 went to Canadian, 48 Australian, 15 New Zealand, 48 South African Conferences, and 21 to the Methodist Episcopal Church of America. There were eight others (three to France, two to West Indies conferences, two to found Independent Methodist Churches in Haiti and Jamaica, and one to join the Wesleyan Methodist Association in the West Indies). In my database only 32 joined other Methodist churches in this country, of whom 10 joined the Methodist New Connexion. This was partly because the MNC was the oldest and had the longest history of co-existence with the Wesleyans. One of these, the great Richard Watson, returned to the Wesleyan ministry. There were 12 who joined the Wesleyan Reformers or the United Methodist Free Church (or in most cases both), five joined the Wesleyan Methodist Association, one the Primitive Methodists, and one each went to the Methodist Unitarians, the Free Methodists, the Independent Methodists, and the Methodist Church in Leith. In each of these last four cases it was someone who founded their own church such as Joseph Cooke of the Methodist Unitarians in

Rochdale. In Ireland Adam Averell established the Primitive Wesleyans.[33]

It is interesting to compare these figures, which are quite large, with Brown's figures for cause of leaving (Table 4.2). Over the whole period he had none who left Wesleyanism to join other churches, a figure which at first made me think my figures of several hundred in this category must be wrong until I realised how he was constructing his samples and that errors there could mean his (too small) samples could miss the (relatively) large numbers found by myself. In addition, large numbers going overseas are appearing among those in my database; British Methodist ministers transferred to other Conferences as they became autonomous, such as Canada or New Zealand, would not appear at all in Brown's samples unless they served in this country first. Many embarked immediately on leaving college, as soon as a boat could be found.[34]

Brown attributed the Wesleyan nil loss to their tighter control. In fact their loss rate was similar to other denominations, not as high as the United Methodists or Primitive Methodists (who for most of the nineteenth century faced more difficult conditions as newer denominations), but comparable with Congregationalists who reduced from 9.5 per cent earlier in the century to a 2.9 per cent loss by 1891-1911. As Brown pointed out, Baptists had a doctrinal problem with other denominations and this is a probable reason why few Baptist ministers joined other denominations. Equally it explains why few departing Wesleyans entered the Baptist ministry, eight (or 0.5 per cent) being a very small proportion of the total number.[35]

---

[33] For the Primitive Wesleyans see Robin Roddie, '"Keeping the Faith". Ireland's Primitive Methodism', *Wesley Historical Society Proceedings,* vol. 57 (2010), 225-45.

[34] Email from Donald Phillips New Zealand, 2 August 2012.

[35] Brown, *Nonconformist Ministry,* chapter 4, especially Tables 4.1 and 4.2.

James N. Knight, e.m. 1876, left 1884.
James Knight appeared in the 1881 Census so more is known about him. The middle name of Nicholas is another help in identification, giving also a place of birth and parentage, making further discoveries about him easier. He was born in Plymouth in January 1853, but not baptized there until February 1854.[36] He trained at Headingley, a long way to travel from his home. His wife came from Lincoln, his first circuit as a probationer, and he married her in 1880 and had a daughter by the time of the 1881 census. After Lincoln he served in relatively wealthy circuits in Birmingham and Nottingham before 'voluntarily retiring from our work' in 1884 to become a Congregational minister. For this he returned to Birmingham, serving the prestigious Ebenezer Congregational church on Steelhouse Lane for the long pastorate of eighteen years (1884-1902), before taking shorter periods at Wycliffe Chapel, Hull (1902-7) and the well-known Albion Chapel, Ashton under Lyne (1907-11). He died in his pulpit in Ashton in early 1911.[37]

Herbert William King, e .m. 1906, left by 1910.
Herbert King served one year as a pre-collegiate in Pontypridd before going to train at Headingley. From college he decided to withdraw his candidature and later became a Unitarian minister from 1911 to around 1920. There is information from Alan Ruston, the President of the Unitarian Historical Society, about his later career.[38] Nothing is known about King's early life or from which circuit he came. There were many in theological colleges who withdrew as students

---

[36] https://www.familysearch.org/search/ (accessed 23 April 2011) for Census and for details of birth and baptism.
[37] *Minutes,* 1884, for the quotation. https://www.surman.english.qmul.ac.uk/ (accessed 20 December 2012).
[38] Email from Alan Ruston quoting *Christian Life,* 10 May 1913.

and most of these do not feature in the database. King is only included because he served in a circuit as a pre-collegiate minister and therefore appeared on the stations in the *Minutes of Conference.*

Thomas H. Leale, e.m. 1860, left 1875.

Thomas Leale was a minister born in Ireland but entering the British ministry, so was somewhat unusual. He trained at Richmond and married a French-born wife. He had four circuits in the southwest (Budleigh Salterton, Bridgwater, Bridport, Taunton) before going north to Barnsley and Derby. His two sons went to Woodhouse Grove School until their father left the ministry, which he did in 1875 in order to become an Anglican priest. By 1881 Leale was curate of St Stephen's, Walworth. Around the time he left he had a second daughter whom he named Cassandra![39]

John S. Ladd, e.m. 1862, left 1868.

John S. Ladd is someone who can probably be identified both before and after he was in the ministry. He could be the John Sam Ladds, baptised at St Luke's Old St. This church is important for those researching Methodist genealogy (seeking baptisms or marriages for Methodists) in London between 1750 and 1850. It is close to Wesley's City Road Chapel and in the late eighteenth and early nineteenth centuries many Wesleyans worshipping at City Road used it for baptisms, marriages and funerals. However, there is the addition of an S to the surname which means identification is uncertain. He could have become an Anglican priest, for in 1881 the rector of West Keal was a John S. Ladds.

---

[39] *Kingswood Register,* 1912; *Minutes,* 1875, p. 35; https://www.familysearch.org/search/ (accessed 3 June 2011) for 1881 Census.

With all the men who joined other churches it is rare for doctrinal differences to be expressly cited. What is more common is to find family connections such as marrying the daughter of an Anglican priest and then becoming a clergyman several years later. On the other hand, in the case of a Unitarian pulpit (as with King) or a High Church Anglican parish, doctrinal questions may well have been crucial even if not documented.

(D) EXPELLED

In Wesleyan Methodism the proportion of those who were expelled among those who left is small. However, the sources do not always agree. Printed *Minutes* had a tendency to say "desisted" or nothing, but reference to the MS Conference Journal show the man was expelled. Only 103 of the total who left were expelled, around 6 per cent. Brown gives no suggested numbers for those who were expelled except to quote the MNC suggestion that for the 59 who left that church's ministry between 1856 and 1888 'dishonourable reasons' were behind about a third. Brown has a paragraph about moral lapses with examples. Four examples are given below. In Wesleyanism there were some who had 'moral lapses'. There were also men who were expelled for political reasons and those expelled because they frequently fell below the standards of ordinary behaviour expected of the ministry. Neither Brown nor I have yet assigned numbers or proportions to these, but it should be possible in a later study.[40] Many were disciplined or even expelled for marrying contrary to the regulations, which did not merely insist that probationers should not marry, but that anyone, probationer or in Full Connexion, who married should first obtain the 'consent of their brethren'. In other words their fellow ministers had a veto on unsuitable fiancées and to marry a woman outside the connexion, that is

---

[40] Brown, *Nonconformist Ministry,* Chapter 4, pp. 133-35.

someone who was not already a Methodist member, was in the words of the Conference of 1823 an instance of 'culpable impudence'.[41]

John Kingston, e .m. 1791, expelled 1807.

John Kingston was an early minister, unusual in many re-spects, not least that he was expelled. A missionary in the West Indies, he spent some time in America recovering his health. When he returned to this country one of the circuits he travelled was Penzance and a Penzance historian, Melissa Hardie, has been my chief informant. Her interest is in the Brontë connection. In January 1800 John Kingston married at Madron in the Penzance circuit Jane Branwell whose sister later married Rev Patrick Brontë and who was thus the future aunt of the Brontë sisters. In 1805 Kingston was in the Shrewsbury circuit. Mary Fletcher, the prominent woman preacher and widow of John, had a dream in which John Fletcher appeared to her and said 'Kingston was a wicked man and that he (Fletcher) would interfere'.[42] Kingston took his family to Baltimore, USA, along with at least £100 of the Circuit's book money.[43] His portrait had appeared in the *Methodist Magazine* in March 1806. At the 1807 Conference he was expelled for embezzlement and sodomy.[44] In 1810 Jane Kingston returned from America with her youngest daughter, leaving the rest of their children with her husband. John Kingston made his living in New York as a printer and publisher, producing books of his own such as the *Popular Life of Washington* and a *Life of Fletcher*, each of which in-

---

[41] Ibid., p.174.
[42] Zechariah Taft to Mr Reson quoted *Methodist Recorder*, Winter No. 6 (1895).
[43] Manchester, John Rylands University Library, Methodist Church Ar-chives MAM Fl 4/9/8 Letter dated 28 September 1807 from G. Lowe to Mary Fletcher & n.
[44] MARC, MS Conference Journal, 1807.

cluded Kingston's reminiscences about them.[45] Melissa Hardie argues that the effect of this family scandal on the young Brontés' imaginations was an important factor in their later literary output. Was truth at least as strange as fiction?

James Lamb, e. m. 1821, left 1835.

James Lamb was excluded for opposing Bunting's control of the Wesleyan Connexion. He was an Irish Methodist minister from Rathkenny in Co. Meath who was called out (expelled) during the year between the Conferences of 1821 and 1822. Having been excluded, in 1834 he moved to Dublin where he set up a women's boot store in Dame Street (until 1842). He was the Irish ringleader for sympathisers of Warren, Dunn and Griffiths and circulated the Fly Sheets in Ireland. He spoke against Bunting at a public meeting in Manchester and brought Griffiths to Dublin. Like Kingston and many who left in the nineteenth century he eventually emigrated, in his case to America.[46]

John Langston, e. m. 1822, expelled 1849.

Langston did fifteen years in the active work before becoming a supernumerary early, almost certainly for disciplinary reasons. Nearly all his circuits were rural ones in the south, (Witney, Banbury, Chichester, Poole) with a single excursion northwards to Skipton for a year. He published three dissertations (totalling 56 pages) in 1834, all at St Albans, against baptism by immersion and in favour of sprinkling and of infant baptism. He based his views on Galatians 3: 16-17 and

---

[45] Emails from Melissa Hardie, 15 October to 17 December 2009. The date they went is not certain since Melissa has found two Atlantic crossings by a John Kingston, one in September 1806 "with family" and one in 1807. Gareth Lloyd has shown that he was present at a District hearing on 1 July 1807, but he could have crossed twice.

[46] Belfast, Edgehill College Library, WHS (Ireland) Library, Robin Roddie's Index of Irish Preachers.

Isaiah 52: 14-15.[47] His two sons went to Kingswood, the younger continuing for two years after his father had left the ministry.[48] He retired first in 1838, to Watlington. There in 1842 he faced charges at his District Meeting and Conference 'directed peremptorily he must leave Watlington' or be expelled. He was ordered by Conference to Oxford to be a supernumerary, but no longer appeared in the printed *Minutes,* another sign he was in trouble with his brother ministers. In 1847 the Chairman of the Oxford District was moved to investigate charges against him. Langston then removed to London where in 1848 he was 'to be informed by his Superintendent (Mr Squance) that he should retire and if he refuse the next Conference will expel him as he is upon the whole unfit for our work'. In 1849 he refused to retire so was expelled.[49]

George Lazenby, e .m. 1804, left 1812.

Lazenby was a preacher who never spent more than one year in any circuit in his eight years' travel and whose problems can be followed through the Conference Journal from 1808, when he was first in trouble, until 1812 when he was finally expelled 'for immoral conduct'. His District Committee in 1808 had originally judged he should be expelled. However, Lazenby at his hearing before Conference appealed for mercy,

---

[47] J. Langston, *Dissertations Demonstrating that Modern Immersion is not Christian Baptism and that Infant Baptism and Baptism by Sprinkling Are the Doctrines of the Bible. Designed to Furnish Methodists with Arguments for the Ordinance as It Obtains among Them* (2nd edn,, St Albans, 1854).

[48] *Register of Kingswood School* (Bath: Kingswood Old Boys Union, 1912). Kingswood was founded by Wesley for the sons of itinerant preachers. The Register also covered Woodhouse Grove, a school near Bradford founded in the north for the sons of the ministers who travelled there.

[49] Hills, 1833; Manchester MARC, Ms Conference Journal 1842, 1848, 1849 (from which the quotations come), *Minutes.* 1842-49; *Kingswood Register,* 1912. Squance was Superintendent of the Fifth London Circuit. If ability was the reason he had to leave, it is not clear why he was expelled. I suspect that he supported Everett and the opposition to Conference, but this is never stated.

expressed contrition, begged for a second chance and was allowed to remain On Trial but was told he must do four more years before he could be accepted into Full Connexion. He wrote a most grovelling letter ('I have been foolish and offensive to a very high degree'). Each year following his case came back to Conference for consideration, presumably because any improvement was limited. In 1810 he received an admonitory letter from the President of Conference. In 1812 Conference finally bit the bullet and expelled him.[50]

(E) OTHER REASONS

This category covers a multitude of different causes. The minister concerned realised he was better suited for some other calling and followed his new call. This probably included most of those who went into business, the large number of 41 in the database being mostly early nineteenth century. Often they were returning to the farming or other work they had had before entering the ministry. Sometimes, as with Knowlson below, they had discovered a new skill which could be put to another use.

A few wanted to teach. The ministry, though it might occasionally permit them to do this, especially abroad, did not allow them to do it permanently so they left the ministry instead; 13 fell into this teacher category. This became a considerable difficulty later. In the whole of the nineteenth century only three Wesleyan ministers left the ministry for teaching, but after 1900 and before 1932 another six left the ministry in favour of teaching: a foretaste of what would happen frequently in the 1950s and 1960s. The increase was partly due to rising educational levels in the ministry in the twentieth century, enabling individuals to do something beyond the competence of many a generation earlier. Partly it was due to the growth in school numbers in conjunction with the attrac-

---

[50] Manchester, MARC, MS Conference Journal, 1808-12.

tiveness of staying in one place rather than perpetually moving every three years as required by the Wesleyan itinerancy.

Brown included those who went into denominational education as having left the ministry: cause 3 in his Table 4.2. For Wesleyans this was a small percentage of the ministry, though one which rose over time, expectedly because Wesleyans began theological education in the 1830s and gradually expanded it in succeeding decades. So the loss of men to this cause increased from 0.8 per cent in his sample for 1831-51 to 3 per cent for 1861-91, and slightly more, 3.7 per cent, for 1891-1911. However, I do not accept his definition of ministerial exiting because some, like Thomas Jackson and John Hannah, Wesleyan Theological Institution tutors, were still active members of Conference. Many Wesleyan Assistant Tutors returned to circuit ministry.

Thomas Sharper Knowlson e.m. 1891, left 1900.

T. Sharper Knowlson, as he was known in the ministry, was an unusual man. His father was a gardener at Bilton Hall near Knaresborough.[51] The son, having left the ministry, became a prolific and much published author, whose work is still selling copies today. He may have left once he had started being published, to make the most of his writing talents, but this is only a surmise. Most of what he wrote went through numerous editions and many are still in print after one hundred years. As a popular author and self-help advocate for the masses he was hard to beat! His titles speak volumes: after the *Art of Thinking* and the *Art of Success* came *Logic for the Million* and its ilk. His *The Origins of Popular Superstitions and Customs* (1910) was *largely* based on Brand's *Popular Antiquities*

---

[51] https://www.familysearch.org/search/ (accessed 2 February 2011) for 1881 Census.

(1841 edition). Knowlson's last book, published in 1944 when he was seventy-seven, was *Put on your Thinking Cap!*[52]

Leonard Ledbrook, e. m. 1793, left 1796.
This man was a farmer in Warwickshire before he entered the ministry. He lasted three years. In his third circuit (it was still the period when young ministers moved every year) he went to Hinckley working under John Beaumont as his Assistant. Within the societies there were quarrels, such as the controversy over whether itinerants should administer communion, and Beaumont wrote bitterly, 'He turned coward, allowed the societies to break up, took his family back to their farm and got in the harvest'.[53] Interestingly, he was one of the many who disappeared with no reference in the Conference Journal.

4 'AN UNSETTLED MINISTRY?'

Brown's Chapter 4, 'An Unsettled Ministry?' signals one of his main findings: Nonconformist ministries were invariably poorly paid, experienced a high turnover, and were therefore unsettling. I do not disagree with this finding for non-Methodist ministries. It was true also for non-Wesleyan Methodists, such as Bible Christians, Primitive Methodists, and United Methodist Free Churches. Under major stress because the connexions were small, their ministers were subjected to more privation than their Wesleyan colleagues. For denominations relatively new in status and ethos the judgement holds. Indeed during the first half of the nineteenth century for the United Methodist ministers covered by Beckerlegge, few in their antecedent bodies (Methodist New Connexion, Bible Christian, and later Wesley Reform or Wesley-

---

[52] *Old Chariot*, Christmas 1911; *Minutes* 1900, 1882 Census via https://www.familysearch.org/search/ (accessed 16 May 2011).
[53] MARC, L. Tyerman MSS, Biographies of Early Methodist Preachers under Beaumont.

an Methodist Association) remained in ministry long.[54] However, for Wesleyan Methodist ministers Brown's methodology is questionable for two reasons. First, as has been shown above, his sample was too small and did not include all the men who entered in the years he was covering. Second, Brown used disputable categories for identifying those leaving the ministry. For him, going into administrative work, teaching at theological college, as well as becoming supernumerary, were all leaving the active ministry. I consider the first two of these categories, at least, as remaining within the on-going ministry of the Church. All three contributed in many ways to active work in the circuits of Wesleyan Methodism. Most Wesleyan administrators and many theological tutors spent their time on trains crossing the country to preach in Wesleyan churches for their 'special anniversary services', often to much acclaim. Supernumeraries were less noticed but still much used especially in rural circuits.[55]

Another category of Brown's leavers were those going into overseas ministry. This assumes they would not return and that the ministry there was somehow different. Both may be true but many of those Wesleyans going overseas in fact returned to active ministry in this country. In my database of men who left there are 1,733 names of whom 544 were missionaries. Of those missionaries 102 returned to serve (or at least retire) in Britain after they had been missionaries abroad. Certainly in the eighteenth century this was not expected by those who sent the missionaries out, but by the twentieth century it was not unusual.[56] Again it depended partly where they went. Missionaries who served in Europe, were likely to return to Britain rather sooner than those who went to Australia, if only because the journey was shorter and cheaper. Once

---

[54] Beckerlegge, *United Methodist Ministers*.
[55] Brown, *Nonconformist Ministry*, pp. 138-39.
[56] By the mid twentieth century it was usual for missionaries to return to Britain after serving abroad.

separate Conferences were established for Australia or elsewhere then ministers were always more likely to remain abroad, possibly because of local marriages and pension arrangements. In the early nineteenth century many missionaries in West Africa died in the first two years but those who survived frequently returned, admittedly with poor health which might force them to retire.

It is not suggested, however, that all or even most of Brown's conclusions were incorrect. His chapter on 'An Unsettled Ministry' rightly pointed to the fact that ministers often found that they had chosen the wrong profession and therefore leaving tended to happen early in ministry. Brown described it as being 'in a constant state of flux'.[57] The Wesleyan Methodist church in this period was a good example of this. The first three years of ministry produced the largest number of leavers, 130 by the end of the first year, 96 more by the end of the second year and another 127 by the end of the third year. At the end of the fourth year another 98 left and then the figures go down steadily, 79, 60, 57, 46, 39 for the successive years. The reason for the rise at the end of the third year in the Wesleyan ministry is easy to determine. For most of this period probation lasted three years. The third year represented the crunch point when Conference often lost patience with the man who refused to learn, to follow the rules (such as on marriage) which others accepted. Ledbrook and King were both examples of men who never got beyond probation as was Lazenby, though Lazenby was much less typical since he received repeated probationary years.

---

[57] Brown, *Nonconformist Ministry*, p. 124.

CONCLUSION

In building up the history of the individual who left the ministry the first clue is the information that the man did leave and this is where any help the reader can give is so useful. It is then relatively easy to trace his college if he had one, his circuits, and when he left. Much more difficult to find are his date of birth, origin, why he left, what he then did, and his date of death. Knowledge about his marriage and children may well depend on whether there is any information from the *Kingswood Register*, donation lists, censuses or a *Who's Who*, if he stayed long enough, or some combination of these. *Crockfords* is very useful, but similar books for other destinations of preachers tend to be lacking. Rarely do former ministers like Thomas Sharper Knowlson leave a trail in print. For overseas churches the website of the United Methodist Church in America is helpful, providing now an online index to all printed obituaries providing, of course, the man remained in his ministry and did not leave again![58] Cornish's *Cyclopedia of Methodism in Canada*, and Australasian and New Zealand indexes have been printed and Berning produced a list for South Africa.[59]

The process of departing is usually opaque.[60] Few leave the kind of official evidence there is for George Lazenby who

---

[58] http://archives.gcah.org/exist/memoirs/memoirs.xq?show-form=yes accessed 20 March 2011.

[59] G.H. Cornish, *Cyclopedia of Methodism in Canada* (2 vols., Toronto: Methodist Book and Publishing House, 1881-1903); J. T. Pinfold (ed.), *An Alphabetical Arrangement of All the Methodist Ministers... in the New Zealand Conference....* (3rd edn., Christchurch: New Zealand Methodist Church, 1913); W. Hunt (ed.), *Methodist Ministerial Index for Australasia and New Zealand* (5th edn., Melbourne: Victoria and Tasmania Conference, 1914); J. H. Berning, *Index to Obituary Notices of Methodist Ministers, 1815-1920* (Johannesburg: Public Library, 1969). There is a CD of the 1896 Australasian Ministerial Index available from www.archivecdbooks.com.au .

[60] For a description of the process see Lenton, *John Wesley's Preachers*, pp. 291-92, 297-300.

appeared so regularly in the disciplinary records of the Conference Journal. Much more usual is the answer to the question: 'Who desisted?' being given as just a name, with no reason attached. 'Going into business' could be for all sorts of reasons, varying from the death of a father so the son was needed back at home, to the minister lacking the health to face the itinerancy.[61] Equally common at all periods (four of these fifteen cases) are those who just 'disappeared' from the Minutes. One year their name was there, the next it had disappeared. No reason was given, nor were the men necessarily even mentioned in the Conference Journal. Leonard Ledbrook is a good example of this process. District Minutes[62] for the year in question can be worth checking but may not have survived and, even if they do, as with Ledbrook, they may not contain any reference to him. Occasionally there is an account from someone, even the minister himself, or in Ledbrook's case his Superintendent. Such an account will, of course, usually be biased and such bias needs to be allowed for. This is shown in the database by putting the reason in quotation marks and giving a source for the judgement, so later users can judge for themselves.

This small subjective sample cannot offer final quantified estimates of reasons for leaving. Three out of the fifteen left for health reasons, undoubtedly the most common cause in this period. The evidence suggests that health, 'to go into business', and 'unknown' are the most often found. Next among motives is wishing to join the ministry of another church, whether overseas or in this country. Exclusions or expulsions are more likely to leave more evidence than other reasons but did not often occur. Four of these fifteen were expelled or excluded: a much higher proportion than average, as was explained above. Doctrinal reasons were very rare.

---

[61] For earlier examples see ibid., pp. 304-5, 327-29.
[62] Gareth Lloyd has produced a useful list of the District Minutes held at the John Rylands University Library in Manchester.

Pierre le Sueur is the only missionary in the fifteen. At the moment between a quarter and a third in the database were at some point missionaries, rather more than their proportion among ministers. This is partly because of their transfer to other Methodist Conferences emerging in the nineteenth century. In addition, the inclusion of names from Albert Mosley's database on missionaries (which he has generously supplied) may bias this database towards missionary ministers.

6

Biographies in Church Monuments: William Smith and Jane Vazeille of Newcastle upon Tyne

Terry Hurst

St Andrew's Church, the oldest of the four Anglican churches in Newcastle upon Tyne, has a number of strong links with the early years of Methodism on Tyneside. The present building dates from the third quarter of the twelfth century although there is evidence to suggest an earlier building on the site. In the churchyard, close to the west door, is a substantial nineteenth century chest tomb bearing the names of William and Jane Smith and other family members. It was within St Andrew's parish that John Wesley's Orphan House was opened in 1743 and many of the rites of passage for Methodist people took place at the church, perhaps most notably the marriage of Grace Murray to John Bennet, conducted on 3 October 1749 by Charles Wesley. The profound effect of this on the relationship between the brothers is well documented and need not figure in this paper. Of more significance here are the marriage of John Wesley to Mrs Mary Vazeille in February 1751 and the subsequent union of one of her four children, Jane, to William Smith, a prominent local businessman and leading member of the Newcastle Methodist society. The inscription on the tomb reads as follows:

The *TOMB of WILLIAM SMITH ESQr*
of HIGH FRIARS STREET IN THIS TOWN
who departed this Life 30th May 1824 Aged 88
Years

and of JANE SMITH, his Wife who died 17th Jany
1820 Aged 83 Years.

Here lie also buried MARY STAMP, their
Daughter
who departed this Life 11th Novr 1794 Aged 25
Years

and Mr THOMAS PRIOR FLANDERS, who died
Septr 1813 Aged 33 Years.

and his daughter JANE VAZEILLE who died 2nd
Jany 1814
Aged 4 Months.

the above named JANE SMITH was the daughter
of
ANTHONY and MARY VAZEILLE the latter
when a widow,
married the Reverend JOHN WESLEY Founder
of Methodism,
and was buried in Camberwell Churchyard on
Oct. 12th 1781. [1]

---

[1] The tomb is in a good state of repair and all the text can be read clearly, to the credit of the vicar and churchwardens who commissioned remedial repair work in 2010

St. Andrew's Church, Newcastle

Illustration 6.1
St Andrew's Church, Newcastle upon Tyne. Image taken from an old black-and-white postcard. (The postcard is marked 'Valentine's Series' and carries the number 46750.) Copyright owner unknown.

The study of church monuments is wide ranging and complex but a vital source of information about the people they commemorate and the age in which they lived. Many situated out of doors deteriorate naturally with the passing of time and even those indoors can be lost as increasing numbers of churches are declared redundant, changed to alternative purposes, or simply allowed to collapse and rot away. From the twelfth century onwards, vast numbers of gravestones, family tombs and other monuments of all shapes and sizes have recorded social history and historical details not always available elsewhere. Although local church records are the primary source of retrieving such information, many of these are thankfully reproduced in local archives, libraries and local history groups, and often available on line or in the form of microfilm and microfiche. The magazines and newsletters of local history groups often contain descriptions and details of

monuments whose significance goes far wider than the immediate constituency, such as memorials to major disasters, min-
ing or otherwise, or to nationally known figures in business,
art, and politics. Speaking of the 'precious heritage' of funer-
ary monuments, and the 'wealth of interest and detail that is
invaluable to our knowledge of a great many aspects of the
past', Professor Brian Kemp observed, 'It is, therefore vital
that this rich legacy should be preserved and handed on to
future generations'.[2]

1   WILLIAM AND JANE SMITH

William Smith (1736–1824) was born in Corbridge, Northumberland, the son of Anthony Smith and Elizabeth Robson.
His father died when he was young and he was brought up by
his mother who was a devoted Anglican, William being confirmed by Bishop Butler at the age of fourteen. Shortly afterwards, he was placed in business with a close relative in Newcastle and began to attend Methodist services at the Orphan
House where he soon became a member of the society. Smith
was made a class leader at 'little more than 20 years of age'[3]
in a 'somewhat arbitrary and unusual' manner.[4] At the end of
a service in the Orphan House, without prior notice or consultation, John Wesley announced that Mr Smith would form a
class and be a class leader. This led William to consider his
mode of dress, fashionably decorated with embroidery and
'frills', and from then on he began to dress more modestly,
with 'plainness and almost elegant simplicity' as befitted his

---

[2] Brian Kemp, *Church Monuments* (Oxford: Shire Books, 2010), p. 4. See
also Trevor Yorke, *Gravestones, Tombs and Memorials* (Newbury: Countryside Books, 2010); and Alex Bruce, *Monuments, Memorials and the
Local Historian* (London: The Historical Association, 1997).
[3] William Wood Stamp, *The Orphan House of Wesley, with Notices of Early
Methodism in Newcastle upon Tyne* (London: John Mason, 1863), p. 121.
[4] Ibid.

new appointment. [5] In business, Smith eventually became a highly successful corn merchant in his own right, so much so that he was able to retire early from business in order to devote himself almost entirely to the work of the rapidly growing Methodist society based at the Orphan House. He was not ordained but preached, baptised, administered Holy Communion, and took a major leadership role in the society; he became a trustee of the Orphan House in 1772 and founder member of Brunswick Methodist Chapel in 1820. William Smith became not only a significant figure in the Orphan House society but a close friend and invaluable assistant to John Wesley, regularly accompanying him when Wesley travelled in the north east using the Orphan House as his base. Wesley visited Newcastle about 50 times during his itinerancy, often staying for periods of several weeks.

William Smith and Jane Vazeille (1736–1820) were married at St Luke's Church, Finsbury, London, though the year is disputed: Stamp gives the date as 7 March 1769,[6] although other sources, including family papers, suggest the wedding took place on the same date two years earlier. [7] The witnesses were her brother Noah Vazeille and her step-father, John Wesley. Jane was the daughter of Anthony Vazeille (c1660-1747) and Mary, nee Goldhawk (1710–1781). She had previously been married to John Matthews, that wedding also taking place at St Luke's Church, on 24 July 1757. The name Vazeille is of Huguenot origin. Anthony, together with his parents, Edouard and Francoise Vazeille and two siblings,

---

[5] Ibid., pp. 121ff.
[6] Ibid., p. 119.
[7] John Wesley's Journal, though not referring to the wedding, favours the earlier date. He arrived in London on the afternoon of Saturday 28 February 1767 and left on Sunday 8 March, but said little of his activities between those two dates. In 1769 he recorded that he preached in Bath on Tuesday 7 March, which arguably rules out his attendance at a wedding in London. Nehemiah Curnock (ed.), *The Journal of the Rev John Wesley* (8 vols., London: Epworth Press, 1909-16), vol. 5, pp.196, 198, 303.

came from Lunel, near Nimes in Provence and settled in a Huguenot community at Portarlington in Ireland, approximately 45 miles south west of Dublin. The Huguenots were subject to severe persecution after Louis XIV of France had revoked the Edict of Nantes in 1685, thus precipitating their relocation. Anthony anglicised his original French Christian name of Antoine and moved to Wandsworth in south London where he set up in business as a hat-maker. It was here that he met and married Mary Goldhawk who later, as a widow, became Mrs John Wesley. The marriage of John and Mary Wesley was not a happy union. She was a jealous and tempestuous lady who enjoyed society life and financial security; he was a single-minded evangelist forever away from home. She may well have seen social advantage in being married to the leader of a national religious movement. It is difficult to learn her true character because, throughout the nineteenth century, most Methodist writers and speakers denigrated her in order to foster the iconic status of her husband. On his side, Wesley's driven nature, his itinerant ministry, and the constant demands of the rapidly growing Methodist movement would not have made him an easy partner for even the most patient of women.

William and Jane Smith had two daughters, Mary and Jane, of whom John Wesley grew very fond. His will included the provision, 'I give the coins and whatever else is in the drawer of my bureau in London, to my dear grand-daughters, Mary and Jane Smith'. [8] William, Jane and their daughters often travelled with Wesley on his journeys in the north east. On 20 June 1774, the horses pulling their carriage became agitated and ran away at high speed. Just as they were approaching a steep fall in the land, Mr. Smith, riding alongside the carriage on his own horse, managed to intervene and stop the carriage horses. Wesley saw this deliverance as nothing

---

[8] Ibid., vol. 8, p. 342.

short of divine guidance. His grand-daughters, who had cried, 'Grandpapa, save us!' had been delivered, 'I am persuaded both evil and good angels had a large share in this transaction; how large we do not know now, but we shall know hereafter', Wesley recorded.[9]

Illustration 6.2

William Smith. Oil portrait; artist and date unknown, approx. 66 x 56 cms; Wesley Room at Brunswick Methodist Church, Newcastle upon Tyne. Photographer Mr Ken Medd, Whickham, Gateshead, Tyne and Wear. Photograph taken 1996.

---

[9] Ibid., vol. 6, p. 27.

The significant role of William Smith in the life of the Wesley family is also highlighted by Smith's attempt during the 1779 Methodist Conference at Coventry to effect reconciliation between Mr and Mrs Wesley. He wrote afterwards, 'I talked freely to both parties, and did all in my power to lay a foundation for future union; but alas all my efforts proved unsuccessful. I had to leave matters no better than I found them. It is indeed a melancholy affair and, I am afraid, productive of bad consequences'.[10] Stamp described William Smith as,

> a man of remarkably placid temper; a lover of peace and not
> infrequently acting as peace-maker; yet, in matters where
> principle or truth was involved, he displayed a firmness
> bordering upon obstinacy. As a preacher, he was much es-
> teemed. His style in the pulpit was affectionate and winning;
> the effect of which was heightened by a pleasing voice and a
> good delivery. He was a sound expositor of Divine truth;
> dwelling chiefly on the leading doctrines of the Gospel.
> Many under his faithful exhortations were brought to a
> 'knowledge of the truth' and added to the church.[11]

After William Smith died, the following obituary was placed in a Newcastle newspaper. It was a glowing testimony to a widely respected citizen. Interestingly, neither Methodism nor the Orphan House was mentioned.

> Sunday evening last, at his house in High Friar's Street,
> aged 88, Mr Wm Smith. An ample competency, realised in
> early life, had enabled the venerable man, agreeably to his
> own benevolent wish, to devote his intelligent mind and ac-
> tivities, with his entire leisure, to the temporal and spiritual
> good of his fellow creatures; and during the greater part of
> half a century, his life had been one prolonged act of benefi-

---

[10] Notes in family papers kindly shared by Professor Nicholas Temperley, Professor Emeritus of Musicology at the University of Illinois at Urbana-Champaign.
[11] Stamp, *Orphan House*, p. 122.

cence in visiting the sick, instructing the ignorant, and re-
lieving the distressed, and, in every practicable form, promoting by his example and influence, the happiness and
well-being of all around him. A protracted confinement
with occasional severe illness, for four years, had been sustained with dignified patience and resignation, and with a
calm unmoved confidence in redeeming love and mercy and
his last end was full of peace and of the hope of the Gospel.[12]

The elder daughter of William and Jane Smith was Mary
(1769–1794) who was baptised in St Andrew's Parish Church,
Newcastle upon Tyne and later married there on 14 August
1790 to John Stamp (1761–1831), a Methodist minister from
Morpeth in Northumberland. They had three daughters: Jane
Vazeille Stamp, Anna Marie Stamp, and Mary Smith Stamp,
but shortly after the birth of their third child, Mary Stamp died
on 11 November 1794 at the age of twenty-five. Her name is
the third one on the tomb in St Andrew's churchyard, following those of her parents. John Stamp was to marry twice more
and in 1824 was appointed Governor (or Headmaster) of
Woodhouse Grove Boarding School near Bradford, founded
in 1812 for the sons of Wesleyan Methodist ministers.

The younger daughter of William and Jane Smith was Jane
Vazeille Smith (1770–1849) who became the second wife of
Christopher Sundius (1754–1835) at St Andrew's Church on
4 July 1798 (his first wife, Anna Richardson of Newent, died
in 1796, having borne him nine children). Sundius, son of
Rev John Sundius, parish minister of Allerum in Sweden, was
educated at university and naval college before securing a
commission in the Swedish army. He came to England,
served in 'several ships and engagements till 1780, when he
received orders from Sweden to enter the French service'. He
refused, resigned his commission, and 'was honoured by King

---

[12] *Tyne Mercury*, 1 June 1824.

George III with his sign manual'.[13] Fluent in several languages, he was appointed a translator for the Admiralty ca. 1799. On a visit to London in 1777, he heard John Wesley preach, hearing views much like his father's. He was converted in 1780 and joined the Methodist society at John Wesley's City Road Chapel in London, where he served on the committee of the Preachers' Friend Society (formed 1799) and became a trustee.[14] In 1804 he became a founder of the British & Foreign Bible Society; was a director of the London Missionary Society (est. 1795); and assisted in forming the Society of Friends of Foreigners in Distress (1807) – all evangelical societies in an age of 'ten thousand compassions'.[15] Personal financial losses in 1815 curtailed his benefactions. He continued as an Admiralty translator until 1829.

Jane and Christopher Sundius had nine children. The memoir of her life in the *Methodist Magazine* suggests she encountered difficult circumstances, but maintained a steadfast faith: 'In her youth she sought and found peace with God; and through the vicissitudes of a chequered life, she exemplified a uniform and consistent piety. Chastened by many afflictions, and sanctified by the grace and truth of God, she attained an eminent maturity of Christian holiness'.[16] The Sundius family (including 13 of his children) were buried in a vault in the graveyard at City Road Chapel, London, near John Wesley's grave.

---

[13] George J. Stevenson, *City Road Chapel, London and Its Associations* (London: George J. Stevenson, 1872), p. 472.
[14] Ibid., pp. 164, 220, 359, 472-76.
[15] Ford K. Brown, *Fathers of the Victorians: the Age of Wilberforce* (Cambridge University Press, 1961), pp. 335, 343-44.
[16] *Methodist Magazine*, 1850, p. 94.

2 THE DAUGHTERS OF JOHN AND MARY STAMP

Of the three daughters of John and Mary Stamp, the eldest was Jane Vazeille Stamp (1791–1875) who was born and brought up in Newcastle and married William Stocks, a businessman from Huddersfield, in St Andrew's Parish Church, Newcastle, on 22 February 1814. They had twelve children, some of whom died in infancy; their eldest boy was baptised William Smith Stocks and their eldest daughter Jane Vazeille Stocks. When their eldest daughter died in infancy, a later daughter was also given the name of Jane Vazeille: she married an Anglican clergyman, Rev James Alfred Boddy. They had several children – including two daughters who became missionaries in Africa, and two sons who became Church of England priests: Alexander Alfred Boddy in Durham and Herbert Anthony Vazeille Boddy, domestic chaplain to the Marquis of Londonderry.

The second daughter of John and Mary Stamp was Anna Marie Stamp (1793-1861) who married Thomas Prior Flanders of Ely in St Andrew's Church, Newcastle, on 18 November 1811; Thomas died in 1813 at the age of thirty-three years and his name is the fourth to appear on the Smith family tomb, followed by that of their infant daughter, Jane Vazeille Flanders, who died in 1814, aged four months. The marriage register of St Andrew's Church records his name as Thomas Flanders Prior but other sources support the name as given on the tomb. Anna Marie later married Thomas Shaw at Bradford in 1817; they had eight children.

The third daughter of John and Mary Stamp, Mary Smith Stamp (born 1794), married the Rev. James Jones and they had two children. Their son, Thomas William Smith Jones (1835-1912), became a Wesleyan Methodist minister who was appointed by the Wesleyan Methodist Missionary Society in 1863 to succeed Rev. Richard Green in Milan, northern Italy. There he met and subsequently married Frances Mary Grafton

(1812-98), the first Principal of the Milan Girls' School, who was originally from Shrewsbury. Letters in the archives of the Wesleyan Methodist Missionary Society show that they had at least two children. After her death in 1898 a tribute in the *Methodist Magazine* stated, 'How much the work in Naples owed to her indefatigable labours will never perhaps be fully known on earth. ... She took a deep interest in Sunday School work and had a class for older girls and women'.[17]

After a few months in Milan, Mr Jones was moved by the WMMS to Naples where he had a very effective ministry for almost forty years; on retirement in 1902 he remained in Naples as a supernumerary minister and made a valuable contribution to the ongoing work. His obituary in the *Methodist Magazine* of 1912 included the following, 'To the end of his life he was recognised officially as Chaplain to Methodist mariners on any occasion of a visit of the British fleet to Naples'.[18] He was musically gifted and published a book of hymns for use in Naples which was used throughout Italy. This drew comment in the official history of the Wesleyan Methodist Missionary Society: 'Mr Jones' book of hymns and tunes appeared just before the occupation of Rome in 1870; it formed a grand accompaniment to our work of evangelization all over the country. There is much in Mr Jones' early contribution, especially in the matter of tunes, which has never been superseded, and never will be'.[19]

The sister of Thomas William Smith Jones, whose Christian name has eluded all research so far, was fully involved in her brother's ministry. The Ladies Auxiliary Committee Report of 1885 states, 'Nor should the assiduous labours of Miss

---

[17] Ibid., 1899, p. 254.
[18] *Minutes of Conference.* (London: Wesleyan Conference Office, 1912), pp. 168-69.
[19] George G. Findlay and W. W. Holdsworth, *The History of the Wesleyan Methodist Missionary Society* (5 vols., London: J.A. Sharpe,1921-24), vol. 4, p. 498.

Jones, Mr Jones' sister, be overlooked. She herself teaches in the schools, as a volunteer and practically gives her life to God in Naples'.[20] The same publication for the following year adds, 'The Ladies Benevolent Society is still in operation under the management of Mrs and Miss Jones'.[21]

Miss Jones died in Naples in 1926 at the age of ninety-three. Shortly before her death she presented to the Wesley Historical Society an oil portrait of William Smith, which she had inherited from her mother. The Rev F. F. Bretherton (1868-1956), who was the General Secretary of the WHS at the time, offered the portrait on behalf of the Society for permanent placement at Brunswick Methodist Chapel where it still hangs in the refurbished Wesley Room as part of a significant collection of paintings, engravings and memorabilia, several of which derive from John Wesley's time in the Orphan House. There is no evidence of the identity of the artist who painted the portrait of William Smith. At Brunswick there are two portraits of John Wesley by Thomas Horsley of Sunderland but professional opinion suggests it is unlikely that the portrait of William Smith is by the same painter.

3   SONS OF JOHN AND ANN STAMP

John Stamp's second wife was Ann Wood (died 1811) with whom he had nine children, two of whom became Wesleyan ministers. Their eldest son, John Sundius Stamp (1799–1848), was for a time Connexional Editor. Their third child William Wood Stamp (1801–1877) became President of the Wesleyan Conference in 1860 and was for many years Editor of the *Wesleyan Year Book*. He was the minister of Brunswick Methodist Chapel between 1854 and 1856 and was instrumental in the replacement of the Orphan House with the splendid

---

[20] Wesleyan Methodist Missionary Society, *Ladies Auxiliary Reports,* 1885, p. 13.
[21] Ibid., 1886, p. 11.

suite of Wesleyan Day Schools on the same site. This latter building, though having many different uses during its lifetime, remained there for almost a century until replaced with modern retail premises. The site, purchased by John Wesley in 1742, remains in Methodist ownership. William Wood Stamp also wrote *The Orphan House of John Wesley* (1863), a major source of information on the history of the Orphan House and the early years of Brunswick Chapel.

A contemporary tribute to W. W. Stamp by Rev. Thomas B. Goodwin describes him as, 'A Methodist of Methodists, and therefore a lover of all good men. He feared God, honoured the Queen and loved the brotherhood',[22] and pays tribute to his gifts of leadership: 'His integrity and singleness of purpose won the confidence of all parties, and his urbane wisdom conciliated many whom authority would exasperate'.[23] John Stamp was married for a third time on 22 January 1813, in St John's Church, Grainger Street, Newcastle upon Tyne, to Mary Ward; there were no children of this marriage.

4 OTHER NAMES ON THE WILLIAM SMITH TOMB

The remaining names on the William Smith family tomb in St Andrew's Churchyard, are those of his wife Jane's parents, Anthony and Mary Vazeille; and that of her famous stepfather: 'Rev. John Wesley, Founder of Methodism'. It is interesting to note how the names of 'William Smith' and 'Vazeille' were repeated by the descendants of Anthony and Mary through several generations. This is a little surprising in view of the unsympathetic way in which Mary has been represented by generations of Methodist writers anxious to pre-

---

[22] *Methodist Magazine*, 1877, p. 149.
[23] Ibid.

serve her husband's iconic status within and outside Methodism.

5 OTHER MEMORIALS IN ST ANDREW'S CHURCHYARD, NEWCASTLE ON TYNE WITH METHODIST CONNECTIONS

There are several other memorials in St Andrew's Churchyard which, although they have no familial relationship to William and Jane Smith, are nevertheless of interest to Methodists because of their links to the Orphan House and Brunswick Chapel. Three of them remain clear and readable, whereas two others can be traced only from church records.[24] One is immediately opposite to the south porch of the church and is dedicated to Edward Avison, a trustee of the Orphan House, and his wife, Margaret. Edward was the son of the celebrated Newcastle-born composer, Charles Avison, and became a trustee of the Orphan House in 1772, at the same time as William Smith. The inscription on the tombstone reads,

> In memory of Edward Avison and Margaret his wife who were eminent for piety and primitive simplicity of manners, having each borne a lingering disease with the most exemplary patience and resignation, they rejoiced at the approach of death and expired with hope full of immortality. He died on October 1776 aged 29. She in November 1777 aged 33.

Edward Avison met his future wife, Margaret (Peggy) Dale, at the Orphan House and they were married in St Andrew's Church on 4 March 1773. John Wesley was fond of Margaret and wrote, '*Miss Peggy is one of the holiest young*

---

[24] *Monumental Inscriptions of St Andrew's Church* compiled by Rev Bernard East, then curate of St Andrew's, in 1873/74. Copies of this are available in several local libraries and archives. Some editions are a later revision by Edwin Dodds in 1906.

women I have any knowledge of.[25] He appears to have an equally high opinion of Edward in writing, *'I do not know where Peggy could have made a better choice'*.[26]

The grave of Charles Avison is immediately adjacent to that of Edward and Margaret Avison. It was Charles Avison's 'Essay on Musical Appreciation', reputedly the first English work of musical criticism, which prompted John Wesley's tract, 'Thoughts on the Power of Music'. Edward's younger brother, Charles Avison Junior, was also a member of the Methodist society at the Orphan House though unlike his brother he did not become a trustee.

Another memorial is the grave of Rev Richard Elliott (1768-1813) who was appointed minister of the Orphan House in 1812 but died less than one year later. His tombstone reads,

> In hope of the Resurrection to Eternal life, here rest the mortal remains of the Rev Richard Elliott, 23 years a zealous, active and useful Preacher of the Gospel in the Methodist Connection. He died (deeply and justly lamented) July 7th 1813 aged 45. Willing rather to be absent from the Body and present with the Lord.

Richard Elliott was born in Derbyshire and entered the itinerant ministry in 1790 following a personal meeting with John Wesley; after some years he took a break from full time work, re-entering in 1809 and was stationed in Newcastle in 1812. His obituary included the following tribute, 'As a divine, he was plain and judicious, and his striking and affecting manner of preaching secured him very great attention. But his highest glory was the abundance of fruit which crowned his labours'[27].

---

[25] John Telford (ed.), *The Letters of John Wesley* (8 vols., London: Epworth Press 1931), vol. 5, p. 49. To Lady Maxwell, 4 June 1767.
[26] Ibid., vol. 6, p. 22. To Christopher Hopper 21 March 1773.
[27] *Methodist Magazine*, 1813, p. 708

A most poignant memorial in St Andrew's Churchyard, Newcastle, is the grave of two small children:

> Sacred to the memory of Timothy J. Grindrod, son of the Rev Edmund and Mary Grindrod, who departed this life March 11th 1818, aged 4 years and 6 months. Also Elizabeth M. Grindrod their daughter who departed this life July 26th 1819, aged 2 years and 8 months.

The Baptismal Register of the Orphan House shows a third child, James Munro Grindrod, born on 29 March 1818 and baptised on 15 June 1818. Edmund Grindrod (1786–1842) was the minister at the Orphan House, 1817-20, during which time Brunswick Chapel was built. In a letter to Jabez Bunting in March 1820 he wrote,

> Much of my time for several months past has been taken up in assisting our friends here to commence building a chapel in lieu of the Orphan House. ... We are going to build on the plan and dimensions of the large chapel at Hull [Waltham Street], with the exception of the vaults and some of its ornaments.[28]

The foundation stone of Brunswick was laid on 5 May 1820 by Mr. Grindrod and the opening services held on the 23 and 25 February 1821. Grindrod became Secretary of the Wesleyan Methodist Conference in 1833, was President of the Conference in 1837 and is buried in the burial ground at Wesley's Chapel, London.

One memorial no longer exists although its approximate position and its content can be ascertained from church records. It is dedicated to Rev Thomas Wood who was appointed in 1825 as both minister of Brunswick Methodist Chapel and Chairman of the Newcastle District. He died following a brief illness in 1826; the inscription on his gravestone read,

---

[28] W. R. Ward (ed.), *The Early Correspondence of Jabez Bunting 1820-1829* (London: Royal Historical Society, 1972), pp. 28-29.

To the memory of Rev Thomas Wood AM who for nearly forty years faithfully and successfully discharged his ministerial duties in the Wesleyan Connection and peacefully terminated his labours in this town January 8th 1826 Aet 61. Also of Catherine, the beloved wife of the above Rev Thomas Wood, who departed this life in peace at Tynemouth, June 25th 1843 aged 72 years. For me to live is Christ and to died is gain.

Thomas Wood was born at Flixton, near Manchester and entered the itinerant ministry in 1787; his obituary records that throughout his ministry he, 'Preached the Gospel of Christ with ability and success in the principal circuits of the Methodist Connexion' and that, 'He was an example of diligence and punctuality, and his piety was deep and uniform'.[29]

6   THE HENRY PERLEE PARKER CONNECTION

A remaining grave whose location is uncertain is listed in church records as, 'The Family Grave of Henry Parker and Ann Parker, and Robert Ballentyne Parker, Son of the above, born July 4th 1824, Died November 8th 1826'. In reporting the death of the child, the local newspaper included the information, 'The boy was the son of Henry Perlee Parker, the painter'.[30] A native of Devonport, Parker spent twenty five years in Newcastle between 1816 and 1841 and became a major figure in artistic circles. He supported Thomas Miles Richardson (1784-1848) in setting up the Northumberland Institution for the Promotion of the Fine Arts in the North of England in July 1822 and for a time acted as its treasurer. Both Richardson and Parker lived in Brunswick Place and the first

---

[29] *Methodist Magazine*, 1826
[30] *Tyne Mercury*, 14 November 1826.

fine art exhibition in the north east of England was opened in Richardson's house there on 23 September 1822.

In Methodist circles, Parker is chiefly remembered as the artist who produced a major iconic painting of Methodist heritage entitled, 'Is not this a brand plucked out of the fire?' The subject is the young John Wesley, at only five years of age, being rescued from the upper storey of the Epworth Rectory which was ravaged by a fire on 9 February 1709. It was painted at the suggestion of the Rev James Everett in 1839 to commemorate the centenary of the beginnings of Methodism, dated from the foundation of John Wesley's first preaching places, in London and Bristol in 1739. It was presented to the Methodist Conference of 1840 during its meeting in Brunswick Methodist Church in Newcastle upon Tyne. Parker painted two copies, one of which hangs in Methodist Church House, Marylebone Road, London; the other, a half size version,[31] can be seen in the Wesley Room at Brunswick, the most significant item in an impressive collection of Methodist heritage and memorabilia. In 1841, Parker became the Professor of Painting at Wesley College, Sheffield and in 1844 moved to London. He was twice married and had 14 children in all but died penniless in Shepherd's Bush, London, on 9 November 1873.

In view of his wife's death in Sheffield and his second wife's death in London, and Parker's latter-end impoverishment, it is highly unlikely that his mortal remains were interred at St Andrew's. Certainly no written evidence has emerged to indicate that anyone other than the infant Robert is buried there. A reasonable assumption is that the grave in St Andrew's was purchased on the death of his young son, who

---

[31] See Illustrations 2.5 and 2.9 above and the back cover of this book. The context of the painting is discussed in David J. Jeremy, '"What Mean Ye by These Stones?" Aspects of Memorialising and Remembering in Wesleyan Methodism' (Chapter 2 above).

was then buried there, and although intended as a family plot, the changes in Parker's career and circumstances made it unrealistic for any further family members to be placed there also. Looking at plans of the churchyard included with some versions of the monumental inscriptions, it is possible that this grave was one of a number which were removed when the road was widened in 1884 and any human remains moved to the St Andrew's Cemetery in Jesmond, a suburb of Newcastle. A further link between the family and the church is the Baptismal Register of St Andrew's Church, which records the baptism of Mary Perlee Parker, daughter of Henry Perlee and Amy Parker on 6 October 1816.

In the church office of St Andrew's is a pastel portrait of a clergyman which has two labels attached to its back, which read, 'The Rev. Henry Deer Griffith, Perpetual Curate of St Andrews, by H. P. Parker 1831' and 'Presented to the Vicar and Churchwardens of St Andrews by R. Y. Green, April 1887'. A large monument inside the church on the south wall of the choir stalls is also dedicated to the life and ministry of the Rev. Henry Deer Griffith.

CONCLUSION

This fine old church, whose effective ministry continues in the twenty first century, has a secure place in the story of Methodism. It is surely a cause for thanksgiving that John Wesley built his northern base within the parish of St Andrew's Church, Newcastle on Tyne, and that historic ties as described here have contributed to the growth, not only of Methodism in the north east of England, but of the wider church. A recently discovered local reference says that the early Methodists paid rent for two pews in St Andrew's Church, John Wesley insisting that, whilst in Newcastle, his itinerant preachers, if not engaged elsewhere, should attend worship there. However, this claim has yet to be substantiated from the records of either church. The final word on St Andrew's is given to the Founder of Methodism himself. On Sunday 22 September 1745, having first preached in Gateshead at 8.00 am; John Wesley worshipped at St Andrew's Church and recorded in his journal, 'I never saw before so well-behaved a congregation in any church in Newcastle as was that at St Andrew's this morning. The place appeared as indeed the house of God'.[32]

Acknowledgements
Thanks are due to Dr Peter S. Forsaith and Michelle Duff for help and specialist advice; to Geoffrey Fisher for help and for creating the family tree diagram; to Professor Nicholas Temperley for access to family papers; and to Rev Glyn Evans and staff of St Andrew's Church, Newcastle upon Tyne

The staff of the following institutions have been unfailingly helpful; my thanks to them all: the Library of the Society of Antiquaries, Great North Museum, Newcastle upon Tyne; Literary and Philosophical Society of Newcastle upon Tyne; Methodist Archives and Research Centre, John Ryland University Library, Manchester; Newcastle Central Library, Local Studies Department, Newcastle upon Tyne; Northumberland and Durham Family History Society; Tyne and Wear Archives Services, Blandford House, Newcastle upon Tyne; Northumberland County Records Office, Woodhorn, Ashington, Northumberland; School of Oriental and African Studies, University of London.

---

[32] Curnock (ed.), *Journal of John Wesley*, vol. 3, p. 212.

Table 6.1
Vazeille family tree

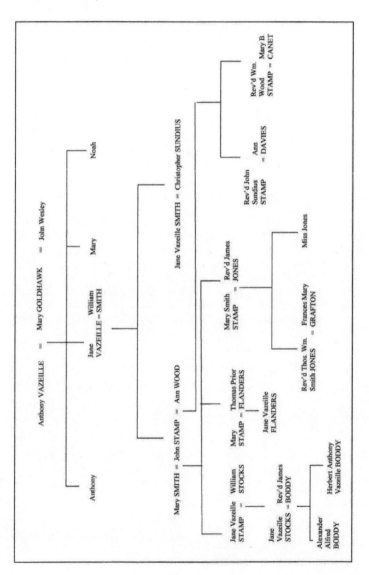

7

Memorials of Motherhood: the Travels and Travails of Preachers' Wives

Janet Kelly

In the autumn of 1823 on the island of Barbados Mrs Hillaria Shrewsbury, the wife of a Wesleyan missionary, faced the impending birth of her first child in desperate circumstances. Hostility towards the Methodists from the local planters was intense and her husband, William, had been particularly singled out, rumoured locally to be an agent of the London Anti-Slavery Society. Things came to a head in October when the Methodist chapel was torn down and the couple fled for their lives. After boarding a small boat for St Vincent, however, their situation then took an even more dramatic turn as Mrs Shrewsbury went into labour. William later described the scene: 'After our departure from Barbadoes, [sic] towards midnight the pains of travail commenced. We knew not what to do. No female was with us, and the vessel was small, manned by the Captain and three sailors'.[1] He went on: 'We could only cry to God in our troubles; and the Captain, who was an exceedingly wicked man, acknowledged, that, though he had never prayed to God before, yet when he saw our distressing condition, he could not help praying also'.[2] Thankfully these prayers were answered. Mrs Shrewsbury survived the voyage. The couple landed safely at St Vincent before noon

---

[1] Rev. William J. Shrewsbury, 'Memoir of Mrs. Hillaria Shrewsbury', *Wesleyan Methodist Magazine,* vol. 61 (1838), 481-95, at 483; [hereafter *WMM*].

[2] Ibid., p. 484.

the following day, and their baby son was born a few hours later.[3]

This striking episode, related in the published account of Mrs Shrewsbury's life in the *Wesleyan Methodist Magazine* of 1838, is a vivid reminder of the difficulties and dangers that could befall the wives of Methodist travelling preachers in the eighteenth and early nineteenth centuries. Relatively little scholarly attention has been paid to the lives of these women and the practicalities of their daily existence as partners of Wesley's roving evangelists, yet their situation presented many challenges.[4] These arose not only from the disciplines of their husbands' office and the hardships that the itinerant way of life frequently involved, but their position in the public eye. Along with their husbands the preachers' wives were expected to embody and uphold Methodist ideals.[5] Moreover, they faced a difficult balancing act in which personal needs, household and family responsibilities, and demands from local folk, both within and outside the Methodist society, had somehow to be reconciled.

---

[3] Ibid.

[4] Edmund Ralph Bates, 'The Wives of Wesley's Travelling Preachers', *Wesley Historical Society (Bristol)*, vol. 15 (1975), 1-3 is one short piece. A number of studies of ministerial life and of the itinerant ministry incorporate discussion of the situation facing the men's wives. See Kenneth D. Brown, *A Social History of the Nonconformist Ministry in England and Wales, 1800-1930* (Oxford: Clarendon Press, 1988), especially Chapter 5; A. K. Lloyd, *The Labourer's Hire: The Payment and Deployment of the Early Methodist Preachers, 1744-1813* (Bunbury, Cheshire: Wesley Historical Society, 1987), especially Chapter 3; John Lenton, '*My Sons in the Gospel': An Analysis of Wesley's Itinerant Preachers* (Loughborough: Wesley Historical Society, 2000), pp. 21-24 and idem, *John Wesley's Preachers: a Social and Statistical Analysis of the British and Irish Preachers Who Entered the Methodist Itinerancy before 1791* (Milton Keynes: Paternoster Press, 2009), Chapters 6 and 7.

[5] See Janet Kelly, 'Presenting a Ministry of Wives: a Moving Picture from the Mainstream Methodist Press', in Norma Virgoe (ed.), *Angels and Impudent Women: Women in Methodism* (Loughborough: Wesley Historical Society, 2007), pp. 7-30.

The present paper seeks to shed new light on the complexities of such females' daily existence. Drawing primarily on analysis of the memoirs of ministers' wives published in the *Arminian/Methodist/Wesleyan Methodist Magazine* between 1780 and 1880,[6] the situation of these individuals is explored, looking in particular at the experiences of women who were wives and mothers. As this evidence reveals, there were particular problems for women of childbearing years who accompanied their preacher husbands into circuit life. Though few ministers' wives faced the dramatic circumstances of Mrs Shrewsbury's first confinement, it is clear that there were many others whose procreative labours were complicated by their husbands' itinerant labours for the Lord.

1 THE TRAVELLING LIFE

For any woman marriage signifies a major turning point in life. For the individuals who became wives of Methodist itinerant preachers, however, the dislocation from former times was particularly acute. Their wedding was usually followed by a rapid farewell to kin, close friends and neighbours, and departure for a completely different way of life. Moreover, the initial separation from familiar scenes was only the first disruption of many similar household moves. Married life for these individuals was characterised by frequent changes of habitation and the upheaval that journeying from place to place entailed.

---

[6] This paper draws on research undertaken for Janet Kelly, '"Model Lives?" The Changing Role and Experience of the Wives of Itinerant Preachers in Mainstream Methodism, 1750-1880' (University of Leeds and Leeds Trinity University College, PhD thesis, 2009). I am very grateful to the Arts and Humanities Research Council for supporting this study. A survey of the longer biographical accounts of women's lives in 50 volumes of the denominational magazine during the period 1780-1880 identified 74 preachers' wives. Information about these women, gathered from their accounts and other sources formed the main database for the study.

Though it was persecution that hastened the Shrewsburys' flight from Barbados – and they later left St Vincent in similar circumstances[7] – there is much evidence that the regular travelling imposed by the itinerant system and frequent changes of domicile could compromise the health and welfare of the preachers' wives and their families. The case of Mrs Ann Taylor is an early example. Ann, who married in 1767, had her first child when stationed with her husband, Thomas in Dublin during February 1769.[8] However, due to a painful breast complaint she was unable to feed her daughter. As Thomas was posted to Cork at the next Conference the couple seem to have had little choice but to move, leaving their infant behind in the care of her wet nurse.[9] In fact it was over twelve months before Ann could be re-united with her daughter: a meeting that took place when the couple returned to Dublin en route for another posting in Manchester.[10] The emotional strain on all involved in this arrangement can only be conjectured.[11]

Travelling from place to place, especially in the era before the advent of the railways, often involved long and difficult journeys for the preachers' wives. The geographical distances covered during these circuit changes could be significant, even for those remaining in the British Isles. Jane Stanley's move from Newbury, Berkshire, to Haverfordwest in south west Wales in 1803 is described as 'a most unpleasant jour-

---

[7] Shrewsbury, 'Memoir of Mrs. Shrewsbury', p. 483.

[8] T. Taylor, 'The Grace of God Manifested in an Account of Mrs. Taylor', *Methodist Magazine,* vol. 35 (1812), 42-57, at p. 46-7; [hereafter *MM*]. The baby was born on 22 February.

[9] Ibid., p. 48.

[10] Ibid., p. 47.

[11] Writing of this period later Mr Taylor noted: 'Though the nurse was a Papist, I have reason to believe she did her duty to the child'. See Thomas Jackson, (ed.), *The Lives of Early Methodist Preachers Chiefly Written by Themselves* (6 vols., London: Wesleyan Conference Office, 1878), vol. 5, p. 41.

ney' due to Mrs Stanley's ill health, the bad state of the roads, and 'very hot weather.'[12] Another memoir speaks of the 'long and painful,' journey made by Frances Derry when going from Swansea to Rotherham in 1808.[13] Elizabeth Rosser, a later preacher's wife, spent 1837 in Aberdeen then went to Maidstone, Kent,
journeying on other occasions to circuits such as the Isle of Man and Alderney.[14] Mary Sykes, who married in 1840, appears to have had a singular introduction to the demands of the itinerant life, being stationed with her husband in England, Scotland and Wales in the space of just three years.[15]

Such transfers were particularly trying for women close to, or recovering from childbirth, and for their offspring. The memoir of Mrs Sarah Benson relates that in 1795 only six weeks after 'a narrow escape from death' in the delivery of her youngest daughter,[16] Sarah was obliged to travel two hundred miles from Bristol to Leeds with her baby and four other children.[17] Another preacher's wife, Sarah Stevens, undertook a similar lengthy journey with her family in 1801 going

---

[12] Jacob Stanley, 'An Account of the Experience and Happy Death of Mrs. Jane Stanley', *MM*, vol. 29 (1806), 225-33 at 230.
[13] 'Memoir of Frances Derry', *MM*, vol. 33 (1810), 396-432, at 430.
[14] William Hill (ed.), *An Alphabetical Arrangement of the Wesleyan Methodist Ministers and Preachers on Trial in Connexion with the British and Irish Conferences* (11th edn., London: Wesleyan Conference Office, 1869), p. 117. Mrs Rosser went to the Isle of Man in 1846 and to Alderney in 1854.
[15] Rev. Joseph Sykes, 'Memoir of Mrs. Mary Sykes', *WMM*, vol. 99 (1876),1057-68, at 1057-8; Hill, *Arrangement* (12th edn. , London, Wesleyan Conference Office, 1874), p. 147. After marriage in 1840, Mary travelled with her husband from her native Lancashire to the Alnwick circuit, going to Perth, Scotland in 1841, and Holyhead, Wales in 1842.
[16] Mr Benson, 'Memoir of Mrs. Benson', *MM,* vol. 33 (1810), 453-61 and 492-98, at 456.
[17] Ibid., p. 457.

from Ripon to Bristol and riding 'six in the same chaise'.[18] In this case Sarah's discomfort at the time is said to have been greatly compounded by being 'near [to] her confinement'.[19] For one woman the difficulties of moving had much more tragic consequences. In a transfer from the Preston circuit to Sowerby Bridge during 1814 Elizabeth McKitrick was forced to complete her journey on foot because of 'the miserable condition of the horses'.[20] Elizabeth was heavily pregnant at the time, and this effort involved a steep climb up the difficult terrain of Blackstone Edge. Her biographer reports that she gave birth to a still-born child shortly afterwards.[21]

2 HUSBAND'S WORKLOAD

On a day to day level, the itinerants travelled round their circuits fulfilling the requirements of the local preaching plan, and this, with their attendance at Conference, meant many periods of separation and loneliness for the preachers' wives. At St Austell in 1801, the extensive circuit is said to have presented 'a fine scope for the exercise of self-denial' for the newly-married Bridget Daniell, as the preachers were absent from home 'six weeks at a time, riding and preaching with little intermission'.[22] The sense of isolation was arguably more acute for those tending young children. Writing of her arrival in Oxford in 1791, for example, Sarah Stevens noted: 'The Society in the city consisted of 24 [sic] members, and we had been here some time before any of them called upon us. My body was exceeding weak, my child troublesome, my

---

[18] Thomas Stanley, 'The Grace of God Manifested in a Memoir of Mrs. Stevens', *MM*, vol. 43 (1820), 46-53 and 126-36, at 129.
[19] Ibid.
[20] J. E., 'Memoir of Mrs McKitrick', *MM,* vol. 39 (1816), 681-90, at 688.
[21] Ibid. It is not clear from the text whether this was a premature labour or not.
[22] 'Memoir of the late Mrs. Daniell', *WMM,* vol.63 (1840), 879-907 at 897.

husband almost always from home, and I had no one to speak to ...'.[23] Mary Entwisle's initial period in the Colne circuit in August 1794, meanwhile, could hardly have been more trying. During the journey from their previous circuit, Leeds, Mary and her husband, Joseph discovered not only that smallpox was very prevalent in Colne but that Mr Harrison, the departing itinerant, had left a child in the preacher's house that was 'dangerously ill in that disorder'.[24] Naturally they were highly alarmed, especially as their son, John, was only seventeen months old, and according to Joseph 'in a habit of body very unfit for the small-pox'.[25]

Despite being inoculated, John became infected and so seriously ill that 'his life was despaired of'.[26] Moreover, Joseph's circuit engagements meant that at the height of John's illness his wife was left alone. Mary herself was heavily pregnant and became 'greatly fatigued' caring for her son.[27] In a personal journal entry Mary described the unfolding events: '... my dear John had not had the Small-pox and was obliged to be prepared and enoculated [sic] immediately. He was severely handled, his life endangered, I in a strange place, my dear husband, true partner of my weal or woe, at a great distance, when the child was at the worst, my trials were great ...'.[28]

Though John subsequently recovered fully, and Mary was delivered of a second son three weeks later, these traumatic

---

[23] Stanley, 'Memoir of Mrs Stevens', p. 51.

[24] J. Entwisle, *Memoir of the Rev. Joseph Entwisle Fifty Four Years a Wesleyan Minister* (London, 1862), p. 119.

[25] Ibid., p. 120.

[26] Ibid., p. 122.

[27] Ibid.

[28] Manchester, John Rylands University Library, Methodist Archive Collection, 'Diary of Mrs Entwisle 1793 - 1798,' MAM L. 613, fols 1-31 at f. 15. Diary entry dated 26 July 1795. This extract and later ones cited are reproduced by courtesy of the University Librarian and Director, the John Rylands University Library, University of Manchester.

events appear to have weighed on the young woman's mind as another change of circuit approached in 1796. Being again in the third trimester of pregnancy Mary faced the upheaval this time even closer to the impending birth. She admitted to her diary that her mind was 'taken up' with 'the thoughts of our removal from this place, [and] of what I have to go thro' before, ...'.[29] The latter words referred to Joseph's departure for Conference, which was evidently another burden. Mary wrote that it was 'painful to part with [her] precious companion' for a period of a month.[30] The clash between this young wife's personal needs and the demands of the connexion are evident once more.

3   THE DANGERS OF PREGNANCY AND CHILDBIRTH

For women in this period, however welcome a pregnancy was, there was bound to be uncertainty about the outcome. Phyllis Mack has written movingly of the dangers of childbirth. Labour itself, she suggests, could be 'a brutalizing experience with horrendous potential side effects'.[31] In the general population although the rate of maternal and infant mortality was falling by the mid nineteenth century, the chance of a woman dying from childbirth or its consequences remained high.[32] It is not surprising to find, therefore, that though sev-

---

[29] Ibid., f. 23. Diary entry dated June [1796].

[30] Ibid., f. 25. Diary entry dated 17 July [1796]. An additional uncertainty was that at this stage, prior to Conference, the couple did not know where they would be going in September.

[31] Phyllis Mack, 'Does Gender Matter? Suffering and Salvation in Eighteenth Century Methodism,' *Bulletin of the John Rylands University Library Manchester*, vol. 85 (Summer and Autumn 2003), 157-76, at 170.

[32] E. Anthony Wrigley, 'British Population during the Long Eighteenth Century, 1680 - 1840', in Roderick C. Floud and P. McClosky (eds.), *The Cambridge Economic History of Modern Britain* (Cambridge: Cambridge University Press, 2004), pp. 79-86, at pp. 81-83. Data on maternal mortality

eral individuals in the survey successfully reared large families,[33] the childbearing histories of many of the preachers'
wives were marked by pain and loss.

4 MATERNAL DEATHS IN PREGNANCY AND CHILDBIRTH

Out of the fifty-six cases in the study providing evidence of
procreation, five women are known to have died either during
childbirth or from related complications. The brief account of
Mrs Bumsted, published in 1786, reports how her husband
flew to her side on hearing that she was in labour, only to wit-
ness her demise.[34] In this case no other details are provided to
explain the circumstances further. Elizabeth McKitrick is
known to have survived earlier pregnancies, but lost her life
suddenly in 1815 due to difficulties at a late stage in gesta-
tion.[35] Evidence provided in the accounts of Mrs Heath,[36]
Margaret Hinson,[37] and Betsy Lofthouse, meanwhile, suggests
that these women died after giving birth to their first child, the
latter wife having been married only a year.[38]

---

cited here suggests a decrease from 9.3 deaths per 1,000 birth events in
1750-99 to 5.8 deaths during 1800-37. The study also suggests that in the
period 1725-1835 childhood mortality was at its height during 1725-50, but
declined thereafter.

[33] At the time of Jane Allen's death she had eight children. See 'Memoir of
Jane, Wife of the Rev. William Allen', *WMM*, vol. 83 (1860), 779-86, at
786. Nine of Sarah Turton's children survived her. See Rev. Isaac Turton,
'Memoir of Mrs. Sarah Turton', *WMM*, vol. 53 (1830), 449-52, at. 450.

[34] D. Bumsted, 'A Short Account of the Death of Mrs. S. Bumsted', *Arminian Magazine,* vol. 3 (1786), 136-37; [hereafter *AM*].

[35] J. E., 'Memoir of Mrs. McKitrick', p. 688.

[36] Mr Heath, 'A Short Account of the Life and Death of Mrs. Heath', *AM,*
19 (1796), 601-3, at 603.

[37] A. Watmough, 'The Experience and Happy Death of Mrs. Margaret Hinson', *MM,* vol. 39 (1816), 370-75, at 372-73.

[38] Rev. A. Farrar, 'Memoir of the Late Mrs. Lofthouse', *WMM,* vol. 63
(1840), 370-75 at 372-73.

The women's worries about the potential danger of child-birth are voiced in several accounts. During her fourth pregnancy, Elizabeth McKitrick repeatedly asked her husband: 'What is your serious opinion? Shall I be spared this time?'[39] The biographer of Margaret Hinson reported that she had a 'strong presentiment' of her death through childbirth, which could not be shaken despite the comfort and advice of female friends.[40] In another case Diana Claxton recorded the impact of news of the deaths of three preachers' wives writing in her journal: 'being myself near the hour of nature's sorrow, and under very unpromising appearances, I was led to examine myself very closely in reference to eternity'.[41]

5   INCIDENCE OF MISCARRIAGE AND CHILD DEATHS

Other evidence indicates that miscarriages and child deaths were common experiences among the preachers' wives. Twenty-eight individuals are reported as suffering such loss. What is quite striking is the number of multiple bereavements that some individuals underwent. Almost half of those suffering child deaths experienced the demise of two or more of their offspring.[42] Sarah Stevens was particularly afflicted in this way. When nearing her own death she is reported as finding comfort in the fact that she would soon be reunited with *seven* of her children.[43] Elizabeth Burdsall is another preacher's wife, who through a variety of circumstances witnessed a

---

[39] J. E. 'Memoir of Mrs. Mc Kitrick', p. 688.
[40] Watmough, 'Experience and Happy Death of Mrs. Hinson', p. 372.
[41] 'Memoir of Mrs. Claxton', *MM,* vol. 41 (1818), 915-25, at 921. Diary extract written at Loughborough, dated 30 July [1809].
[42] Miscarriages are recorded in four accounts. Available evidence suggests that twenty-five wives experienced the death of a young baby or older children. Twelve of these lost two or more of their offspring.
[43] Stanley, 'Memoir of Mrs Stevens', p. 134.

similar level of loss, in this case comprising her entire family of eight.[44]

At a time when the mortality rate for infants within the general population was falling,[45] these findings underline the precariousness of children's lives. While some of the child deaths recorded relate to newborn or very young babies,[46] the danger of childhood diseases and epidemics to older children is also clear. Summoned from Woodhouse Grove School because of his father's death from typhoid, Jane Vasey's eldest son, Samuel was struck down by the same disease.[47] After her husband was transferred to an East London circuit in the 1820s, Elizabeth Burdsall endured the death of several of her children in quick succession, in circumstances suggesting some prevalent disease.[48] Paradoxically, Jane Allen's two eldest children survived the family's time in Africa, but Jane suffered the death of a later newborn baby after her return to English shores.[49]

There is evidence of the pain that such bereavements caused and the women's attempts to make sense of their loss.

---

[44] Rev. John Burdsall, 'Memoir of Mrs. Elizabeth Birdsall', *WMM*, vol. 51 (1828), 148-58, at 153.

[45] See note 32 above.

[46] See, for example Rev. John Brown, 'Memoir of Mrs. Mary Finch Walker', *WMM*, vol. 69 (1846), 1145-55, at 1153, and Rev. Robert Willcox, 'Memoir of Mrs. Leach, Late of Wakefield', *WMM*, vol. 89 (1866), 865-75, at 870.

[47] Rev. Thomas Vasey, 'Memoir of Mrs. Jane Vasey', *WMM*, vol. 83 (1860), 577-83, at 581; Mary Jane Vasey, *The Life of Thomas Vasey by His Widow* (London: Elliot Stock, 1874), p. 2.

[48] Burdsall, 'Memoir of Mrs. Burdsall', pp. 152-3. Elizabeth's husband reported that he had: 'received (much against my judgement and inclination) an appointment to travel in the London East Circuit', saying also that both he and his wife '[depreciated] greatly our destination ...especially at this time'.

[49] 'Memoir of Jane', p. 784. Jane's biographer observed that 'though the English have been on the coast of Guinea for upwards of three hundred years, [Jane] was the only European lady that ever gave birth to two children there, and afterwards returned with her offspring'.

In a cruel irony Mary Entwisle's second son Marmaduke, 'a sweet, affectionate child',[50] succumbed to an outbreak of smallpox in 1797 at the age of two and a half. Writing in her journal Mary recorded her prayer: 'Lord help me constantly to say thy will be done, knowing thou can'st not err, thou doest all things well, however contrary to our feelings, ... I trust I shall go to him but he shall not return to me'.[51] In a similar way, after losing her baby of a few weeks old, Ann Leach tried to come to terms with this situation, asking: 'Why should I murmur to give him back to Him who lent him to me for a short time?'[52] Both these women clearly felt the death of their infants to be a bitter blow, attempting to reconcile their own anguish with the will of God. To add to the heartbreak of such bereavements the constant moves that the itinerancy imposed meant a child's final resting place often had to be forsaken due to the pressing need to travel on.[53]

6 FINANCIAL HARDSHIPS

The Methodist approach to funding the movement's itinerant preachers developed in a haphazard fashion,[54] and despite the fact that Conference laid down minimum allowances for the support of the preachers and their wives and families from the

---

[50] 'Diary of Mrs Entwisle' f. 27, entry dated 7 May [1797].
[51] Ibid.
[52] Willcox, 'Memoir of Mrs. Leach', 870. Diary entry dated 1 March 1819.
[53] William Stevens, the husband of Sarah Stevens, noted that the couple's time in Yorkshire (1799-1802) had been marked by three child deaths. They left the county for Bristol in 1802 and never returned. See Thomas Stanley, 'Memoir of Mr. William Stevens' *MM,* vol. 37 (1814), 722-27, at 726.
[54] See, for example, Lloyd, *Labourer's Hire,* especially chapters 2 and 3. A succinct and more recent summary of the complexities of the developing allowance system for wives and children in the eighteenth and nineteenth centuries is given in Lenton, *John Wesley's Preachers,* pp. 95-97 and 109-10. Lloyd, *Labourer's Hire,* p. 9 notes that as late as 1753 Wesley declared 'We have barely the first outlines of a plan with regard to temporals'.

1750s,[55] available funding in the circuits, which was raised from the class money of local society members, varied from place to place.[56] In some circuits there was a great reluctance to accept married preachers because of the extra expense. Circuit stewards are said to have viewed married preachers and the prospect of large families with something of an 'evil eye'.[57] Financial instability, therefore, was another factor affecting the daily experience of the preachers' wives.

In view of this economic uncertainty it is pertinent to ask whether low standards of living, and especially a meagre diet, contributed to the poor outcome of some of the pregnancies of the preachers' wives. Information given in the records of the short-lived Preachers' Friend Society clearly reveals, for example, that as the itinerants were travelling around their circuits, the heaviest burden of managing the family budget fell on their wives at home.[58] One man described his spouse's tears 'on reviewing the disproportion of our Income and Expenditure' noting that this was *after* she had made significant sacrifices '... by lopping off Butter, Sugar, Wheat Flour etc...'.[59] In another touching case a preacher suggested that 'a want of proper nourishment' was the reason for numerous family afflictions and the rapid decline of his wife.[60] The lat-

---

[55] Ibid., pp. 10-13. In 1752 an allowance was fixed for the preachers of £12 a year. At the same time maintenance for any wife in need was decided at £10 yearly with an additional allowance for children.

[56] Ibid., p. 13. In newly formed societies, thinly populated areas, or places where Methodist membership was low, for example, such funds were often difficult to find.

[57] Ibid., p. 20; Lenton, *John Wesley's Preachers*, p. 109.

[58] Lloyd, *Labourer's Hire*, pp. 14-15; Lenton, *John Wesley's Preachers*, p. 109. The Preachers' Friend Society was a benevolent fund for the relief of itinerant preachers set up in 1799.

[59] *MM*, vol. 24 (1801), 367-68.

[60] *MM*, vol. 25 (1802), 337.

ter seldom got any dinner, he added, except when he was at home, and that was usually only four days a month.[61]

The expenses incurred during childbirth were undoubtedly an added burden on circuit finances in some cash-strapped areas. Writing of his time in Ireland, Thomas Taylor commented bitterly about the meagre allowances, noting that the stewards provided for his wife during her lying in, 'but as soon as she could crawl out, that ceased'.[62] Meanwhile there is other evidence of more general hardship from the sources of this study. Sarah Stevens, whose husband was not a popular preacher, was required to move frequently, and went to some of the poorest circuits.[63] She is said to have endured 'great poverty and want' throughout her married life.[64] However, even the Entwisles, who were posted in some prosperous circuits, saw fluctuations in their income. They were lucky to be subsidised by Mary's father until his death in 1798.[65] Shortly afterwards Joseph had to plead for an increase in the 'scanty' allowance at York simply to feed his growing family.[66] Whilst frugality was enjoined upon all Methodist members, therefore, it appears to have been obligatory for the preachers' wives.

7 THE PREACHERS' WIVES AND THEIR CHILDREN

When describing the relationship between the preachers' wives and their offspring, the accounts typically allude to the subjects' kindness, tenderness and affection. The biographer of Mrs Gartrell, for example, reflected: 'Perhaps there never

---

[61] Ibid.
[62] Taylor, 'Account of Mrs. Taylor', p. 48.
[63] Stanley, 'Memoir of Mrs. Stevens', p. 49.
[64] Ibid., p. 50.
[65] J. Entwisle, *Memoir,* p. 169.
[66] Ibid.

was a more kind and affectionate mother'.[67] In another case Mr Roadhouse described his wife, Harriet as 'most tender-hearted',[68] observing in a poignant phrase, that her two sons: 'had always been lovely in her eyes, and entwined around her heart'.[69] The wives' unfailing attention to their offspring and concern for their welfare is also stressed. Sarah Benson is said to have insisted on feeding her children herself, despite personal health problems, refusing a wet nurse.[70] Ann Hardcastle is reported to have made the health and comfort of her children 'her constant care'.[71] Significantly, these examples promulgate an idea of the selfless home-oriented mother, focused upon the needs of her offspring. This was an ideal that was gaining prominence in wider society during the period of the study, and one that accorded well with the growing conservatism of Methodist leaders.[72]

8 EXPECTATIONS OF THE PUBLIC

However, other evidence within the accounts suggests that there were general expectations that these women would embrace a public role: a fact that prompted anxiety in some individuals. The biographer of Mary Ann Cusworth, who married in 1813, for example, noted that at first she 'shrank from the duties pictured on her mind, as *imposed* on the wife of a

---

[67] J. Brougham, 'Some Account of the Christian Experience and Happy Death of Mrs. Gartrell', *MM*, vol. 41 (1818), 676-80, at 677.

[68] J. Roadhouse, 'Memoir of Harriet Hammont Roadhouse', *MM* vol. 43 (1820), 843-49, at 849.

[69] Ibid., pp. 846-47.

[70] Benson, 'Memoir of Mrs. Benson', p. 455.

[71] Philip Hardcastle, 'The Grace of God Manifested in a Short Account of Mrs Ann Hardcastle', *MM*, vol. 35 (1812), 764-79, at 779.

[72] As Ruth Perry has argued, this ideal of maternity emerged in wider society during the eighteenth century. See her 'Colonising the Breast: Sexuality and Maternity in Eighteenth Century England', *Journal of the History of Sexuality*, vol. 2 (1991), 204-34, at 209, 212-13 and 214.

Christian Minister'[My emphasis].[73] A later member of the study, Mrs Dernaley, complained that there were 'people everywhere who make the most unreasonable demands upon a minister's wife' and that there was a 'constant call for visiting ...'.[74] Details in Mary Entwisle's memoir reveal that she faced forthright criticism during one class meeting when a person 'bluntly [blamed] her ... for not acting in a public way'.[75] Undoubtedly some strength of character was required to stand up to such pressures.

9   FACTORS INFLUENCING THE WIVES' INVOLVEMENT IN PUBLIC SERVICE

It is clear that factors such as personal conviction, traits of personality, health problems, and family commitments all helped to determine the wives' decisions about the scope of service they could tackle.[76] Some women undoubtedly felt it

---

[73] See Mr Peter Kruse, 'Memoir of Mrs. Mary Ann Cusworth', *WMM* vol. 59 (1836), 414-23, at 419.   Speaking of clergy wives in the Anglican Church, Jeremy Gregory has pointed out that 'ideas about ... wifely behaviour came not only from the Church but also from the laity's expectations.' See his 'Gender and the Clerical Profession', in R. N. Swan (ed.), *Gender and Christian Religion, Studies in Church History* vol. 34 (Woodbridge: Boydell Press, 1998), pp. 235-71, at 260.

[74] S., 'Memoir of the Late Rev. Abel Dernaley with Notices of Mrs. Dernaley', *WMM*, vol. 91 (1868), 1057-64, at 1063.

[75] Joseph Entwisle, 'The Grace of God Manifested in a Brief Account of the Life and Death of Mrs Entwisle', *MM*, vol. 27 (1804), 368-76, at 372.

[76] Elizabeth Burdsall and Mrs Jennings, for example, are both said to have believed that their roles as wives and mothers should be paramount. See Burdsall, 'Memoir of Mrs. Elizabeth Burdsall', p, 151, and Rev. Edward Jennings, 'Memoir of Mrs. Jennings', *WMM*, vol. 67 (1844), 105-12, at p.109. Duncan McAllum wrote that his wife, Elizabeth 'never ventured to act in any public capacity' because of her timid disposition and 'weak voice'. See his 'The Grace of God Manifested in a Short Account of Mrs Elizabeth McAllum', *MM*, vol. 37 (1814), 207-12, at 209. Health problems and family commitments were cited by Mary Entwisle as reasons for focusing on her family. See Entwisle, 'Account of Mrs Entwisle', p. 370.

right to channel all their efforts into their homes. But there are hints too of the tensions others experienced as increasing family responsibilities limited their opportunities for more public work. As a young wife Mary Walker complained: 'I have been much taken up with domestic concerns. I frequently feel much at doing so little for the good of others; but I am almost fully occupied with my two young children, and am not to choose my own work, but to do what is set before me'.[77] In a similar vein the biographer of Harriet Roadhouse remarked that having her children 'so near together' prevented her 'from going amongst our people ... as often as she desired to do ...'.[78]

10 RECONCILING HOME AND PUBLIC WORK

In fact many preachers' wives did succeed in combining home responsibilities and other active work, both within and outside the Society. Moreover, the women's willingness to rise to the challenges of their situations in spite of personal difficulties and sorrows is often evident. Shortly after losing her first baby in 1789, for example, Sarah Stevens formed a society for the relief of the sick and poor, visited hospitals, prisons, and the soldiers' barracks.[79] Two years later, despite the gloomy start to her husband's appointment in Oxford, she was soon busy leading early morning prayer-meetings in various parts of the city, an enterprise that brought many into the Society.[80] When stationed in the Bridlington circuit in 1796, and even with a growing family, she reported: 'At present my hands are

---

[77] Rev. John Brown, 'Memoir of Mrs. Mary Finch Walker', *WMM*, vol. 69 (1846), 1145-55, at 1152. This undated diary entry appears to have been written shortly after arrival in the Sandhurst circuit in 1818.
[78] Roadhouse, 'Memoir of Harriet Roadhouse', p. 845.
[79] Stanley, 'Memoir of Mrs Stevens', p. 49.
[80] Ibid., pp. 50-51. Letter to Thomas Coke from Mr Stevens dated 12 December 1791.

full. With two classes, three bands, a prayer-meeting every morning at six o'clock, and the publick [sic] bands on the Saturday evening'.[81] This was truly a prodigious range of duties.

Other women showed similar resilience. Mary Ann Cooke was confined to home because of ill health, but still managed to pass religious literature to local railway workers from her garden, her philosophy being that 'it was much more agreeable to be able to work for God, and to serve him in active duties'.[82] A later preacher's wife, Ann Leach, is said to have suffered 'yearning maternal grief' when a circuit move to Bristol from Darlington separated her from some of her older children.[83] In spite of this and various other personal difficulties she began work visiting the sick, teaching, distributing tracts, and eventually taking up the role of a class leader, a job she fulfilled for many years.[84]

CONCLUSION

In the memoir of Charlotte Rowland, published in 1822, Charlotte's husband described the couple's trip from Gravesend to London in February 1821, undertaken, it seems, to seek urgent advice about Charlotte's rapid decline from tuberculosis.[85] 'After being in town with her for a few days, during which she seemed to improve a little', Mr Rowland wrote, 'the work of my circuit imperiously called me home ...'[86] Despite the

---

[81] Ibid., p. 127. Diary entry dated 6 February 1796.

[82] Rev. Corbett Cooke, 'Memoir of Mary Ann, Wife of the Rev. Corbett Cooke', *WMM*, vol. 75 (1852), 1149-55, at 1153-54. This was at Macclesfield, between 1847 and 1849.

[83] Willcox, 'Memoir of Mrs. Leach', pp. 871-72.

[84] Ibid.

[85] Rev. Thomas Rowland, 'Memoir of the Late Mrs. Rowland', *WMM*, vol. 45 (1822), 213-16, and 282-86, at 282-83. The trip was made on the advice of 'two medical gentlemen.'

[86] Ibid., p. 283.

gravity of Charlotte's situation, and her longing to see her husband, the couple were not reunited until the middle of the following month, by which time Charlotte's condition was considerably worse.[87] As this instance again well illustrates, the imperatives of institutional Methodism and the personal health and wellbeing of the preachers' wives often clashed. The discussion above has also shown that this conflict was particularly acute for women in their reproductive years and their offspring. Some of the family sorrows experienced by Elizabeth McKitrick, Elizabeth Burdsall, and Mary Entwisle, for example, were demonstrably exacerbated by their husbands' work commitments within the connexional system.

Given the additional pressures of the travelling life for women who were mothers, it is not surprising that some individuals, such as Mrs Jennings, decided to channel all their energies into their homes and families.[88] Indeed, the fact that several of the study's subjects successfully managed to rear large broods seems a cause for celebration.[89] Examples given above show that a number of the women did manage to strike a balance between their home lives and other forms of active service, both within the Methodist movement and in their wider communities. Moreover, as the cases of Sarah Stevens and Ann Leach reveal, private sorrows could prompt a new engagement in public work. Such evidence clearly indicates that existence as a preacher's wife and a mother was never plain sailing. But in the midst of their travels and travails, many individuals wrought personal triumphs too.

---

[87] Ibid. At their reunion Mr Rowland was shocked at his wife's 'fearfully wasted' appearance, and she 'shed tears of joy'.
[88] See note 76 above.
[89] See note 33 above.

8

Methodist Prosopography: Sources and Exemplars of Collective Biography in British Methodism

Clive D. Field

Prosopography derives from the Greek word *prosopon*, initially denoting face or mask in a theatrical context, but later acquiring a technical theological meaning, translating as person. In historical research, it is the name given to the aggregate study of the lives of a group of individuals with common background characteristics, collective biography as many would understand it (or multiple career-line analysis, in social scientific jargon). It combines the techniques of genealogy, onomastics, and demography. There is a long tradition of prosopographical studies, especially in secondary works on ancient and medieval history, but the concept has especially caught on for early modern and modern history thanks to a seminal article written in 1971 by Lawrence Stone,[1] who had applied prosopographical techniques in his magisterial survey of the crisis of the English aristocracy, 1558-1641.[2] Another

---

[1] Lawrence Stone, 'Prosopography', *Daedalus*, vol. 100 (1971), 46-79. Cf. idem, 'Prosopography', in Felix Gilbert and Stephen Graubard (eds.), *Historical Studies Today* (New York: W. W. Norton, 1972), pp. 107-40.
[2] Lawrence Stone, *The Crisis of the Aristocracy, 1558-1641* (Oxford: Clarendon Press, 1965).

major exponent of the approach was Gerald Aylmer, with his trilogy on the seventeenth-century civil service.[3]

In Britain a *de facto* co-ordinating and dissemination function for prosopography during the 1990s and 2000s was discharged by the Prosopographical Centre at the University of Oxford's Modern History Research Unit, with an extensive website[4] and an impressive range of print publications, among them a newsletter (*Prosopon*) and a substantial handbook.[5] Prosopography is increasingly synonymous with quantification and automation, particularly through the development of collective biographical databases. Once applied mainly to research into elites, prosopography has extended into a tool for investigating the lives of ordinary folk. Similarly, although many initial applications were in a politico-historical environment, exemplars in the ecclesiastical historical field have emerged in recent years, such as the *Clergy of the Church of England Database*[6] and the *Who were the Nuns?* project.[7]

At first glance, prosopography is not a concept which features much in the study of the history of British Methodism, but that is not to say that prosopographical techniques have been entirely absent, for they have sometimes been used without being explicitly described as such. In this essay two as-

---

[3] Gerald Aylmer, *The King's Servants: the Civil Service of Charles I, 1625-1642* (London: Routledge & Kegan Paul, 1961); idem, *The State's Servants: the Civil Service of the English Republic, 1649-1660* (London: Routledge & Kegan Paul, 1973); idem, *The Crown's Servants: Government and Civil Service under Charles II, 1660-1685* (Oxford: Oxford University Press, 2002). Cf. idem, 'Prosopography and Seventeenth-century England', in Jean-Philippe Genet and Günther Lottes (eds), *L'état moderne et les élites, XIIIe-XVIIIe siècles* (Paris: Publications de la Sorbonne, 1996), pp. 19-26.
[4] http://prosopography.modhist.ox.ac.uk/ [this, and all subsequent URLs, accessed 15 August 2012].
[5] Katherine Keats-Rohan (ed.), *Prosopography Approaches and Applications: a Handbook* (Oxford: Unit for Prosopographical Research, University of Oxford, 2007).
[6] http://www.theclergydatabase.org.uk/
[7] http://www.history.qmul.ac.uk/wwtn/the_project.html

pects of the topic are considered. First, there is a survey of the range of primary resources which would support the prosopographical analysis of Methodism, as regards both ministry and laity, and including evidence which might be termed born-prosopographical as well as material which can be retrospectively assembled. Reference is also made to significant secondary studies which have deployed these resources.[8] It must be stressed, however, that this is a more focused exercise than reviewing Methodist genealogical tools as a whole.[9] Second, by way of case study, four illustrations are provided from the author's own research of how quantitative collective biography can shed light on the history of British Methodism in the opening decades of the twentieth century.

---

[8] It should be noted that only the original edition of each work has been cited. In some cases, printed reprints or digital surrogates may be available, which can be traced through library union catalogues or search engines. Moreover, a large number of the out-of-copyright Methodist reference works cited were republished on microfiche as part of Clive Field (ed.), *The People Called Methodists: a Documentary History of the Methodist Church in Great Britain and Ireland on Microfiche* (Leiden: Inter Documentation Company, 1989-98). See the catalogue of this collection at http://www.idc.nl/pdf/151_titlelist.pdf

[9] See William Leary, *My Ancestors were Methodists* (rev. edn., London: Society of Genealogists, 1999); Richard Ratcliffe, *Basic Facts about Methodist Records for Family Historians* (Bury: Federation of Family History Societies Publications, 2005); and three new and, as yet, relatively undeveloped websites: http://www.mymethodisthistory.org.uk, http://www.myprimitivemethodists.org.uk, http://www.mywesleyanmethodists.org.uk. Also out of scope are prosopographical tools for other Free Church denominations, although they may be useful for tracing former Methodists; these are dealt with in Clive Field, 'Sources for Protestant Nonconformity in England and Wales since 1662: a Structured Bibliography', in Robert Pope (ed.), *The T&T Clark Companion to Nonconformity* (London: Bloomsbury, 2013), pp. 495-531, at 510-21.

1 PROSOPOGRAPHICAL RESOURCES FOR THE STUDY OF METHODISM

We are relatively well-served with collective biographical information about the Methodist ministry, at three levels: a) minutes of Conference and derivative publications, sometimes augmented by obituaries in magazines and other sources; b) contemporary who's who directories; and c) biographical reference works, often compiled after the event and selective in their coverage.

At the top level, the minutes of the annual Conferences of the various branches provide lists of preachers' names, their year of entry to the ministry and their stations, although they do not constitute a complete record of those who desisted or were expelled from the Methodist itinerancy. The minutes also include obituaries from 1777, but, in the early days, these were often cursory, lacking in factual detail and majoring on the deceased's piety, often in a rather stylized way. Wesleyan ministerial obituaries until 1840 were reprinted by Joseph Hall,[10] but a second volume mooted for later years never appeared. From the minutes several scholars have undertaken quantitative analyses of the Methodist ministry in the nineteenth and twentieth centuries, often by means of randomly-drawn samples. The most accessible and, in terms of the evidence base, largest-scale work in this category is by Kenneth Brown, who investigated the origins, training, retention, and public and private lives of Wesleyans, Primitive Methodists and United Methodists entering their respective ministries during the period 1830-1930.[11] Other examples include Clive

---

[10] Joseph Hall, *Memorials of Wesleyan Methodist Ministers; or, the Yearly Death Roll from 1777 to 1840* (London: Haughton & Co., 1876).

[11] Kenneth Brown, 'Ministerial Recruitment and Training: an Aspect of the Crisis of Victorian Nonconformity', *Victorian Studies*, vol. 30 (1987), 365-83; idem, 'College Principals: a Cause of Nonconformist Decay?', *Journal of Ecclesiastical History*, vol. 38 (1987), 236-53; idem, 'An Unsettled Ministry? Some Aspects of Nineteenth-century British Nonconformity', *Church*

Field, who studied the career patterns of 1,500 Wesleyan, Primitive and United Methodist ministers born between 1781 and 1900;[12] and Timothy Allison, who examined issues of socio-economic status and lifespan in relation to four cohorts of Wesleyan and Primitive Methodist preachers born in the 1850s and 1880s.[13]

From the Conference minutes a number of cumulative listings of ministers have been compiled.[14] The earliest were by John Pawson (1795),[15] William Myles (1799, 1801, 1803, 1813),[16] Charles Atmore (1801),[17] an anonymous writer

---

History, vol. 56 (1987), 204-23; and idem, *A Social History of the Nonconformist Ministry in England and Wales, 1800-1930* (Oxford: Clarendon Press, 1988).

[12] Clive Field, 'Methodism in Metropolitan London, 1850-1920' (DPhil thesis, University of Oxford, 1974), pp. 23-60.

[13] Timothy Allison, 'An Historical Cohort Study of Methodist Ministers, Examining Lifespan and Socioeconomic Status' (MSc thesis, University of Manchester, 1995); Allison and Selwyn St Leger, 'The Life Span of Methodist Ministers: an Example of the Use of Obituaries in Epidemiology', *Journal of Epidemiology and Community Health*, vol. 53 (1999), 253-54.

[14] Bernard Sheldon, '"Hill's arrangement"', *Wesley Historical Society Proceedings*, vol. 30 (1956), 134-5; Kenneth Garlick, '*Ministers and Probationers of the Methodist Church*: "Hill's arrangement"', *Wesley Historical Society Proceedings*, vol. 40 (1975), 2-5.

[15] John Pawson, *A Chronological Catalogue of all the Travelling Preachers now in the Methodist Connexion* (Liverpool: printed by J. M'Creery, 1795).

[16] William Myles, *A Chronological History of the People called Methodists* (4th edn., London: printed at the Conference-Office by Thomas Cordeux, 1813), pp. 445-64. Lists of preachers also appeared in the second (1799) and third (1803) editions, as well as separately: Myles, *A List of All the Methodist Preachers Who Have Laboured in Connexion with the Late Rev. John Wesley and with the Methodist Conference* (Bristol: printed for the author by R. Edwards, [1801]).

[17] Charles Atmore, *The Methodist Memorial* (Bristol: printed by Richard Edwards, 1801), pp. 43-512 (biographies of deceased ministers), 531-6 (ministers then itinerating). The list of preachers was also separately published as Atmore, *A Chronological List of the Itinerant Preachers in the Connexion of the Late Rev. John Wesley* (Manchester: printed at the Office of W. Shelmerdine & Co., 1801).

(1814),[18] Jonathan Crowther (1815),[19] and James Holroyd (1819),[20] Atmore additionally providing 199 biographical sketches of deceased preachers. Deficiencies in these records were subsequently made good by Kenneth Garlick[21] and, even more authoritatively, by John Lenton, who significantly augmented the information contained in the Conference minutes. Lenton constructed a database of the eighteenth-century itinerant preachers and then subjected it to statistical interrogation, in order to establish a group profile, especially from the perspective of geographical, social class, educational, and religious backgrounds and of their family lives and careers in the ministry.[22] Lenton is now undertaking a parallel project, building a database of the 2,000 or so men who left the Wesleyan ministry from 1791 to 1932.[23]

The first edition of the work popularly known as 'Hill's arrangement' (named after William Hill), which became *Ministers and Probationers of the Methodist Church* after the 1932 reunion, appeared in 1819, with a further 31 editions

---

[18] *A Chronological and Alphabetical List of All the Itinerant Methodist Preachers in the Connexion of the Late Rev. John Wesley* (Exeter: printed by E. Woolmer for A. B. Seckerson, [1814]).

[19] Jonathan Crowther, *A Portraiture of Methodism* (2nd edn., London: Richard Edwards, 1815), pp. 442-50 (ministers then itinerating), 451-54 (deceased), 454-56 (departed or expelled).

[20] James Holroyd, *A Chronological and Alphabetical List of All the Itinerant Preachers that Have Been and now Are in the Wesleyan Methodist Connexion* (Haslingden: J. Walton, 1819).

[21] Kenneth Garlick, *Mr Wesley's Preachers* (London: Pinhorns for the World Methodist Historical Society British Section, 1977).

[22] John Lenton, '*My Sons in the Gospel': an Analysis of Wesley's Itinerant Preachers* ([Wolverhampton]: Wesley Historical Society, 2000) and idem, *John Wesley's Preachers* (Milton Keynes: Paternoster, 2009). A cut-down version of the database is available at http://www.gcah.org/site/c.ghKJI0PHIoE/b.3945307/.

[23] See John Lenton, 'Men Who Left the Wesleyan Methodist Ministry, 1791-1932: a Database in Progress' (Above, Chapter 5).

thereafter, until the last in 1968.[24] This covers Wesleyan ministers before 1932 and Methodist ones thereafter. The appendix to the 1968 edition, detailing ministers and probationers who had died in the work to that point, is now available online.[25] The only relevant publications to have appeared since 1968 are William Leary's list of ministers who died between 1968 and 1989,[26] Eric Edwards's accounts of those who entered the Methodist itinerancy from Welsh districts since the commencement of Methodism,[27] and Ian Henderson's record of Irish Primitive Wesleyan preachers.[28]

There was never any contemporary Primitive Methodist equivalent to 'Hill's arrangement', but William Leary created one retrospectively in 1990-93.[29] This has been elaborated by Dorothy Graham in respect of the female travelling preachers of early Primitive Methodism.[30] Lists of Methodist New Connexion ministers and their circuits were prepared by William

---

[24] William Hill, *An Alphabetical Arrangement of all the Wesleyan Methodist Preachers and Missionaries* (Bradford: printed and sold by T. Inkersley, 1819 [with 24 further editions to 1926]); *Ministers and Probationers of the Methodist Church* (London: Methodist Publishing House, 1933 [with six further editions to 1968]).

[25] http://www.library.manchester.ac.uk/specialcollections/collections/method ist/using/ indexofministers/.

[26] William Leary, *The Methodist Church: Ministers who have Died, 1968-1989* (Peterborough: printed by Methodist Publishing House, [1990]).

[27] Eric Edwards, *Yr Eglwys Fethodistaidd* (Llandysul: Gwasg Gomer, 1980), pp. 76-132, supplement, 1987, pp. 19-24. Cf. Edwards, *O gylchdaith i gylchdaith: cronicl o daith un gweinidog yng ngweinidogaeth yr Eglwys Fethodistaidd, 1932-1975* ([Caernarvon: Methodist Church, 2001]).

[28] Ian Henderson, 'Primitive Wesleyan Methodist Preachers', *Bulletin of the Wesley Historical Society (Irish Branch)*, vol. 8 (2002), 55-62.

[29] William Leary, *Ministers & Circuits in the Primitive Methodist Church: A Directory* (Loughborough: Teamprint, 1990, supplement, 1993).

[30] Dorothy Graham, *Chosen by God: a List of the Female Travelling Preachers of Early Primitive Methodism* (2nd edn., Evesham: Wesley Historical Society, 2010).

Gunstone in 1896[31] and William Townsend in 1899,[32] while William Boyden and Edwin Askew were responsible for the equivalents for the United Methodist Free Churches in 1877, 1887 and 1899.[33] Henry Smith, John Swallow and William Treffry compiled the record for the United Methodist Church between 1907 and 1932.[34] All these United Methodist efforts were superseded by Oliver Beckerlegge in 1968, who brought in the Bible Christians and other smaller branches of the United Methodist family, as well as adding biographical notes derived from obituaries.[35]

The importance of these variants of 'Hill's arrangement', based upon Conference minutes and amplified by the obituaries therein, is that they cover the total universe of serving Methodist ministers and those who died in the work or as supernumeraries. They may sometimes be supplemented by biographical information contained in the membership registers of the various Methodist ministerial annuitant societies (a largely unexplored source)[36] and in connexional magazines

---

[31] William Gunstone, *Companion to the Minutes of Conference; Being an Alphabetical Arrangement of the Ministers of the Methodist New Connexion* (Dewsbury: Darley Terry, 1896).

[32] William Townsend, *A Handbook for the Methodist New Connexion* (London: Geo. Burroughs, [1899]), pp. 5-26.

[33] Edwin Askew (ed.), *Free Methodist Manual* (London: Andrew Crombie, 1899), pp. 76-117. Equivalent lists were included in the 1877 and 1887 editions, which were entitled *Handbook of the United Methodist Free Churches* and authored by William Boyden.

[34] Henry Smith, John Swallow and William Treffry, *The Story of the United Methodist Church* (London: Henry Hooks, [1932]), pp. 230-308.

[35] Oliver Beckerlegge, *United Methodist Ministers and Their Circuits* (London: Epworth Press, 1968).

[36] These are all held at the Methodist Archives and Research Centre, John Rylands Library, University of Manchester and relate to the nineteenth and twentieth centuries. They comprise the records of the Wesleyan Methodist Preachers Annuitant Society (accession number 2008/019, boxes 1 and 2); the Primitive Methodist Itinerant Preachers' Friendly Society (accession number 1977/121, boxes 2 and 3); and the United Methodist Church Super-

and newspapers.[37] Although, as regards the latter, the principal printed indexes are to obituaries in the *Arminian Magazine*
and *Wesleyan Methodist Magazine* between 1778 and 1839,[38]
and to writings about ministers in the Welsh Wesleyan magazine from 1809 to 1983,[39] several other unpublished indexes
to 1932, compiled by William Leary and others, are available
at the Methodist Archives in Manchester. These indexes naturally cover laity, not just ministers, but somewhat serendipi-
tously, thereby falling well short of a scientific sample. Notwithstanding, some scholars have used biographical data in
the magazines as the core evidence for investigating hybrid
groups of ministers and laity, for instance, quantification of
the spirituality of eighteenth-century Methodists by Tom Albin,[40] and of mid-nineteenth-century Wesleyans and Primitive
Methodists by Linda Wilson.[41] Janet Kelly has also employed

---

annuation and Beneficent Society (accession number 1986/001, boxes 1 and
2).
[37] Methodist newspapers, like newspapers in general, are especially poorly
indexed, if at all, making obituaries or biographies difficult to locate. Obituaries were also far less a feature of nineteenth-century Methodist newspapers than they were to become in the twentieth century. At present, only *The
Watchman* newspaper is available online (on a payment basis) via
http://www.ukpressonline.co.uk.
[38] [Francis Marris Jackson], *An Index to the Memoirs, Obituary Notices and
Recent Deaths ... in the 'Arminian Magazine', 1778-1797, the 'Methodist
Magazine', 1798-1821, and the 'Wesleyan Methodist Magazine', 1822-
1839, Wesley Historical Society Proceedings*, supplement to vol. 7 (1910).
[39] Lionel Madden, *Yr Eurgrawn (Wesleyaidd), 1809-1983: mynegai i
ysgrifau am weinidogion* (Aberystwyth: Yr Eglwys Fethodistaidd,
Cymdeithas Hanes Talaith Cymru, 2006).
[40] Thomas Albin, 'An Empirical Study of Early Methodist Spirituality', in
Theodore Runyon (ed.), *Wesleyan Theology Today* (Nashville, TN: Kingswood Books, 1985), pp. 275-90.
[41] Linda Wilson, *Constrained by Zeal: Female Spirituality amongst Nonconformists, 1825-75* (Carlisle: Paternoster Press, 2000). Despite the title,
her sample of obituaries included both men and women.

them to investigate the lives of the wives of itinerant preachers between 1750 and 1880.[42]

For Wesleyan Methodist missionaries there are additionally memorials, by William Moister, of all who died in the work to 1885.[43] A long-standing component of the *Methodist Missionary Society History Project* is the production of a register of all British Methodist missionaries from 1769 to 2003, which will cover non-Wesleyan besides Wesleyan missionaries and laity as well as ministers. The database is not yet available online, but preliminary printouts can be consulted.[44]

A second tier of information, but only for Methodist ministers alive at the time of their compilation, is to be found in who's who directories. The earliest of these was *The 'Christian World' Year Book*, published between 1883 and 1886, which comprised a single alphabetical listing of Nonconformist ministers from 21 denominations in Britain and Ireland, including Wesleyan, Primitive, Free, New Connexion, Bible Christian, and Wesleyan Reform Union Methodists. It was based upon the skeletal information which responding ministers had provided to enquiries from James Clarke, the publisher.[45] Rather better known is *The Methodist Who's Who*, issued annually between 1910 and 1915 by the Wesleyan Methodist Book Room.[46] It covered all branches of British Methodism,

---

[42] Janet Kelly, 'Model Lives: the Changing Role and Experience of the Wives of Itinerant Preachers in Mainstream Methodism, 1750-1880' (unpublished PhD thesis, University of Leeds and Leeds Trinity University College, 2009); idem, 'Memorials of Motherhood: the Travels and Travails of Preachers' Wives' (Above, Chapter 7).

[43] William Moister, *Missionary Worthies* (London: T. Woolmer, 1885). An earlier edition, covering deaths to 1860, appeared as *Heralds of Salvation* (London: Wesleyan Conference Office, 1878).

[44] http://www2.div.ed.ac.uk/other/mms/mmsresearch.htm. Cf. Albert Mosley, 'The Methodist Missionary Database Project', *Wesley Historical Society West Midlands Bulletin*, vol. 9 (2011), 129-36.

[45] *The 'Christian World' Year Book* (London: James Clarke, 1883-86).

[46] *The Methodist Who's Who* (London: Robert Culley, 1910-15).

including the Wesleyan Reform Union and the Independent Methodist Church. Laymen (but virtually no women) were listed as well as ministers, in a merged alphabetical sequence, with the latter in a slight majority. Foreign missionaries were added from 1911, and Methodists from the colonies and the United States from 1912. The criteria for selection were not explained, other than that the biographees were 'prominent', nor was the response rate clarified. There were about 1,600 entries in the 1910 edition with a peak of 3,800 in both 1914 and 1915. The volume for 1915 also recorded the deaths of those included between 1910 and 1914. The First World War then put paid to the enterprise.[47]

Who's Who in Methodism followed in 1933, as a celebration of Methodist reunion, and under the aegis of the *Methodist Times and Leader*.[48] Its content was restricted to the Methodist Church in Great Britain and Ireland, and its foreign missions, with separate sections for ministers and laity. The number of ministers included, at 5,200, was very close to the actual total, but the information for some of them was fairly skeletal, probably derived from the minutes of Conference. 'Later editions' of *Who's Who in Methodism* were promised but never materialized, and it was to be 18 years before another attempt was made to compile an alphabetical directory of British Methodism's ministers and leading laity, in the Methodist part of *Who's Who in the Free Churches* (1951).[49]

---

[47] A small number of Methodists also appeared in the who's who section introduced to the *Free Church Year Book* in 1911: *Free Church Year Book & Who's Who, 1911* (London: National Council of Evangelical Free Churches, 1911), pp. 298-314. The section was only published for a few years, until 1916 (pp. 249-73), after which the *Year Book* was drastically reduced in length.

[48] *Who's Who in Methodism, 1933* (London: *Methodist Times and Leader*, 1933), pp. 1-258.

[49] Leslie Pine (ed.), *Who's Who in the Free Churches (and Other Denominations)* (London: Shaw Publishing Co., 1951), pp. 177-321.

This contained about 4,500 Methodist entries, ministers and laity combined, but a large number of the ministerial ones were very brief, often confined to contact (address and telephone) information obtained from Church sources, denoting that the individuals concerned had failed to reply to the publisher's enquiries. *Who's Who in the Free Churches* was a commercial venture, which was four years in the planning and execution. Notwithstanding expectation of a 'next edition', it was never repeated, an ostensibly successor publication, the *Free Church Directory* (issued thrice between 1965 and 1970) simply reprinting the names and addresses of Methodist ministers from the minutes of Conference.[50] Meanwhile, an American publisher had issued *Who's Who in Methodism* in 1952, but, despite the volume's professed international scope, its non-United States coverage was rather pitiful.[51] Much more ambitious in the British and Irish context was Kenneth Garlick's *Methodist Registry* of 1983, which included mini-biographies of 2,758 ministers, 78 per cent of the total at that time.[52]

Although not as comprehensive as the 'Hill's arrangement' type of listing, because they were dependent upon their subjects' co-operation, these various who's who compilations are still, so far as Methodist ministers are concerned, sufficiently broad and representative in coverage to be a suitable basis for prosopographical analysis. Other biographical reference tools, our third level of information, cannot be used in this way, being restricted to a tiny minority of the ministerial universe, and not even constituting a cross-section of it. Unlike the two other source genres, which mostly take the form of primary evidence, they may be only secondary or tertiary works. Nev-

---

[50] *Free Church Directory* (Morden: Crown House Publications, 1965-70).
[51] Elmer Clark (ed.), *Who's Who in Methodism* (Chicago, IL: A. N. Marquis, 1952).
[52] Kenneth Garlick, *Garlick's Methodist Registry, 1983* (London: Edsall, 1983).

ertheless, they may still have value in fleshing out the detail for particular individuals cited in the primary literature.

Among the secular exemplars to feature Methodists, the *Oxford Dictionary of National Biography*,[53] *Who was Who* (covering those who died from 1897),[54] and Frederic Boase's *Modern English Biography* (restricted to persons dying between 1851 and 1900)[55] are the best-known, but it is important not to overlook the *British Biographical Index*, which aggregates into a single sequence a large number of specialist topographical and/or professional who's who volumes.[56] Wales is served by a dedicated online resource,[57] while there is a printed *Dictionary of Irish Biography*.[58] Foremost of the modern religious collective biographies are the dictionaries of evangelicals edited by Donald Lewis in 1995[59] and Timothy Larsen in 2003.[60]

---

[53] Brian Harrison et al. (eds.), *Oxford Dictionary of National Biography* (60 vols., Oxford University Press, 2004-); http://www.oxforddnb.com/. Cf. John Vickers, 'Methodist Entries in the *Oxford DNB*', *Wesley Historical Society Proceedings*, vol. 57 (2009), 1-4.

[54] *Who Was Who* [1897-2005] (11 vols., London: A&C Black, 1920-2006). This is also available online, to subscribers, at http://www.oup.com/whoswho/.

[55] Frederic Boase, *Modern English Biography* (6 vols.,Truro: Netherton & Worth, 1892-1921)

[56] Tommaso Nappo, *British Biographical Index* (3rd edn., 8 vols., Munich: K. G. Saur, 2008) and *British Biographical Archive on Microfiche* (Munich: K. G. Saur, 1984-2003). This is now subsumed within the *World Biographical Information System Online*, for which see http://www.degruyter.de/cont/fb/nw/nwWbisEn.cfm.

[57] *Welsh Biography Online*, http://yba.llgc.org.uk/en/index.html.

[58] James McGuire and James Quinn (eds.), *Dictionary of Irish Biography* (9 vols., Cambridge: Cambridge University Press, 2009). The 78 Methodist-related entries are identified in *Wesley Historical Society in Ireland Archives & Study Centre Newsletter*, no. 6 (Spring, 2010), 7.

[59] Donald Lewis (ed.), *The Blackwell Dictionary of Evangelical Biography, 1730-1860* (2 vols., Oxford: Blackwell, 1995).

[60] Timothy Larsen (ed.), *Biographical Dictionary of Evangelicals* (Leicester: Inter-Varsity Press, 2003).

For Methodism alone, *The Encyclopedia of World Methodism*[61] and, especially, *A Dictionary of Methodism in Britain and Ireland* (which has over 2,400 person entries)[62] are indispensable general sources of biographical data, while the online *Methodist Archives Biographical Index* is also worth noting.[63] More focused and recently-published Methodist collective biographies include those by Samuel Rogal on the eighteenth century[64] and William Leary on Lincolnshire.[65] Older compilations can sometimes have continuing value but, through authorial bias, may not always offer balanced perspectives. In Wesleyan Methodism *The Lives of Early Methodist Preachers*, which is mainly autobiographical, is much-quarried,[66] with other accounts of ministers appearing in James Everett's *Wesleyan Takings* (1840-51),[67] Robert West's

---

[61] Nolan Harmon (ed.), *The Encyclopedia of World Methodism* (2 vols., Nashville, TN: United Methodist Publishing House, 1974).

[62] John Vickers (ed.), *A Dictionary of Methodism in Britain and Ireland* (Peterborough: Epworth Press, 2000) and, in a greatly expanded edition, at http://dmbi.wesleyhistorical society.org.uk. Cf. Lionel Madden, 'A Dictionary of Methodism Online', *Cylchgrawn Hanes*, vol. 33 (2009), 187-94.

[63] Gareth Lloyd, *The Methodist Archives Biographical Index*, http://www.library.manchester.ac.uk/searchresources/guidetospecialcollecti ons/methodist/using/biographicalindex/

[64] Samuel Rogal, *A Biographical Dictionary of 18th Century Methodism* (10 vols., Lewiston, NY: Edwin Mellen Press, 1997-99).

[65] William Leary, *Some Lincolnshire Methodists* (Loughborough: Teamprint, 1998); idem, *Musical Methodists in Lincolnshire* (Loughborough: Teamprint, 1999); idem, *The Early Methodist People of Lincolnshire* (Loughborough: printed by Teamprint, 2000); idem, *For All the Saints: Lincolnshire Methodists of the Twentieth Century* (Loughborough: printed by Teamprint, 2000); idem, *Lincolnshire Born Methodist Ministers* (Loughborough: printed by Teamprint, 2001).

[66] Thomas Jackson, *The Lives of Early Methodist Preachers* (3rd edn., 6 vols., London: Wesleyan Conference Office, 1865-66).

[67] [James Everett], *Wesleyan Takings; or, Centenary Sketches of Ministerial Character* (2 vols., London: Hamilton, Adams & Co., 1840-51).

Clive D. Field, Methodist Prosopography

Sketches of Wesleyan Preachers (1849),[68] and *Wesley and His Successors* (1891),[69] also in John Jones (1866)[70] and John Davies (1884)[71] on Welsh Wesleyanism.[72]

The Primitive Methodist equivalents are by Edward Barrass (1853),[73] George Herod (1855),[74] F. H. Hurd (1872),[75] Samuel Smith (1872),[76] Joseph Pearce (1932-35),[77] and Arthur Wilkes and Joseph Lovatt (1942),[78] with a further volume of obituaries of ministers who died between the Conferences

---

[68] Robert West, *Sketches of Wesleyan Preachers* (London: Simpkin, Marshall & Co., 1849).

[69] *Wesley and his Successors* (London: Charles H. Kelly, 1891).

[70] John Jones, *Y Bywgraffydd Wesleyaidd* (Machynlleth: J. Williams, 1866).

[71] John Davies, *Pregethau yr Uwchrifiaid Wesleyaidd Cymreig yn 1881-82* (Machynlleth: Adam Evans, 1884). This comprises sermons by supernumeraries, preceded by short autobiographies.

[72] It should be noted that sketches of only two Welsh Wesleyan ministers are included in John Vyrnwy Morgan (ed.), *Welsh Religious Leaders in the Victorian Era* (London: James Nisbet, 1905), at pp. 391-443.

[73] Edward Barrass, *A Gallery of Deceased Ministers* (London: T. Holliday, 1853). Described as vol. 1, but no further volumes appear to have been published.

[74] George Herod, *Biographical Sketches of Some of those Preachers Whose Labours Contributed to the Origination and Early Extension of the Primitive Methodist Connexion* (London: T. King, [1855]).

[75] F. H. Hurd, *Earnest Men: Sketches of Eminent Primitive Methodists* (London: F. H. Hurd, 1872).

[76] Samuel Smith, *Anecdotes, Facts and Biographical Sketches Connected with the Great Revival of the Work of God in Raising up and Progressing the Primitive Methodist Connexion* (Douglas, Isle of Man: Matthew Glover, 1872).

[77] Joseph Pearce, *Dinna Forget: a Souvenir of Primitive Methodist Soul-Winning Personalities* (Leominster: Orphans' Printing Press, 1932) and *Burning and Shining Lights: a Souvenir of Primitive Methodist Radiant Personalities* (Halesowen: H. Parkes, 1935).

[78] Arthur Wilkes and Joseph Lovatt, *Mow Cop and the Camp Meeting Movement: Sketches of Primitive Methodism* (Leominster: Orphans' Printing Press, [1942]).

of 1888 and 1889.[79] For the various branches of United Methodism there was a *Ministerial Portrait Gallery of the United Methodist Free Churches* in 1860,[80] Henry Smith's sketches of Methodist New Connexion ministers (1893),[81] and William Michell's biographies of Bible Christian ministers and laymen (1906).[82] The principal inter-Methodist enterprise was George Stevenson's multi-volume *Methodist Worthies* (1884-86).[83]

This three-fold typology of biographical data naturally does not hold good for the laity. Clearly, no single source, or set of sources, can offer a systematic inventory of all the millions of people who have been members of, or worshipped with, Methodism since its origins. While several of the biographical reference works, of the sort we have just mentioned in connection with the ministry, feature some lay Methodists, the number of entries is relatively few and usually restricted to those who played a role in connexional affairs, almost by definition excluding women until comparatively recent times.[84] Other modern reference tools useful for following up Methodist laity who contributed to national life *beyond* Methodism

---

[79] William Brownson, John Gair, Thomas Mitchell and David Prosser, *Heroic Men: The Death Roll of the Primitive Methodist Ministry* (London: Joseph Toulson, [1889]).
[80] *Ministerial Portrait Gallery of the United Methodist Free Churches* (Manchester: John Heywood, [1860]).
[81] Henry Smith, *Sketches of Eminent Methodist New Connexion Ministers* (London: J. C. Watts, [1893]).
[82] William Michell, *Brief Biographical Sketches of Bible Christian Ministers and Laymen* (2 vols., Jersey: Beresford Press, 1906).
[83] George J. Stevenson, *Methodist Worthies: Characteristic Sketches of Methodist Preachers of the Several Denominations* (6 vols., London: Thomas C. Jack, 1884-86).
[84] There is, of course, quite an extensive modern secondary literature, by Paul Chilcote and others, on the contribution which a select band of women made to the formative years of Methodism. This is too voluminous to list here. The classic study is Zechariah Taft, *Biographical Sketches of the Lives and Public Ministry of Various Holy Women* (2 vols., London: published for the author, 1825-28).

comprise *Dictionary of Labour Biography*,[85] *Dictionary of British Temperance Biography*,[86] *Who's Who of British Members of Parliament*,[87] *Biographical Dictionary of Modern British Radicals*,[88] and *Dictionary of Business Biography*.[89] David Jeremy, editor of the last-named project, has used it as the basis for prosopographical research into Methodist business leaders,[90] while Geoffrey Milburn attempted a similar but

---

[85] Joyce Bellamy and John Saville (eds), *Dictionary of Labour Biography* (12 vols., London: Macmillan, 1972-2005).

[86] Brian Harrison, *Dictionary of British Temperance Biography* (Coventry: Society for the Study of Labour History, 1973).

[87] Michael Stenton, *Who's Who of British Members of Parliament* (4 vols., Hassocks: Harvester Press, 1978-81). Even more detailed biographies of Members of Parliament for 1832-1945 are in the process of preparation by the History of Parliament Trust; its volumes for 1660-1832 are already available – see http://www.histparl.ac.uk

[88] Joseph Baylen and Norbert Gossman (eds.), *Biographical Dictionary of Modern British Radicals* (3 vols., Hassocks: Harvester Press, 1979-88).

[89] David J. Jeremy and Christine Shaw (eds.), *Dictionary of Business Biography* (5 vols. and supplement, London: Butterworths, 1984-86).

[90] For example, David J. Jeremy, 'Religious Links of Individuals Listed in the *Dictionary of Business Biography*', in David J. Jeremy (ed.), *Business and Religion in Britain* (Aldershot: Gower, 1988), pp. 188-205; idem, *Capitalists and Christians: Business Leaders and the Churches in Britain, 1900-1960* (Oxford: Clarendon Press, 1990); idem, 'Late-Victorian and Edwardian Methodist Businessmen and Wealth', in David J. Jeremy (ed.), *Religion, Business and Wealth in Modern Britain* (London: Routledge, 1998), pp. 71-85; idem, 'Businessmen as Preachers among Methodists in the Early Twentieth Century', in Anthony Cross (ed.), *Ecumenism and History* (Carlisle: Paternoster Press, 2002), pp. 302-25; idem, 'Twentieth-century Protestant Nonconformists in the World of Business', in Alan Sell and Anthony Cross (eds.), *Protestant Nonconformity in the Twentieth Century* (Carlisle: Paternoster Press, 2003), pp. 264-312; idem, 'Methodists and Business, 1860-1960' in William Gibson, Peter Forsaith, and Martin Wellings (eds.), *The Ashgate Research Companion to World Methodism* (Farnham, Surrey, 2013), pp. 431-60; idem,' Nonconformist Business Leaders, ca 1880-1940: the Uses and Abuses of Wealth', in Robert Pope (ed.), *T&T Clark Companion to Nonconformity* (London: T&T Clark, 2013), pp. 407-36.

independent enterprise for the North-East.[91] Clive Field mined these and other business sources to document Methodist involvement in the building society movement.[92] Among older collective biographies of continuing value for the laity are Peter Winskill's *Temperance Standard Bearers* (1897-98)[93] and Charles Howes's *Free Church Musicians* (1909).[94]

Who's who-type publications reach a broader circle of Methodist laity, including many active in chapel and circuit affairs, but they still constitute something of an elite and are largely office-holders in some shape or form. Other than a survey in *The Watchman* of the first lay representatives to the Wesleyan Conference in 1878,[95] nothing substantive appears to exist for the nineteenth century. For the early twentieth century *The Methodist Who's Who* and, particularly, *Who's Who in Methodism* (which lists about 4,000 'lay officers')[96] are invaluable. There was also *The Methodist Local Preachers' Who's Who, 1934*, a commercial venture.[97] This volume purported to offer 'a complete record of the lives and careers of Methodist local preachers', although it actually contained the

---

[91] Geoffrey Milburn, 'Piety, Profit and Paternalism: Methodists in Business in the North-East of England, *c*. 1760-1920', *Wesley Historical Society Proceedings*, vol. 44, no. 3 (December, 1983), 45-92 (including, at 70-92, a biographical appendix).

[92] Clive Field, 'Safe as Houses: Methodism and the Building Society Movement in England and Wales', in Peter Forsaith and Martin Wellings (eds.), *Methodism and History* (Oxford: Applied Theology Press, 2010), pp. 91-139.

[93] Peter Winskill, *Temperance Standard Bearers of the Nineteenth Century* (2 vols., Manchester: printed by Darrah Bros., 1897-98). There is also extensive biographical information in the same author's *The Temperance Movement and its Workers* (4 vols., London: Blackie & Son, 1891-92).

[94] Charles Howes, *Free Church Musicians* (London: Novello, [1909]).

[95] *The Watchman and Wesleyan Advertiser*, 24 July 1878, 241; 31 July 1878, 249; 7 August 1878, 253; 14 August 1878, 267.

[96] *Who's Who in Methodism, 1933*, pp. 259-433.

[97] *The Methodist Local Preachers' Who's Who, 1934* (London: Shaw Publishing Co., 1934).

names and particulars of the 21,100 local preachers (20,660 accredited and 440 on trial) who had eventually (after three reminders) taken the trouble to complete the publisher's postal questionnaire, a response rate of 57 per cent. Non-respondents appear to have disproportionately been ex-Primitive Methodists. As will be discussed later, the present author drew a 5 per cent random sample of entries to construct a prosopography of Methodist local preachers in the aftermath of the 1932 reunion, with special reference to occupation.[98] John Lenton has also used it as a key source in tracing Wesleyan female preachers.[99] Apart from two late-Victorian anthologies,[100] and a few volumes of contemporary reminiscences,[101] there is little else by way of collective biographies of local preachers, while circuit plans are mainly of use for the aggregative analysis of their deployment.[102] For Methodist women there is a

---

[98] Clive Field, 'The Methodist Local Preacher: an Occupational Analysis', in Geoffrey Milburn and Margaret Batty (eds.), *Workaday Preachers: The Story of Methodist Local Preaching* (Peterborough: Methodist Publishing House, 1995), pp. 223-42, 324-27, especially 231-35, 240-42.

[99] John Lenton, '"Labouring for the Lord": Women Preachers in Wesleyan Methodism, 1802-1932 – a Revisionist View', in Richard Sykes (ed.), *Beyond the Boundaries: Preaching in the Wesleyan Tradition* (Oxford: Applied Theology Press, 1998), pp. 58-86. Cf. Lenton, 'East Anglian women Wesleyan Methodist preachers to 1910', *Wesley Historical Society East Anglia District Journal*, no. 112 (Winter, 2008), 1-10 and idem, 'Support Groups for Methodist Women Preachers, 1803-1851', in Geordan Hammond and Peter Forsaith (eds.), *Religion, Gender and Industry: Exploring Church and Methodism in a Local Setting* (Eugene, OR: Pickwick Publications, 2011), pp. 137-55.

[100] [William Lawson], *Wesleyan Local Preachers* (Newcastle-upon-Tyne: William D. Lawson, 1874); and David Whiteley (ed.), *Illustrious Local Preachers* (Bradford: Thornton & Pearson, 1891).

[101] For example, Angela Davis (ed.), *Called to Preach: Local Preachers in Cornwall and their Testimonies* (Truro: Southleigh Publications, 1995).

[102] The only national listing, now out of date, is Alan Rose, *A Register of Methodist Circuit Plans, 1777-1860* [with supplements to 1907] (6 vols., [Manchester]: Society of Cirplanologists, 1961-80). There are also a few county listings.

simple listing of all the Sisters of the National Children's Home between 1875 and 1985, with year of 'ordination',[103] with Dorothy Graham's directory of Methodist deaconesses a forthcoming Wesley Historical Society publication.

There are extensive records of chapel trustees, especially in the Chancery Close Rolls at The National Archives,[104] but, notwithstanding multiple instances of their use for the analysis of Methodist social status (such as by Rodney Ambler for Lincolnshire),[105] the nature of the functions and obligations of trustees means that they will not have been typical of ordinary chapelgoers. Much the same will have been true of lay signatories of Methodist returns in the 1851 religious census, recently examined by Kate Tiller for Berkshire.[106] They perhaps tell us something about the background of local Methodist leadership but cannot be taken as proxies for the rank-and-file. A similar limitation applies to nineteenth-century printed Methodist donation lists;[107] inevitably biased towards wealthier Methodists, they are generally less useful for prosopographical than genealogical purposes. The best-known of

---

[103] Alan Hamblin, *Alverstoke* (Kings Langley: printed by Alpine Press, 2011), pp. 33-50.

[104] The National Archives, C 54, J 18. Cf. Edwin Welch, 'Nonconformist Trust Deeds', *Journal of the Society of Archivists*, vol. 3, no. 8 (1968), 397-403; Rodney Ambler, 'Enrolled Trust Deeds: a Source for the History of Nineteenth-century Nonconformity', *Archives*, vol. 20, no. 90 (October, 1993), 177-86.

[105] Rodney Ambler, 'The Social Composition of Church Leadership: Nonconformist Trustees in Lincolnshire, 1800-1870', *Bulletin of the John Rylands University Library of Manchester*, vol. 75, no. 1 (Spring, 1993), 133-56.

[106] Kate Tiller, 'Chapel People in 1851: the Example of Berkshire', in Chris Skidmore (ed.), *Chapels and Chapel People* (Chapels Society Occasional Publications, 5, London: the Society, 2010), pp. 1-12.

[107] John Lenton, 'Sources for the History of British and Irish Methodism and Genealogy: Some Printed Donation Lists', *Wesley Historical Society Proceedings*, vol. 55, no. 2 (May, 2005), 43-52 and idem, 'More Information on Methodist Donation Lists', *Wesley Historical Society Proceedings*, vol. 55, no. 3 (October, 2005), 121-22.

these is the Wesleyan Twentieth Century Fund,[108] some local sections of which are available in print, microfiche or CD-ROM.[109] Registers of pupils at the various Methodist residential schools will be equally socially unrepresentative.[110] Of course, this is not to deny the value of elite Methodist prosopography, in its own right, a striking example of which exists in David Jeremy's group profiles of Vice-Presidents of the Primitive Methodist Church and the Methodist Church.[111]

For collective investigation of the lives of 'ordinary' lay Methodists, we must look elsewhere. Until the 1830s membership registers are a major source, while not forgetting that members would have been heavily outnumbered at this time by non-member adherents. The present author has studied these early membership registers most systematically, from the point of view of gender, marital status and (until 1800, when this information ceases) occupation.[112] Thereafter, far

---

[108] Richard Ratcliffe, *Basic Facts about the Wesleyan Methodist Historic Roll* (Bury: Federation of Family History Societies Publications, 2005).

[109] Online genealogy stores offer the best means of identifying the sections which have been transcribed, in particular http://www.genfair.co.uk/ and http://www.parishchest.com/

[110] Some of these are published, in a variety of formats. For instance, the retrospective register of Kingswood School was originally printed in 1898, as a supplement to the history of the school by Arthur Hastling, Walter Addington and Walter Workman; further editions were then issued in 1910, 1923 and 1952 (taking the record to 1950). In the case of the Leys School, lists of Old Leysians are included in a *Handbook and Directory* which has appeared every few years since 1884, the latest in 2009. For other schools, the record may be embedded in the school's published history, as with Josiah Slugg, *Woodhouse Grove School: Memorials and Reminiscences* (London: T. Woolmer, 1885), pp. 237-329.

[111] David J. Jeremy, 'Laity in Denominational Leadership: Vice-Presidents of the Primitive Methodist Church, 1872-1932', *Wesley Historical Society Proceedings*, vol. 57 (2010), 246-72; and idem, 'Laity in Denominational Leadership: Methodist Vice-Presidents, 1932-2000', *Wesley Historical Society Proceedings*, vol. 58 (2011), 12-33.

[112] Clive Field, 'The Social Composition of English Methodism to 1830: a Membership Analysis', *Bulletin of the John Rylands University Library of*

fewer lists of members have survived, and alternative sources have to be explored, especially for social status. Baptismal registers fill the gap for the Wesleyans between the 1790s and 1837 (when the denomination introduced a new form of register, with no column for occupation) and, in the case of Primitive Methodism, often right up to Methodist reunion in 1932. In recent years, these manuscript documents have increasingly been transcribed through local efforts and made available in surrogate form, either in print, on microfiche or on CD-ROM.[113] The occupational content of the pre-1837 Methodist registers for England and Wales has been comprehensively tabulated on a county basis by Michael Watts, for Wesleyan, Primitive Methodist, Methodist New Connexion, Bible Christian, and Methodist Unitarian traditions.[114]

Occupational data are also recorded in Methodist marriage registers, which commence in some cases from 1837, although it was not until after the First World War that most Methodists married in chapel and the majority of Methodist chapels became licensed to conduct weddings. In part, this reflects a continuing tendency of, in particular, Wesleyan Methodists to look to the Church of England to provide the rites of passage. It is also the case that, in both baptismal and marriage registers, the strength of the parties' affiliations with Methodism would have been variable. The later baptismal and marital evidence for Methodist social status has again been synthesized by Field.[115] Despite deficiencies, this still represents a sounder and more cost-effective methodology for gauging Methodism's occupational profile than the hugely

---

Manchester, vol. 76, no. 1 (Spring, 1994), 153-78, summarized in Field, 'Zion's People: Who Were the English Nonconformists?', *Local Historian*, vol. 40 (2010), 96-97, 104 and vol. 40 (2010), 292-93.

[113] Again, online genealogy stores offer the best means of identifying the registers which have been transcribed. See n. 109.

[114] Michael Watts, *The Dissenters, Volume II: the Expansion of Evangelical Nonconformity* (Oxford: Clarendon Press, 1995), pp. 718-88.

[115] Field, 'Zion's People', pp. 293-300.

labour-intensive nominal linkage alternative, which involves the matching of names in Methodist sources with household schedules in the decennial population census. That said, the census naturally permits correlations with a potentially wider range of demographic factors than just occupation. Barry Biggs was one of the first Methodist historians to make use of the civil census (for 1841 and 1851) in building up his Methodist Personnel Index for North Nottinghamshire in the early nineteenth century.[116]

Additional sources open up for the prosopography of the twentieth-century Methodist laity, including a Conference roll of honour of Wesleyan armed service deaths during the First World War.[117] Life stories and oral history are naturally also important, and there has been significant (but frequently uncoordinated) effort since the 1970s to record the reminiscences of elderly Methodists, with much Methodist audio material now available at the British Library and in local audio-visual archives.[118] However, apart from the limitation of being generally confined to lifelong Methodists (as opposed to those whose attachment was more transitory), this evidence is mostly of a qualitative nature, and highly specific to the individual subject, making it an uncertain basis for producing corporate profiles. Some time ago, the present writer tried the alternative approach of using self-completion questionnaires to collect more structured information about Methodist home and congregational life between 1900 and 1932, from a broad (but

---

[116] Barry Biggs, 'Methodism in a Rural Society: North Nottinghamshire, 1740-1851' (PhD thesis, University of Nottingham, 1975).
[117] *Roll of Honour and Memorial Service for Methodist Sailors and Soldiers* (4 vols., London: Methodist Publishing House, 1915-[20]). Cf. Clive Field, 'Remembering Methodism's Great War Dead', 2012, http://www.mymethodisthistory.org.uk/page_id__43_path__0p24p25p.aspx
[118] Regrettably, there is currently no national union catalogue of audio-visual material in the British Isles. However, the Religious Archives Group is planning to work with The British Library and The National Archives in carrying out a survey of religion-related oral history collections.

still not scientifically-drawn random or quota) sample of 33
ministers and 73 laity. Respondents were, in effect, asked to
act as proxies for their peers, as well as providing information
about themselves, and this permitted a degree of generaliza-
tion and quantification, which we will explore further later.[119]

This experiment has never really been built upon in an oral
historical sense, but there have certainly been some social
surveys undertaken among Methodists, which report results in
an anonymized and aggregated fashion (data protection legis-
lation obviously being a constraint in studying living individuals). Many of these have been of a local nature, since the
numerical decline of Methodism has meant that, in most representative samples of the adult population, Methodists will
be too few to warrant independent analysis. The principal exception to this has been a recent pooling of data from the British Social Attitudes Surveys for 1983-2008, which has permitted a group portrait of professing Methodist laity in respect of
gender, age, marital status, ethnicity, education, social class,
and housing tenure.[120] The British Religion in Numbers
source database[121] is a useful initial guide to Methodist surveys, some of which deal with the Methodist laity (including a
large-scale study of local preachers by John Sawkins in
2000)[122] and others with the ministry (such as John Haley's

---

[119] Clive Field, 'A Sociological Profile of English Methodism, 1900-1932',
Oral History, vol. 4 (1976), 73-95. More qualitative and unstructured information was also collected, a selection of which was published in Field,
'Vignettes of London Methodism in the Early Twentieth Century', *Wesley
Historical Society London and South East Branch Journal*, no. 77 (2008), 6-
19 and no. 78 (2008), 12-22.
[120] Clive Field, 'The People Called Methodists Today: Statistical Insights
from the Social Sciences', *Epworth Review*, vol. 36 (2009), 16-29. Cf.
Field, 'Zion's People', pp. 99-100, 102-3, 105-8, 300-2.
[121] http://www.brin.ac.uk/sources/
[122] *Over to You, 2002: Reports from Conference, 2002* (Peterborough:
Methodist Publishing House, 2002), pp. 57-73; John Sawkins and Margaret
Batty, 'Methodist Local Preachers in Great Britain: a Millennial Profile',
Epworth Review, vol. 29 (2002), 48-55.

survey of 1997).[123] A more contemporary example is the profile by gender, age, ethnicity, and disability of presbyterial and lay delegates to the 2010 Methodist Conference.[124]

2 CASE STUDIES OF METHODIST PROSOPOGRAPHY

In the second half of this paper, an attempt will be made to demonstrate how prosopographical techniques can transform our understanding of British Methodist history. Four complementary case studies will be discussed, each relating to the opening decades of the twentieth century. Although these research projects were actually completed some considerable time ago, their findings have only been partially reported before.

Our first case study, which examines afresh the evidence about Methodism before the 1932 reunion provided by 106 elderly Methodists in the early 1970s,[125] reveals the centrality of the chapel to everyday life. Sunday was a day generally kept apart for religious worship, with many secular activities taboo, especially games and sport (which were banned from 71 per cent of Methodist households). Most committed Methodists would have attended services each Sunday, with 'twicing' (attendance in both morning and evening) widespread. However, the size of congregations did vary somewhat week-by-week, the holiday season, bad weather and (in urban chapels) the planning of a local preacher usually causing decreases and visiting ministers or special services an in-

---

[123] John Haley and Leslie Francis, *British Methodism: What Circuit Ministers Really Think* (Peterborough: Epworth, 2006).
[124] http://www.methodist.org.uk/downloads/stats-Demographics-of-Representatives-Attending-Conference-2010-0910.pdf.
[125] This section draws on the author's unpublished tabulations and analyses which underpin Field, 'A Sociological Profile of English Methodism, 1900-1932', pp. 73-95.

crease. Sermons and hymns were the most popular components of worship, well ahead of prayer and scripture-reading. Many Methodists were additionally involved in teaching in Sunday school or attending prayer meetings, Bible classes or Pleasant Sunday Afternoon meetings, making Methodism a full-time Sunday occupation for a very large number.

During the week, there was a plethora of religious and social activities at the chapel, notwithstanding the progressive decline of the class meeting, whose slow demise commenced well before the First World War. It was a very common occurrence for Methodists to be at the chapel on two or three weekday evenings, and for most friendships, particularly for the young, to be based on the chapel circle.[126] As one veteran recalled, it was 'the pivot around which their life revolved', secular alternatives (such as theatres, cinemas, dance-halls, and – of course – public houses) still being viewed with some suspicion. Attachment to the chapel was also far stronger than to the circuit, with connexional affairs attracting limited interest, sometimes regarded 'as giving an opportunity to place seekers'. Fellowship, religious and social, was identified by this sample as by far the single most distinctive and attractive feature of Methodism.

Pre-union Methodism was thus 'rather clannish' in nature, as one Wesleyan minister expressed it. It was similarly quite ancestral. Although there were several recruitment pathways, the children of Methodist parents were the preponderant one, Sunday Schools suffering a high rate of leakage. Seven-tenths of respondents cited birth and upbringing as their principal reason for being Methodist. More than four-fifths of this sample and their parents were nurtured in Methodism, with a similar proportion marrying fellow Methodists. In roughly

---

[126] For an illustration of the centrality of Methodist chapel life during the inter-war period, see Lily Field, *Lutonian Odyssey: Reminiscences of Lily Field for 1915-52*, ed. Clive Field (Birmingham: the editor, 2008), pp. 46-56.

two cases in every three there was even continuity within the same pre-union branch of Methodism. While nine in ten had supported Methodist union, this was often for reasons of pragmatism or inevitability, rather than out of genuine enthusiasm, 'somewhat apathetically with the head but hardly at all with the heart', as one Primitive Methodist reminisced. Unsurprisingly, three-fifths reported some disillusionment with the outcomes of Methodist union.

Recruitment from other Christian denominations was confined to the Free Churches, usually in connection with removals, and the Church of England, but relations with the latter were not especially close, neutrality being the normative outlook on Anglicans. Some blamed this stand-off on Anglican arrogance: 'Primitive Methodists were frowned on by the Church of England parson who used to say going to chapel was like going to heaven in a muck cart, but going to the Church of England was like going to heaven in a chariot'. At least this position was better than in the case of Roman Catholicism, where there were few signs of friendliness and more hostility than neutrality. Catholics were remembered by these elderly Methodists as beyond the pale, sometimes as not true Christians. Genuine converts from the outside world were very few indeed, apart from in some central missions, and could often fall away quite quickly.

This dependence upon autogenous growth (from children of the church), as distinct from allogenous or conversion growth, forms the link to our second case study, which is, in turn, a component of a preliminary investigation into Methodist demography.[127] The subject has both intrinsic interest and relevance as a potential explanation for the numerical decline

---

[127] This section draws upon the initial research by Field, 'Methodism in Metropolitan London', pp. 275-93 and upon subsequent extended research reported in the first two of the author's trilogy of articles on 'Demography and the Decline of British Methodism', *Wesley Historical Society Proceedings*, vol. 58 (2012), 175-89, 200-15.

of British Methodism in the twentieth century. In circumstances where recruitment had become so internalized, it is
naturally important to understand the extent to which Methodists got married and raised children, thus helping to perpetuate
institutional Methodism. Evidence for this was sought by constructing a national sample of male Methodists (the sources
used included insufficient women for study). This was necessarily an elite sample, of ministers and lay office-holders (in
roughly equal numbers), and therefore cannot be claimed to
be statistically representative of worshippers in the pews.

The sample comprised persons alive in 1913 (practically
all entries in that year's edition of *The Methodist Who's Who*),
1933 (all entries for surnames A-G inclusive in both ministerial and lay sections of *Who's Who in Methodism*), and 1934
(a booster sample of 250 local preachers drawn from *The
Methodist Local Preachers' Who's Who*). In all, data were
manually processed for 3,660 individuals, mostly born between 1831 and 1890, with analysis by ecclesiastical status
(ministers or laymen), pre-union Methodist denomination
(Wesleyan, Primitive or United), and (for the laity) social
class. Social class breakdowns had to be limited to Registrar
General's groups I-III, corresponding to non-manual and
skilled manual workers, since the who's whos listed only a
handful of semi-skilled or unskilled manual workers (classes
IV and V, respectively). However, since the backbone of
Methodist congregations at this time was provided by classes
II and III combined,[128] this is not necessarily so great a draw-
back as might be imagined.

The data revealed that Methodists of these generations
overwhelmingly got married. Just 3.0 per cent of ministers
and 3.5 per cent of laymen appear not to have done so, about
one-third of the figure for all males aged 45-54 in the civil
censuses. United Methodists were more likely to stay single

---

[128] Field, 'Zion's People', pp. 294-300, 305.

265

than either Wesleyan or Primitive Methodists, while for ministers the proportion of unmarried rose somewhat between the 1831-50 and 1871-90 birth cohorts and for the laity it peaked in social class I (professional and higher managerial staff, at 4.9 per cent). Of those Methodists who did marry, about one in eight (12.3 per cent of ministers and 13.4 per cent of laymen) never had children, even taking account of children who had pre-deceased their parents by 1913 and 1933-34. This was a somewhat higher ratio than in society at large. There was no obvious pattern by Methodist denomination, but among the laity the figure was higher in social classes I and II than in III (routine non-manual and skilled manual workers). Age cohort also made a difference: for ministers the percentage of infertile marriages rose from 8.5 in 1831-50 to 15.0 in 1871-90, the increase for the laity being from 9.6 to 14.9 per cent.

Across the entire sample, mean Methodist family size generally halved between the 1831-40 birth cohort of fathers and that for 1881-90, the last to be considered in the analysis (to minimize the risk of distortion arising from the inclusion of families which were still incomplete in 1913 and 1933-34). For instance, ministers born in 1831-40 had an average of 4.38 children, but their successor cohort of 1881-90 had only 1.93. Similarly, lay Methodists born between 1831 and 1850 had 4.49 children each, and those born in the 1880s had 1.94. This reduction in Methodist fertility was visible in each of the denominations and all social classes. Among ministers Wesleyans had the most children and United Methodists the least, but the gap closed over time, from 0.73 in 1831-50 to 0.34 for the 1871-90 birth cohort. For laity, Primitive Methodists had the most children throughout and United Methodists the fewest until 1870 and the Wesleyans thereafter, the denominational gap reducing from 1.60 to 0.39 between 1831-50 and 1871-90. Primitive Methodist laymen consistently had larger families than their ministers, but there was no such trend in Wesleyanism. Family size fell in direct relationship to a rise in occupational status. Methodists in class I had the fewest children and, in this sample (which excluded classes IV and V), class III the most, although the difference narrowed from 1.05 in the 1831-50 birth cohort to 0.43 in 1871-90.

This halving of Methodist family size in the space of sixty years largely mirrored what was happening in the population as a whole, so might be dismissed as unremarkable. On the other hand, Methodists in this particular sample always had fewer children than the national average, one less by the 1881-90 birth cohort and one and a half for laity born in the 1830s and 1840s. Nor is the variation explicable by the disproportionate concentration of Methodists in the higher classes of society by the early twentieth century and the relative absence of classes IV and V, which had the greatest fertility. Even within the same social class Methodists had smaller families than the norm. The cause is partly to be found in the pursuit of prudence and responsibility in Methodist family life. Perhaps in response to the Church's informal social teaching, Methodists postponed marriage (as a separate analysis of marriage registers demonstrated) and delayed raising a family until they were economically able to support first a wife and then children. Contemporary calculations showed that family size was reduced by 0.25 to 0.33 children for each year that a marriage was postponed. However, there are also suspicions that Methodists may have increasingly been practising family limitation, whether by natural (including self-restraint) or artificial means, albeit the evidence is fragmentary. Certainly, by the 1930s there are clear signs of liberalizing attitudes in Methodism on the subject of birth control, fuelled in some measure by Leslie Weatherhead's hugely successful book on *The Mastery of Sex* (1931). But, whatever the reasons, Methodists were clearly having fewer children, and this impacted negatively on their ability to sustain membership levels in the Methodist Church.

Our third case study focuses on Methodist local preachers, revisiting the 5 per cent random sample (corresponding to 1,055 individuals) from *The Methodist Local Preachers' Who's Who* (1934), to which reference has already been made. Although the occupational data have been printed in some detail,[129] those for the twenty-one other variables which were recorded have remained unpublished, and a selection of results will help to give a better feel for the attributes of British Methodist local preachers in the 1930s.

Only 5 per cent of the sample were women, a fraction more than in the connexional return of local preachers for the year, despite the significant female majority in most Methodist congregations. Of those who gave their ages, 30 per cent were under forty, 34 per cent in their forties or fifties, and 36 per cent over sixty (including 16 per cent over seventy). The majority (84 per cent) was married or widowed and 16 per cent single. Of the married, 21 per cent had no children, 53 per cent between one and three, and 26 per cent four or over. Rather more than two-thirds (68 per cent) had only been educated to elementary level, with 16 per cent to secondary level, 8 per cent at college, 5 per cent at university, and 3 per cent privately. Social class background was more elevated than for the male population generally, with 83 per cent (21 per cent above the norm) belonging to Registrar General groups II and III, comprising intermediate and skilled occupations. Dealers or retailers (12 per cent) and farmers (8 per cent) particularly stood out. If telephone ownership was one mark of affluence, then the social advancement of Methodist local preachers still had some way to go: just 11 per cent were on the telephone in 1934.

Ninety-eight per cent of these local preachers were on full plan and 2 per cent on trial. Of the fully accredited, 12 per

---

[129] This section draws on the author's unpublished tabulations and analyses which underpin Field, 'The Methodist Local Preacher', pp. 231-35, 240-42.

cent had been appointed in their teens, 59 per cent in their twenties, 19 per cent in their thirties, 7 per cent in their forties, and 4 per cent in later life. Twenty-four per cent had served for less than ten years, 21 per cent from 10 to 19 years, 17 per cent each for 20-29 or 30-39 years, 14 per cent for 40-49 years, and 8 per cent for 50 years or more. Virtually all had combined local preaching with one or more other church offices at some stage in their religious life, the positions most often cited being Sunday School teacher (49 per cent), trustee (31 per cent), class leader (23 per cent), society steward (22 per cent), Wesley Guild or Christian Endeavour leader (16 per cent), circuit steward (11 per cent), and chapel steward (8 per cent). Surprisingly, given this huge commitment of time and effort to local Methodism, one-quarter still found the energy for some form of public office, about half of these as a local government councillor, at parish, district, borough or county levels. Other common offices held were school governorships and justice of the peace. Information was also captured on leisure interests, with gardening, cricket, and reading being most frequently mentioned in a predictably varied list.

Six per cent of this 1934 sample of local preachers comprised teachers or lecturers, a proportion which, if anything, has grown since, partly in response to the rising number of female lay preachers.[130] Through the Wesleyan tradition, Methodism has maintained its own schools and training colleges, and this prompted the present writer to investigate (as our fourth case study) the prosopographical potential of the registers of male Wesleyan schoolteachers trained at the Glasgow Normal Seminary and at Westminster College in the later nineteenth and early twentieth centuries (women were excluded because the convention was for them to withdraw from the profession on marriage).[131] This endeavour was not wholly

---

[130] Ibid., pp. 237-38.
[131] Oxford, Oxford Centre for Methodism and Church History, Oxford Brookes University, Westminster College Archives [WCA], B/1.

satisfactory, since there are some gaps in the registers and, more importantly, the authorities of Westminster College had variable success in keeping track of their students' careers subsequent to leaving college – a familiar problem in alumni management today. For example, one of the author's aspirations had been to use this community of 'graduands'[132] as a basis for analysing Methodist longevity, but this was frustrated by the almost total absence of birth dates (which could not have been guessed with sufficient accuracy, since students served pupil-teacher apprenticeships in elementary schools before going to college), and the minority recording of years of death (for example, in only 35 per cent of cases for entrants between 1841 and 1860). In the end, no useful conclusions could be reached about this aspect of Methodist demography from the available data, other than for the rather obvious mortality of former students arising from active service in the First World War, an aggregate 8 per cent of the intake between 1898 and 1916.[133]

All was not lost, however, since a couple of discoveries were made. The first was about a progressive weakening of Westminster College's links with Wesleyan schools. Whereas in the 1860s, 82 per cent of its students had been pupil-teachers at these schools, the proportion had fallen to 32 per cent in 1888-1902 and to 12 per cent in 1903-20, following implementation of the Education Act 1902, which established local education authorities. Similarly, on leaving college, diminishing numbers of students found appointments in Wesleyan schools, 23 per cent in 1891-1902 and 15 per cent in

---

[132] The term is used loosely, since students were not awarded degrees for studying at the College at this time.

[133] Westminster College Roll of Honour, 1914-19, WCA. This also gives details of the total number of staff and former students who served with the colours, recipients of medals or other distinctions, and those who were disabled or captured.

1903-7.[134] A second revelation was about leakage from the teaching profession of Wesleyan-trained students. Of men who completed the course at Glasgow between 1841 and 1851, 39 per cent later withdrew from teaching in the Wesleyan or (with school boards) public sectors (9 per cent on grounds of misconduct or incapacity), 6 per cent emigrated (some of whom would have been lost to teaching), and 15 per cent ended up in other, mostly private, schools. A further 8 per cent died within ten years of entering college and thus had truncated teaching careers. Far less evidence is extant for Westminster College entrants from 1851 to 1880, but at least 12 per cent eventually withdrew from teaching (including 3 per cent for religious ministry and 8 per cent for other secular employment), with 2 per cent emigrating and 1 per cent dying within ten years of college entry. The true losses (allowing for relatively weak tracking of former students) were, almost certainly, far higher than this.

It is salutary to end on a cautionary note. Prosopographical techniques are not the answer to every Methodist historian's prayer. But the case studies do serve to illustrate how, through the application of prosopography, fresh light can often be shone on to old research questions and new agendas opened up. As the first half of this paper has shown, there is a wider range of prosopographical sources available for the study of British Methodist history than might be imagined, with their exploitation now rendered much easier through computer-based tools in general and databases in particular. Go to it!

---

[134] Calculated from lists in *The Westminsterian*, vols. 2-6 (1892-95) and 10-17 (1899-1907).